ANDREA OPPENHEIMER DEAN

Bruno Zevi
on
Modern Architecture

Rizzoli, New York

Published in the United States of America in 1983 by
RIZZOLI INTERNATIONAL PUBLICATIONS, INC.
712 Fifth Avenue, New York, New York 10019

Designed by Abby Goldstein
Typeset by Western Publishing Company, Inc., Missouri
Printed by Lucas Litho Inc., Maryland

To Kaethe Oppenheimer

Library of Congress Cataloging in Publication Data

Dean, Andrea Oppenheimer.
    Bruno Zevi on modern architecture.

    Includes essays, articles, and speeches by Zevi.
    Bibliography: p.
    1. Architecture, Modern—20th century.   I. Zevi,
Bruno, 1918–   II. Title.
NA680.D4   1983   724.9'1   82–42914
ISBN 0–8478–0487–9 (pbk.)

Contents

Acknowledgments

Among the many people for whose help I am grateful, I want especially to thank Bill N. Lacy, President of the American Academy in Rome in 1977–79 and now President of The Cooper Union, for his abiding encouragement and good counsel; Joanna Cohen, Nathaniel Cohen and Lisa Cohen, my children, for their support and affection in all circumstances; Donald Canty, Editor of the *AIA Journal,* without whom I would not have entered the field of architectural writing; Wolf von Eckardt, architecture critic for *Time* Magazine, for his initial suggestions for this project; and Kenneth Frampton and Stanley Abercrombie, critics and wordsmiths, who applied their talents and time to greatly improve the final text.

Foreword

Not many writers on architecture and related matters, in this century, have had a significant impact on the shape of the man-made environment. Some of us spend our time amusing ourselves, and sometimes our readers, with clever comments on the passing parade, hoping that this year's comments will never catch up with next year's readers. Some of us spend our time serving as flacks for small cliques of designers who are expert at using the media to promote the latest esoterica (and themselves). And some of us take up arms in the defense of a landmark here, or a community there, hoping usually against hope that the barb will turn out mightier than the bulldozer— knowing, full well, that as critics, we have nothing to lose fighting for a lost cause: regardless of how things turn out in the end, we will have been on the side of the angels.

Among the few 20th century critics of architecture whose words have made a difference, there are two who strike me as totally admirable: the first is the American, Lewis Mumford; the second is the Italian, Bruno Zevi.

What has made them so effective is that both have always stood slightly above the daily battle, and for a constant, unshakable set of principles more important than any or all the issues of the moment. That set of principles can be described in two words: humanity and democracy. In Mumford's case, it was humanity that usually seemed in greater peril, and there were times when he seems to have taken a less than charitable view of democracy. In Zevi's case—because he grew up an anti-Fascist in the declining years of Mussolini's empire— democracy was usually his governing passion. But in either case, both Mumford and Zevi have stood for principle, and above fads and fashions. And so they were listened to, and their words made a difference.

Mumford's vision of a humane society— once considered rather charmingly naive by the young hotheads of the modern movement—seems to us today more luminous than a hundred Radiant Cities. And Zevi's vision of a modern, democratic architecture—so clear, so pure, so delightfully utopian—seems to us today more radical than ever, especially when compared with the latest manifestations of neo-fascism, formalism, and nouveau-riche elitism, in the United States and elsewhere.

The last time I saw Bruno Zevi, in a little restaurant near his house on the Via Nomentana, in Rome, he had just completed his 26th year of writing a column, week after week, without fail, for the Roman journal *L'Espresso*. That comes to about 1,350 columns; and it is probably just as well that Bruno Zevi is a man of unshakable principle; otherwise he might have been expected to pronounce something very different every Monday morning.

Zevi's position has never been more relevant than it is today. He has always believed that there was a certain ethic to modern, democratic architecture that made it much

7

Lewis Mumford, introduced by Zevi, speaks to Roman architects after receiving an honor-ary degree from the University of Rome, 1965.

more than just another style: it was, in his view, an expression of a free, unrestricted society, dedicated to equality and social justice.

Out of this basic conviction came his view that classicistic formalism was a kind of straightjacket that inhibited freedom—and that Wright's and Aalto's "organic architecture," with its determination to create a humanistic environment, was the only valid expression for a democratic society.

Out of Zevi's commitment to freedom, equality and social justice came his view that a democratic architecture had to express society's preoccupations—the creation of free communities with equal opportunities for all. The means to achieve all this were of interest to him, of course: architectural forms that bore no relation to the technology that shaped them were as false as those that bore no relation to the kind of society Zevi felt they should serve.

Why are these idealistic, utopian, faintly naive convictions of such interest to us today? The reason is that the ideas and the ideals of the modern movement have been corrupted—largely in the United States—and that this corruption is growing into a cancer that threatens contemporary architecture everywhere.

Modern European architecture—this passionately idealistic, socialistic, utopian movement— came to America in 1932, courtesy of New York's Museum of Modern Art. That year MOMA put on a most important exhibition of what it called then (and has called ever since) the "International Style."

It was, of course, not a "style," though it was fairly "international." It was about as much a "style" as socialism was a "style"; but to the Rockefellers, Whitneys, et al, who financed MOMA, the idea that this radical, revolutionary movement was merely another "style" (like Art Nouveau or Art Deco) was, clearly, very comforting: what made the "International Style" (as presented by MOMA) different from Art Nouveau, for example, was that all the international buildings had lots of glass and flat roofs.

Lewis Mumford was hauled in to contributing a separate section on "Housing" to the MOMA exhibition; but the fact that his contribution was treated as a parenthetical afterthought, rather than as the very core of any presentation of the Modern Movement, simply reinforces my argument.

Ever since 1932, modern architecture in America—and, by extension, throughout the modern world—has been viewed as a "style," and as a style that was, somehow, closely associated with American capitalism. Its monuments were the headquarters of international banks and cartels, or the "cultural centers" built for the entertainment of the wealthy; and its most spectacular demonstrations of "housing" theory were expensive villas for the same elite that commissioned the corporate headquarters and the cultural centers. Housing for the vast majority was left to others to design and build—it was of limited interest to those who considered Architecture primarily an Art.

To a few observers, like Bruno Zevi, this corruption of a pure and noble ideal into an expensive toy for the rich was clearly appalling. And it was predictable to Zevi, and to the very few like-minded observers, that the Modern Movement, so corrupted by dilettantes, would soon fall prey to formalism and other vagaries of fashion. If the Movement was merely another "style" for the enjoyment of the rich, with flat roofs and lots of glass the principal distinguishing features, then why not have a new "style" every year? Why not have arches next year, and broken pediments the year after that, and cuckoo clock towers, and applied pilasters and fake facades after that? And why, for that matter, not try slicked-up, polychrome neo-classicism . . . in the manner of Mussolini Modern, anno 1930?

All of this was predictable, and all of it has come to pass. The fact that some of these flights of fashion, these exercises in exterior decoration for the nouveau riche, are labelled "modern" does not disguise the truth that they are profoundly reactionary, in the manner of the Ecole des Beaux-Arts at its most elitist. They are expensive exercises in ostentatious fashion for the rich, and promoted by their institutions. They have nothing to do with the vast majority of mankind—its needs, its hopes, and its aspirations. And they have nothing to do with the kind of democratic society and its architecture that Zevi has written about for more than 40 years.

Nothing makes clearer how topical Zevi's writings have remained over all these years than a comparision of the first and the last essays reproduced in this book.

The first was written by Zevi when he was a student at the Harvard Graduate School of Design, in 1941. It was an attack on the emerging formalism in modern architecture, and Zevi saw it coming almost 40 years before the debut of the likes of Robert Stern and Michael Graves. He said then: "Modern architecture faces the danger of becoming a style that we like better than others . . . the school faces the danger of becoming a workshop of mannerism, or a playhouse of individualistic preference."

The last speech in this book was written in 1982, for a conference held at Harvard, and entitled "The International Style: Architecture since 1932." Zevi had come from Rome to deliver his paper, and he said: "The modern language of architecture still has to be explored in all its complex and splendid implications. It can and must be codified in an anti-classical, anti-Beaux-Arts manner, based on disorder, choice and participation, so as to become . . . really democratic . . ." And he added that, reading his essay of 1941 made him "feel 41 years younger, still restless . . ."

Zevi has remained topical for almost half a century—topical, restless, consistent, and totally relevant to our day.

Peter Blake
Washington, D.C.
December 1982

Introduction

A generation of American students of architecture and architectural history has grown up on Zevi's *Architecture as Space,* which the now 65-year old Italian critic and historian of architecture published at the age of 30 in 1948. The book was translated into English in 1957 and finally issued in paperback in 1979. It followed his earlier *Towards an Organic Architecture,* whose English translation appeared in 1950. Zevi is widely regarded as the foremost European interpreter of the American tradition of Richardson, Sullivan and Wright and among the handful of most influential post-World War II critics of modern design—albeit an always acerbic and combative one.

As such, he has been a familiar and respected presence at American design conferences since the mid-1940s, presenting the opening address to the first conference held after the Second World War by the American Institute of Planners; providing the highlight, in the form of a discussion with Lewis Mumford, of the American Institute of Architects' 1961 convention; and giving keynote speeches at conventions of the International Federation of Landscape Architects in 1962 and the International Congress of Industrial Designers in 1977. A paper delivered by Zevi at the 1964 American Institute of Architects/Association of Collegiate Schools of Architecture (AIA/ACSA) seminar held at Cranbrook, entitled "History as a Method for Teaching Architecture," was published in the 1965 book, *History, Theory and Criticism of Architecture,* by MIT Press, edited by Marcus Whiffen; and his bicentennial address at the Smithsonian Institution, "Two Hundred Years of American Architecture: What Difference Did It Make?" was released last year by Greenwood Press in *For Better or Worse: The American Influence in the World,* edited by Alan F. Davis.

Zevi has long been known for his impassioned advocacy of modern architecture in Italy, a battle he led beginning in 1944 and for many years thereafter when fascist styles and attitudes still dominated his country. As forums for his crusade, Zevi first launched and edited the magazine *Metron* in 1945, and then a decade later *L'Architettura,* of which he is still the editor. Italy's popular weekly, *L'Espresso,* began publishing his architecture column in 1955, and it still appears each week. Organizations founded by Zevi have also left an imprint outside his native country, most notably the Association for Organic Architecture (1945–50) and In/Arch (Italian Institute for Architecture) initiated in 1959.

Yet, Zevi's most recent book, *The Modern Language of Architecture,* and his thinking about contemporary design are not well known in the United States. A partial explanation, perhaps, is to be found in a 1958 editorial he wrote for *L'Architettura,* which voices a position he has never abandoned:

The instinct that characterizes our period is of evasive nature. We have a morbid fear

11

Zevi and Pier Luigi Nervi at the founding of the National Institute of Architecture (In/ Arch), 1959. "The figure of Pier Luigi Nervi rises well above national boundaries." (Appendix, p. 112)

of aging. We fear the true liberty that derives from being faithful to a choice
. . . We increase our so-called ideas without really dedicating ourselves to thought
. . . Thus we betray our cultural directions without first having thoroughly sounded
them out, consolidated them and lived them. The result is we fall into . . . a nervous
vitality intrinsically conformist. (*L'Architettura,* no. 38, Dec. 1958)

Zevi has remained "faithful to a choice" he made as a very young man who fought
for acceptance of the modern revolution as a hope for nations physically and spiritual-
ly devastated by the First World War, then crushed by Fascism. Unnerving similari-
ties can be drawn between the 1930s and our own time, as economies lurch drunkenly
toward the brink and democratic-centrist governments retreat before demagogues of
the left and right. But today there is no single foe like Fascism to blame, much less
to fight; there is, instead, a pervasive feeling of uncertainty. What we *are* sure of is
that we do not like what the commercial products of modernism have left us and that
we have neither its impassioned faith in the future nor in the perfectability of man
and his institutions. We take refuge in nostalgia (even for the 1930s) and in postmodernism, a catchall that, in Philip Johnson's words, means that "anything goes." There
is, as a result, "rejoicing among the philistines and recanting among the faithful," as
Ada Louise Huxtable has written. (*Architectural Design,* 1/81, p. 10)

In this climate of opinion, Bruno Zevi retains his faith in modernism, and, the
farther contemporary architects depart from it, the more tenacious becomes his
defense. He views today's architecture and the controversies surrounding it as reactionary, escapist and cynical—his ideas are unfashionable and unpopular and therefore often ignored. There are, however, at least four reasons why Zevi deserves an
attentive hearing.

1. Ironically, perhaps, he anticipated by decades today's criticism of the tedious glass
boxes that litter our landscape as a perverse heritage of the 1930s. Zevi was by far
the strongest and most influential opponent of Sigfried Giedion's *Space, Time and
Architecture,* which held a virtual stranglehold on architectural thought for dozens
of years. It served as fount and nourishment for the International Style, now widely
regarded as synonymous with modern architecture. Unlike the critics of today, however, Zevi aimed not at denuding or reversing the revolution in architecture, but at
preventing its precepts from being distorted and enlisted in the service of mediocrity.
Modern architecture, he believed, was conceived not as a style but in reaction to all
preconceived styles, and derived primarily from the lessons of the Arts and Crafts
movement of the mid-19th century, from late-19th century Art Nouveau and, most
crucially, from Frank Lloyd Wright, who anticipated the innovations of Expressionism and the De Stijl movement. For Zevi, Wright's functionalism was far richer than
that of the International Style, because, as he wrote in 1945 in *Towards an Organic
Architecture,* it included

a reliance on nature, the use of warm, natural and frequently of local materials and,
above all, an experimental approach and a constant search for new solutions, instead
of ready-made recipes, to both practical and psychological problems. (p. 125)

Zevi regarded—and still regards—the International Style as "reactionary academicism, because of its concepts, classical notions of symmetry, modular proportion,
frontal perspective and rigidity." For Zevi, the issue today is not whether modern

architecture may be dead, as has been rumored, but rather that, even before reaching maturity, it was transformed into a tyrannical changeling. In essence, then, Zevi, has for 35 years waged a crusade *against* modernism, as we think of it, but *for* modern architecture as it was conceived by Wright and such Germans and Scandinavians as Hugo Häring, Alvar Aalto and Gunnar Asplund.

2. As an architectural historian of unquestioned erudition and breadth, Zevi brings to his work on the modern period the perspective of a critic who is steeped in history but views the past through the eyes of a modernist. Thus, his analyses of Michelangelo's 1529 fortifications of Florence employ methods he refined while "reading" Frank Lloyd Wright's houses for Paul Hanna, the works of Rudolph Schindler and Greene & Greene of California. Zevi's huge book on Biagio Rossetti, the 15th century town planner of Ferrara, evinces no less fervor than his essay on the Garden City movement or on Broadacre City or on recent landscape architecture.

3. Zevi recognized the existence of modern mannerism 15 years before Robert Venturi published *Complexity and Contradiction in Architecture* in 1966. Zevi's 1950 studies of Renaissance architects, most notably Alberti and Palladio, revealed to him analogies between the developments—mannerism and revival—that followed such innovators as Michelangelo, Raphael and Leonardo and developments of our own time. "In the 16th century," he says, "mannerism lost its battle; its efforts to popularize the language of the masters were rejected by the Baroque and lost to history." The influence of mannerism, he concluded, is positive, but ultimately limited.

4. Unlike the majority of critics who accept mannerism and its ultimate rout by academicism as simply an inevitable though unfortunate fact of history, Zevi undertook an almost 20-year-long search for an antidote that would immunize architecture against recurrent bouts of mannerism and revivalism. *The Modern Language of Architecture* is the product of that quest. The book developed, Zevi explains, from the following premise:

> If architecture is a "language," an instrument of communication, it would have to follow the normal rules of language. English cannot be learned only by reading Shakespeare, Byron or Shelley. To be spoken as a language, it had to undergo a process of simplification; it had to be codified. The same is true of architecture. Unless it is codified, only an elite will be able to use it, while all the rest remain unable to express themselves in a modern way. They will, instead, use the old language, the language of the Beaux-Arts, making glass boxes instead of stone boxes. The Seagram Building, for example, is nothing but a refined Beaux-Arts box.

Zevi looked to modern architecture itself, rather than semiotics or linguistics, for what he calls invariable principles that could be codified into a comprehensible tongue. What he found in exploring the modern movement from Philip Webb's Red House of 1859 to the present were "seven invariables" which he says "are not rules but anti-rules, seven no's to the seven principles of classical, authoritarian architecture. A language of architectural emancipation, free of restrictions." Zevi regards these invariables, as developed in *The Modern Language of Architecture,* as his most important contribution to architectural criticism. They are also his most controversial.

Zevi firmly believes, with Frank Lloyd Wright, that there is a direct relationship

Zevi with Frank Lloyd Wright in Venice, 1951, after Wright was given the degree honoris causa *by the University.*

between political, civic and social patterns and architectural concepts and forms. Says Zevi:

> Architecture can serve as prophesy of a freer world. Einstein, Freud and Schönberg are my heroes—all dissidents. Everybody thought they were crazy, because they stood common sense on its head. I believe in the dynamism of Biblical Judaism, as against static Greece and all its followers (Fascists, neo-Rationalists) up and through the Enlightenment.

Polemical as this stance may sound, it is key, as will be made clear in later pages. Let us simply note here its succinct expression of Zevi's refusal to make peace through compromise, to give up fighting for ideals he has held since his youth, despite apparent evidence that the struggle may be doomed.

Such, in brief, are some of the beliefs of Bruno Zevi. He is a man as complex and often contradictory in character as was his mentor, Frank Lloyd Wright. It is all but impossible, I believe, to read Zevi's more recent essays without experiencing a strong resistance. In his hatred of dogmatism, he becomes emphatically dogmatic. While lashing out at all "isms" and ideologies, he ineluctably creates his own.

In 1979, at the founding session of the International Committee of Architectural Critics, held in Barcelona, Zevi fought his colleagues for three days straight, accusing them variously, as is his wont, of tautology, Beaux-Artsism, agnosticism, postmodernism and so on. Characteristically, he refused all compromise: there would be no agreement on the basis of vague generalities. And yet, when it came time for choosing a president, the group unanimously elected Zevi.

This book was written at the American Academy in Rome during the winter of 1979–80 when I was privileged to spend long hours in conversation with Zevi over a period of five months discussing his major writings and ideas on modern architecture. Except where otherwise noted, statements by Zevi that appear in this book are from tapes or notes from our discussions. My intention here is not to attempt a definitive study, but simply to make clear Zevi's principal contributions to the criticism of modern architecture. Omitted, therefore, is most of his work in architectural history of earlier periods and all his activities as a designer. Biographical material, though plentiful in the first chapter, is used primarily to illuminate the development of his attitudes toward contemporary design. Often the material is presented in Zevi's own words in order to permit the reader to arrive at his or her own conclusions. This text is therefore a presentation, not a critical evaluation of his thinking.

CHAPTER

1

A struggle against Fascism, a battle against Giedion

Towards an Organic Architecture was Zevi's first and smallest book. Today, 38 years after its Italian publication, he still adheres to the conclusions of this 'manifesto' which served as foundation for each of his subsequent volumes on modern architecture: Architecture as Space (1948); Storia dell'Architettura Moderna (1950); The Modern Language of Architecture (1978); and Spazi dell'Architettura Moderna (1973). The last revised, updated and transposed Storia dell'Architettura into an encyclopedia of contemporary design with over 3,000 illustrations.

Towards an Organic Architecture was, above all, an attack on Sigfried Giedion's Space, Time and Architecture, whose guiding ideas Zevi considered myopic and detrimental to future building activity. He intended the book, which he wrote in London during the winter of 1943– 44, as a form of tribute to his native Italy after four years of exile. Zevi was just 25 years old at the time and able to work on the book only at night. During the day he was employed by U.S. Army Headquarters in London, helping to design military camps for the invasion of France. As he recalls, unmanned V-1 bombers blitzed the city daily.

> The V-1s flew overhead each night, sometimes every five or ten minutes. They made a terrific noise, like the banging of huge iron chains against each other. Then, all of a sudden, when it seemed as though one of these self-propelling machines was just over your head, you felt a strange stillness, there was complete silence. A few seconds later, came a terrific crash and whole buildings crumbled. Every night I had to make the choice: to go to the underground refuge or to remain in my top floor apartment at Oslo Court and write.

Zevi completed the book in three months' time, consumed with the idea that its principles, if adopted, could have a profound influence on the course of Europe's reconstruction after the war.

Among his co-workers at U.S. Army Headquarters in London was Gordon Bunshaft, future star of the New York office of Skidmore, Owings & Merrill, the world's largest architectural firm of distinction. According to his own account, Zevi began his

17

Bruno Zevi

lifelong attack, then and there, against what he calls SOMism, which he regards as an embodiment of Giedion's pernicious influence with its emphasis on technology and "isms." During that winter, he recalls, Bunshaft was sketching an ideal house, for relief from the tedium of everyday work.

> It was a fully Miesian structure: a square prism suspended over a pond. I was furious, lambasting him with: "How can you do that after Fallingwater? You are making static everything that is dynamic in Wright's work. The water at Bear Run is not a pond or lake, but a cascade, moving dramatically. In Wright, there is no elementary geometry, no simple squares, no simple rectangles, no boxy volumes, but a full interpenetration between interior and exterior space. The countryside enters into the house; the space explodes violently outward. Gordon, I must tell you frankly that you are three or four centuries behind Wright. Your house has an anonymous physiognomy; it cannot grow; it cannot change. What kind of people do you expect will live there? At bottom my objections are not based on questions of taste or even design, but on social and political principles. Here we are in this dreary, awful job of planning military camps, because we are fighting Fascism, and your sketch is for a house that isn't democratic in principle."

This struggle against Fascism is the historical backdrop against which Zevi wrote *Towards an Organic Architecture* and it still influences his reactions to today's events.

Sixty-five years old, Zevi still works and lives in the spacious house where he was raised, the only son of a prosperous, respected Jewish family that had for centuries resided in Rome. His office and the spaces occupied by *L'Architettura,* of which he has been publisher and editor for 29 years, occupy the ground floor; and it is here that Zevi spends most of his time, surrounded by books, working 12 hours out of every 24. The second story apartment, austere and sparsely furnished, reflects in feeling and appearance its owner's essential asceticism. Zevi remains a lean, dark, youthful-looking man with a full head of straight, unparted black hair. He pays scant attention to his appearance and claims to be intimidated by mirrors, which, he says, he avoids even when shaving. His everyday clothes are casual, generally somber, except for one colorful touch, the ever-present American bow tie. When he is tranquil, his gestures have a sense of gravity, even grace. It is more usual, however, to find him vigorously conversing, protesting, inveighing, imprecating, gesticulating, his hands and facial muscles in constant motion as in a mime. Zevi has shed none of the partisanship and idealism of his youth, though it has been tempered, if only slightly, by a long life of experience and study. In addition to being a scholar and critic, he is also a shrewd entrepreneur, yet quite uncomprehending of such everyday, mechanical matters as how to operate the photocopying machine. He is a spellbinding performer, but a very private human being. Though highly disciplined and meticulous in his work, he can be impetuous and intolerant in everyday human interchange, frequently overbearing, occasionally vain, yet often vulnerable, easily moved, profoundly generous. He is quick to anger, slow to forgive and, over time, has remained more attached to ideas than people. ("People change, ideas do not.") He is a man inclined to action—for better or worse.

Zevi's salient characteristics as a person coincide almost too neatly with his lifelong attitudes toward modern design and architectural history. What shaped both, he is convinced, was his experience with Fascism, for Mussolini came to power when Zevi was four-years old. Thus, before examining *Towards an Organic Architecture* and its assault on Giedion's modernist orthodoxy, it is appropriate to review, mostly in Zevi's own words, some of the events that shaped his first book as well as his life.

Like many of Italy's brightest and best young students of his time, Zevi early opposed Fascism on intellectual and aesthetic grounds under the influence of Benedetto Croce.

> I learned to think on the books of Benedetto Croce. I used to say, only half humorously, that I became anti-Fascist after having read the *Aesthetics* of Croce. Basically, it was true. For Croce was the dominant anti-Fascist figure among Italian intellectuals. His aesthetic conception implied the independence of art from political bias, which was an idea flatly opposed to Fascism, since Fascism saw art as an instrument of the regime. I thought to study art history. My father, who was an engineer, wished me to study engineering. We compromised and I became an architect.

It was an uncharacteristic way for this man who has been almost fanatically uncompromising throughout to make what was doubtless the most important decision of his life, one to which he has single-mindedly devoted himself. Zevi's respect for Croce also bore uncharacteristic traces of ambivalence.

> Especially now that the term has become unfashionable, I still define myself as a "Crociano." But there are several areas where I disagree with Croce, some where I always disagreed, which does not diminish my respect for him. A few examples of my disagreement: Croce felt that one aesthetic could be applied to all the arts; I soon developed the idea that architecture has its own aesthetic, which is the treatment of space. Croce had an optimistic view of history as progress; I think, instead, that history is a series of lost occasions, or opportunities, with many periods of regression. Croce believed that art is form; I believe that form is significant only when it expresses functions and contents. Croce made a clear distinction between poetry and non-poetry even in a single work of art; I believe that such distinctions are useful as an exercise, but that in the end the non-poetry belongs to the work of art as much as the poetry and cannot be separated from it. Croce had no understanding whatever of modern art; I loved it from the beginning. Croce did not believe in psychology; I was interested in psychoanalysis since I was a student. Politically, Croce was a liberal (in the Italian sense), while from the start, I was a "liberal Socialist"—something quite different and more complicated.

Politics dominated Zevi's thoughts and activities from 1935, which was his last year at the *liceo,* up to the time that he wrote *Towards an Organic Architecture,* which was in large part shaped by political considerations.

In 1935 Mussolini was at the peak of his power, having invaded Ethiopia and proclaimed the Third Roman Empire. In the following year, during which Zevi began his architectural studies at the University of Rome, the Spanish Civil War began. He recalls that about four dozen first and second year students at the University went to fight for Republican Spain. Others affiliated themselves with Communist parties abroad, of which he says he was suspicious from the start because he saw Communism as "the reverse side of the Fascist coin." Still other anti-Fascist youths established contacts with the Italian refugee organization in France, called *Giustizia e Libertà,* the socialist movement founded by Carlo Rosselli, who was killed by the Fascists after returning from Spain. Zevi would soon become a refugee himself and ally himself with *Giustizia e Libertà.* For the moment, however, he joined the university's anti-Fascist group and quickly became one of its leaders.

> I remember our political activities in Rome as most splendid from a human point of view. We knew that our very life depended on the honesty of all the members of the group. When you met a new member, you did not ask yourself whether you liked him or not, because your life depended on this new friend. It was a time of total solidarity, rather than compromise as usual. Total honesty on all levels. For instance, very often when it was too dangerous to meet, we would communicate through our girlfriends. It never happened that one of us made an approach to somebody else's girl. Ethics and politics coincided.

As repugnant as Italian Fascism patently was, it never attained the rapacious and sweeping control of its counterpart in Germany. Two examples of the regime's apparent tolerance of opposition, or impotence to suppress it, experienced by Zevi may illustrate. He recalled that just after Hitler's *Anschluss* of Austria in 1938, students at Rome University took to the streets demonstrating against German expansionism. The authorities were apparently unable to quell the protest. The same year, Zevi participated in the regime's annual *Littoriali della Cultura* held at Palermo. His speech at the session on Fascist architecture was dramatic.

> I proclaimed that such architecture could have no meaning, and to the astonishment even of my friends, I affirmed the virtues of modern architecture in opposing all totalitarianism and serving as prophesy for a democratic world. A speech of this kind, on any occasion, would have meant immediate arrest, but I risked jail calculating that if my speech was received with enthusiasm, the regime would have to compromise, because they could not accept the idea that the "Fascist generation" was anti-Fascist. And this is what happened at Palermo. Though I was only 20 at the time, my speech was greeted by a roar of approval—the crowd was enormous. The Fascist leaders, not knowing what to do, declared their opposition to my thesis, pronounced the meeting adjourned and left the great hall, hooted and jeered by the public.

However it may have been embroidered by Zevi's memory, such a scene could hardly have occurred in Nazi Germany, where he would probably have been expelled from the lecture hall at the beginning of his exhortation.

In late 1938 Mussolini's anti-Semitic campaign was launched in ernest. Zevi recalls:

> I was glad about it, because pro-Jewish Fascism was a contradiction in terms. Mussolini's rather liberal policy toward German Jewish refugees since 1933 irritated me, because it made many Italian Jews pro-Fascist. However, difficulties arose that I had not foreseen.

He was clearly not aware of the terrible consequences the campaign would have for the Jews as a people, and for himself. One day, Paolo Bufalini, a leader of the anti-Fascist group, warned Zevi that his underground activities had become too dangerous, for him personally and for the organization. He advised Zevi to emigrate and continue his fight from abroad. For Zevi this was a terrible shock, for as far as he knew his family has been Roman for centuries, possibly even since the time of Titus.

By the beginning of 1939, Zevi agreed to go to London, though only for a visit; shortly thereafter he made his first trip to the Paris headquarters of the overseas Italian resistance movement, *Giustizia e Libertà*. The political situation took an alarming turn just as he was preparing to return to Rome, with the result that he decided to stay and enter the Architectural Association School at Bedford Square. A few months later the Second World War began.

During this first stay in London, Zevi felt restive: the anti-Fascist organization with which he worked was insufficiently active for his tastes, nor was he satisfied with the AA School. He soon left and journeyed again to Paris to seek advice from the leaders of *Giustizia e Libertà.*

> We formulated the following plan: I would try to obtain an American student visa, and once in the United States would be met by Franco Venturi, son of the art historian Lionello Venturi. Together we would publish an anti-Fascist magazine *Quaderni Italiani,* which would be smuggled into Italy via France. I was urged to return briefly to Italy, before leaving the continent, in order to strengthen old anti-Fascist contacts and forge new ones.

As he remembers it, the plan was put into effect, almost to the last detail. Zevi wrote to Walter Gropius, he says, asking to be admitted to the Harvard Graduate School of Design. The request was granted, and he obtained a student visa. Zevi's father then gained permission for his son to spend two weeks in Italy without being harrassed by the police, and young Zevi returned to his native country for what he describes as a jam-packed fortnight.

> I travelled to Turin, Florence and other cities to help forge a renewed sense of commitment among anti-Fascist groups and to establish contacts with couriers for disseminating the proposed magazine. In addition, I completed an essay on Brunelleschi, which I had begun in London; while in Italy, I edited, corrected and checked my text against actual Florentine monuments. My passion for Borromini also took root during these 14 days.

> While in Rome, every morning I would go to San Carlino alle Quattro Fontane, a little church whose interior was Borromini's first work, whose facade was his last.

In Rome, Zevi also discovered that three of his political friends had been jailed, which finally convinced him that he had no alternative but to emigrate. In March of 1940, he boarded ship at Naples for New York.

During his first night in New York, Zevi went to see Lionello Venturi, assaulting him, according to his own account, with questions about his son Franco, with whom Zevi was to produce the magazine, *Quaderni Italiani.* The elder Venturi explained that his son was still in France, and would soon leave for the United States. But in June 1940, Fascist Italy entered the war and Franco Venturi was arrested by the Nazis when they invaded France, sent to Italy and jailed. And so, Zevi ended publishing his small anti-Fascist magazine alone, in Boston, while attending the Harvard Graduate School of Design. The publication appeared in two editions, one for Italian emigrés in America, the other— concealed behind a false cover—was mailed to France and smuggled from there to Italy.

Zevi remembers the academic year 1940 – 41 at Harvard as a strange, unsettling period. Among his fellow students was Philip Johnson who, after his influential curatorship at the Museum of Modern Art, had just decided to become an architect.

> It did not take me more than five minutes to begin quarreling with Johnson, who was sympathetic to America First and was favorably inclined toward Germany. I clashed with him over both politics and architecture, for he was more Miesian than Mies.

Though Zevi admired Mies' European work, especially his 1929 German Pavilion at Barcelona, he believed that the reductionism of Mies' American work plus his abandonment of the syntax of the De Stijl movement was leading him toward a classicism in steel and glass.

From all accounts, Zevi unleashed his combative temperament not only against Johnson, but against the Graduate School of Design in general and Walter Gropius in particular. Among the forms this criticism took was a pamphlet, written by Zevi and signed by ten other students, entitled, "An Opinion on Architecture." It was an attempt to demonstrate the shortcomings of Gropius both as an architect and pedagogue. The text opened with the following critique:

> We find the training in our school to be: unclear from a social point of view . . . We too often have a settled attitude towards modern architecture. As a consequence the school faces the danger of becoming a workshop of mannerism, or a playhouse of individualistic preference. The school is unclear from an aesthetic point of view . . . As far as aesthetic tools are concerned, is there the great difference we have always taken for granted between our system and the Beaux-Arts? Have we substituted for the "art for art's sake" of the "rendered project," the "art for art's sake" of the "abstract model?" In addition, the school is inadequate in its teaching of engineering, construction materials and methods, professional practice, landscaping, regional planning and furniture design.

While Zevi called in "An Opinion on Architecture" for collective work and collaboration among all disciplines involved in building activity, he included in it a section on genius, which made it plain, in his opinion, that the methods of Gropius discouraged real creativity.

> We must recognize the existence of the genius as a philosophical necessity. Outside and above collective work, and group movements, there has been in the past, and there will be in the future the man of self-sufficiency in analytical and comprehensive work: the man of synthesis and creation. We call for collaboration but a Leonardo could work alone.

Among contemporary geniuses the pamphlet called attention to the achievement of Wright, who was to be Zevi's lifelong mentor.

> This obscure genius has a deep interest in social problems, but, in their solution, he is overshadowed by his own personality. We regard him, as he probably will be regarded by history, as a genius able to free himself from the conventions of the outside world, but never able to free himself from himself.

His fascination with Wright began long before Zevi came to the United States, though it was certainly strengthened by his American experience. Wright's work had, of course, been widely published in Europe years before he emerged from obscurity in his native land. The influential critic Edoardo Persico, had publicized his buildings in Italy in the early-1930s, and, according to Zevi, Persico regarded Wright's work as the principal source for modern architecture. Even in the 30s Zevi had been deeply impressed with Wright's ability to meld together people, buildings and landscape. He went to the States in 1940 already opposed to the International Style, regarding it as a classicization of functionalism. He was, therefore, more than ever open to Wright. At the time he thought that Borromini and Wright had many traits in common. As

Norris Kelly Smith points out in *Frank Lloyd Wright, A Study in Architectural Content,* Wright's intuitive inclination was toward Hebraic rather than Greek attitudes and ways of thinking. The same can be said of Zevi. Drawing heavily on Thorlief Boman's book, *Hebrew Thought Compared to Greek,* Smith characterizes Hebraic (and Wright's) approach as dynamic, vigorous, passionate and sometimes explosive, as compared to the Greek, which he describes as static, peaceful, moderate and harmonious.[1] Like Wright, Zevi's view of functionalism was diametrically opposed to the problem-solving approach of anonymous specialists.

In 1941 after completing a final project for the degree from the Harvard School of Design, Zevi worked briefly for Stone & Webster in Boston. Among his co-workers was I.M. Pei, who was already oriented towards the large American corporate-type design firm, which he wanted to reproduce in China. Zevi, in the meantime, was bored and unhappy, since no work he admired was being produced by the firm.

He soon returned to New York to immerse himself, once again, in political work. In 1942, politics still took precedence over architecture for Zevi. Once in New York, he requested permission, along with three other members of *Giustizia e Libertà,* to return to Italy and work there for the resistance. Obtaining it took months of negotiations with American intelligence, British intelligence and the Italian underground movement in France. Zevi's eventual return to Italy was arranged through the mediation of Emilio Lussu, a well-known writer and leader of *Giustizia e Libertà,* who travelled from France to London and then to the United States to meet with Zevi and his compatriots and represent their case before American and British intelligence officials. Finally, in March of 1943, Zevi found himself crossing the Atlantic on what he says was America's largest convoy of World War II, with an armored division of 15,000 men aboard.

> Soldiers were packed in three layers below sea level, virtually sleeping one on top of another in the corridors. We could hardly see the sky, because armored cars were piled some 20 meters high. Among this incredible crowd of officers and enlisted men, only four of us were civilians: Alberto Cianca, later a minister of the Italian government, Alberto Tarchiani, who would become Italian ambassador to the United States, Aldo Garosci, a historian who had participated in the Spanish Civil War, and myself. All four of us insisted upon wearing civilian clothes, though we knew what that meant. If we were taken by the Germans, we would be shot on sight as Italian traitors, instead of being treated as prisoners of war. But that was our attitude, our spirit; we saw ourselves as representing free Italy and going back to fight Fascism. The "puritanism" of the Italian anti-Fascists prevailed. Our ship followed a zig-zag route to avoid detection by German submarines, and arrived finally in Glasgow, where it was welcomed by an American general.

Upon arrival in England, the four Italians started their clandestine activities, Zevi's taking the form of two daily radio broadcasts to Italy in the name of *Giustizia e Libertà.* His three friends soon left for Sicily and then Salerno to join newly organized democratic movements. Within months and without warning, Zevi was ordered by the British to cease his broadcasts. Perplexed, he rushed to British intelligence headquarters, where, he says, he was shown a cable signed by General Eisenhower. According to his recollections, the cable conveyed the following message:

> If you have any control over the radio transmissions of *Giustizia e Libertà,* stop them immediately, as they are dangerous to Allied policy.

For Zevi the meaning was clear: it was obvious that the Allies had decided to support the Italian monarchy and the Badoglio semi-Fascist government, and since the anti-Fascists were all Republicans, they had to be silenced. There ensued a conversation between Zevi and British intelligence in which the officials resisted his demand to join the underground in Italy, adding that if they could recall his colleagues they would do so. They asserted that the underground had already become a nuisance, as far as British policies were concerned. Zevi then pleaded to be allowed to go back to the United States and help the Italian underground from there. But this was also refused on grounds that Zevi would at once start an anti-British campaign attacking the Allied pro-monarchic stance. When Zevi asked if he should consider himself a prisoner of the British Empire, he was told:

> What a brutal way of putting it, Mr. Zevi. You are our guest; you will allow us to take care of all your needs while in London.

Zevi recalls concluding the conversation with the words:

> Wonderful, a golden prison. I will be a tourist paid by British intelligence. I prefer to starve rather than accept your money. Don't be offended; you know we are puritan. We are the new free Italy: no military dress, no money, not even from our natural allies.

His underground anti-Fascist activities thus put to an abrupt end, Zevi turned his energies to a battle in print, the writing of *Towards an Organic Architecture.* Its goal was to encourage a post-war reconstruction of Europe along democratic architectural principles. As already mentioned, it was written in London at night while V-1 bombers buzzed the city; during the day, Zevi worked as a planner of sorts for the U.S. Army. The book was as much a political and social as an architectural manifesto. The basic premises from which its architectural positions sprung—and which continue to inform Zevi's thinking today—are similar to conclusions drawn by the painter, writer and physician, Carlo Levi, from his years of exile as an anti-Fascist in a small and backward southern Italian village. In the well-known book, *Christ Stopped at Eboli,* Levi wrote:

> We cannot foresee the political forms of the future, but in a middle-class country like Italy, where middle-class ideology has infected the masses of workers in the city, it is probable, alas, that the new institutions arising after Fascism, through either gradual evolution or violence, no matter how extreme and revolutionary they may be in appearance, will maintain the same ideology under different forms and create a new State equally far removed from real life, equally idolatrous and abstract, a perpetuation under new slogans and new flags of the worst features of the eternal tendency toward Fascism.

> . . . We must make ourselves capable of inventing a new form of government, neither Fascist, nor Communist, nor Liberal, for all three of these are forms of the religion of the State. We must rebuild the foundations of our concept of the State with the concept of the individual, which is its basis. For the juridical and abstract concept of the individual we must substitute a new concept, more expressive of reality, one that will do away with the now unbridgeable gulf between the individual and the State.

The individual is not a separate unit, but a link, a meeting place of relationships of every kind. This concept of relationship, without which the individual has no life, is at the same time the basis of the State. The individual and the State coincide in theory and they must be made to coincide in practice as well, if they are to survive.

. . . The State can only be a group of autonomies, an *organic* federation . . . the autonomy of the factory, the school, and the city, of every form of social life. This is what I learned from a year of life underground. (Italics added)[2]

While following very different paths, Carlo Levi and Bruno Zevi were firm friends until Levi's recent death.

One of Zevi's principal purposes in writing *Towards an Organic Architecture* was to do battle with Sigfried Giedion's position which then dominated modern architecture. Zevi feared it would undermine the ability of architects to tackle, efficiently and democratically, the massive task of rebuilding post-war Europe. He believed:

If Giedion's vision of the development of modern architecture was accepted, the result would be a perpetuation and strengthening of the mechanistic International Style, which would be followed by a chaotic revolt against it.

As he now describes it:

In this revolt, a lot of architects would discover a lot of different umbrellas, unconscious of the fact that such devices had already been discovered and belonged to the patriomony of the modern movement itself.

Partly in jest, Zevi told members of a CIAM (International Congress for Modern Architecture) meeting in 1948:

All I did was translate *Space, Time and Architecture* with one modification: I transposed the chapter on F.L. Wright so that it followed the one on Le Corbusier. But this was a variation of no little importance. It changes the whole historical perspective and the development of modern architecture appears in a new light. To speak of Fallingwater or the Johnson Building of Wright 50 pages before the description of the Bauhaus and 75 pages before Villa Savoye and the Swiss Pavilion at the University of Paris is chronologically, scientifically and historically incomprehensible. One can understand when Giedion may see fit to ignore Asplund; it is inconceivable, however, even within a tendentious historical interpretation, that he considers Wright merely a predecessor of Le Corbusier and Gropius.[3]

For Zevi, Wright's work, more than that of any other architect, was the formative influence on European modern architecture, and took it several steps further. It contained the lessons of the Arts and Crafts movement and Art Nouveau ("though his taste in decoration was often questionable"), of Expressionism, Cubism and the De Stijl group. Wright's form of functionalism, deriving from Sullivan, is to Zevi's mind much richer than that of the European International Style, for it included a multitude of elements ignored by that style.

The term "organic architecture," with which both Wright and Zevi's names remain inextricably linked, is still regarded by most as vague and was dismissed by Giedion as being associated primarily with the romantic. In *Towards an Organic Architecture,* Zevi quoted Giedion as saying:

Frank Lloyd Wright with Zevi and painter, writer and physician Carlo Levi during a reception in honor of Wright, Rome, 1956.

From the beginning, F.L. Wright has faced toward an organic perception of the world. Wright's whole career has been an endeavor to express himself in what he calls "organic architecture," whatever that may be.[4]

What it meant for Zevi when he wrote his first book, and still means for him today, can be gleaned from such passages as the following from *Towards an Organic Architecture:*

> . . . We must admit that organic architecture has a place of its own—not in the aesthetics of architecture, but in the psychology, in the social interest and in the intellectual premises of those who are practising architecture. The distinction, then, between organic and inorganic architecture appears not to be absolute but one of degree and emphasis.

> . . . In Le Corbusier's architecture, and still more in that of Gropius, form derives from function and changes with changed conditions. But the important thing is to see whether we are to relate this "function" to some theoretic, classic and predetermined plan or to the natural growth of things from the essential nucleus. We have to decide whether there is a difference—not, I repeat, in artistic value, but in the mentality and the psychological outlook of architects on their work—between Greek and Gothic, between Le Corbusier and Aalto, and between the first and second generation of modern architects. In many European countries, when a peasant decides to build a house, he immediately thinks of it as a cube or as some other simple geometric form: and he builds it larger than he needs, and shuts off a couple of rooms which will only come into use when his children are older. In his mind the *growth* of the house is subject to a definite program and is limited to the framework of a geometric design. Now a laborer in America follows a different principle: he builds one room and then as time goes on, a second and a third to meet his progressively changing requirements. The European peasant's way of looking at the matter is theoretic, inorganic, and, if you will, classic. The American's attitude is, on the other hand, more evolutionary and closer to natural growth—in a word, organic: the exterior forms are derivations of the interior space.[5]

In the main, the salient characteristics of organic architecture, for Zevi, lie both in what it opposes, and also in what it surmounts. Thus, he referred to it as:

> something equally opposed to the theoretic and the geometrical, to the artificial standards, the white boxes and the cylinders which distinguish so much of the first modern architecture and to its general nudism.[6]

And he concluded his chapter on the subject as follows:

> The interest which organic architecture (unlike the academic and the stylistic) manifests in man and his life, goes far beyond reproducing physical sensations either directly or indirectly. If for example organic architecture has a feeling of movement and a dynamic quality, this is not achieved through the walls being covered in the Art Nouveau manner with neurotic linear patterns which evoke recollections of movement, nor through the composition being such as to necessitate ocular movement before it is intelligible (as we saw in the case of the plan of the Bauhaus). The reason is that the spatial arrangement corresponds fundamentally to the actual movements of the man who inhabits it; organic architecture is not abstractly utilitarian but, in the integral sense of the word, functional. We are still too much in the habit of looking at a house as though it were a picture, and even the best critics are often better at analysing plans and sections and elevations than the total structure and the spatial conception of a building. The organic architect concentrates upon the structure, and

he regards it not merely from a technical point of view but as the complex of all the human activities and feelings of the people who will use it.

Architecture is organic when the spatial arrangement of room, house and city is planned for human happiness, material, psychological and spiritual. The organic is based therefore on a social idea and not on a figurative idea. We can only call architecture organic when it aims at being human before it is humanist.[7]

For Zevi there was never any question but that Wright's organic architecture came *after* functionalism. It came to maturity in the United States following the functionalist period of the Chicago School, with its slogan of "form follows function," which was reinterpreted some 50 years later in Europe, in the 1920s and 30s. Zevi was certain when writing *Towards an Organic Architecture* that functionalism in Europe would yield, as it had in America, to a more mature stage in architecture dominated by organic principles.

The first generation in order to find their feet—to create a real movement—and to impose their views in spite of traditionalism had absolutely no choice but to develop rigid theories and to invent, if not a set of clichés, a restricted figurative vocabulary and to insist on its use as a matter of discipline. The five canons of Le Corbusier and the other dogmas of functionalism were bound to remain for many an absolute rule; in actual practice, they were never that for Le Corbusier himself . . . However, the second generation was born in the atmosphere of functionalism, and for them it constituted something achieved and won, a base to be used in the next advance. The effort to free themselves from dogmatism was natural and right.[8]

As far as Zevi was concerned, Giedion could not see this because his notion of history culminated in the supreme achievements of the Bauhaus and in Le Corbusier's villa at Poissy. What came before was seen as an immature attempt; what came after was viewed as decadence. In such a misinterpretation of history there was, to Zevi's mind, nothing to be learned about the future of the modern movement. Giedion's fundamental mistake, the one, for Zevi, upon which all his other errors hinged, was that he viewed the history of architecture as evolving from only two sources: from technics, on the one hand, abstract and figurative "isms," on the other.

He ignored everything that did not fit into these two parameters. As a consequence, when Giedion reviewed the first age of modern architecture (1850–1915), he almost completely ignored the Arts and Crafts movement of William Morris, together with its fundamental social implications, as was clearly recognized by Nicholas Pevsner's *Pioneers of Modern Architecture* of 1936.

Zevi further charges Giedion with neglecting the whole of British architectural development (as exemplified by C.F.A. Voysey and the Scotsman, Charles Rennie Mackintosh), ignoring at least two of Art Nouveau's most important architects (the Austrian Josef Hoffman, designer of the Stoclet Palace in Brussels and Joseph Maria Olbrich, architect of the Vienna Palace of the Secession and of the Darmstadt Colony) and omitting from his history such notables as Antoni Gaudí and Frank Furness.

The reason for these omissions was that in the name of Le Corbusier and Gropius—more the former than the latter—the elements which were taken up and developed in the rationalistic period of 1917 to 1933 are more heavily accented than those elements which, for various reasons, Rationalism had abandoned.[9]

Still more misleading, says Zevi, was Giedion's interpretation of the period between the two world wars. He gave appropriate importance to the "isms," but selectively, as Zevi wrote:

> Giedion also gives enormous importance to the 'isms.' And this too is proper. But what 'isms' are these? Only those abstract visual ones which do form an essential component of modern culture, but not the only one. Take the case of Expressionism. Giedion notes in passing that it was a transitory phenomenon and not a constituent element of modern architecture; but whoever among you lived in the Germany of 1918–22 can bear witness that such a judgment is quite superficial. To declare, as Giedion does, that Futurism was a more constructive phenomenon than Expressionism, sounds fallacious even to those who, like the writer, recognize the authenticity of the art of Umberto Boccioni. The truth is that Giedion occupies himself only with visual media, with the mechanical formula of a plastic composition much more than with the moral world and the inner inspiration of artists. Expressionism is concerned with psychology, not with abstract visual media, and treats of sorrow, of the moral fracture, and of the despair in the world, things which seem much less interesting to Giedion than grammatical instruments.[10]

In the 1967 edition of *Space, Time and Architecture,* Giedion added chapters on Aalto and Jørn Utzon, but still omitted Gunnar Asplund and such Expressionist masters as Gaudí and Mendelsohn, Patrick Abercrombie's 1943 plan for London and the architects of the California Bay Region. While Giedion portrayed architecture between the wars as fairly homogeneous and monotonous in character, Zevi in *Towards an Organic Architecture* saw it quite differently. He viewed Gunnar Asplund's Stockholm exhibition hall as having marked a turning point, "the initiation of a new season, marked by 'organic' architecture." Of Asplund Zevi wrote:

> The buildings he designed were truly functional and utilitarian, but he had succeeded in broadening the functionalist attitude and in giving to the simple forms of modern building a sense of novelty and gaiety and playfulness which was a revelation to Europe, very different from the monotony of flat roofs and naked walls.[11]

Zevi also regarded Aalto's work as marking a similar watershed and remarked that Aalto once wrote:

> The wrongness lies in the fact that the rationalism has not gone deep enough. Instead of fighting rational mentality, the newest phase of Modern Architecture tries to project rational methods from the technical field out to human and psychological fields . . . The present phase of Modern Architecture is doubtless a new one, with the special aim of solving problems in the humanitarian and psychological fields.[12]

Rather than denying functionalism Aalto, according to Zevi, used lessons of the past for new research into the use of everyday elements ("a door handle, a chair of biological form"), into color and into the specific (as opposed to the universal) uses of space.

For Zevi, "the recognition of space as the protagonist of architecture" was the determining difference between the International Style and "organic" architecture. Speaking of Wright's concept of interior space, Zevi wrote:

> This is without a doubt the greatest of his contributions and also the most difficult to explain in words . . . A cube has no spatial reality in the human organic sense: it is a purely stereometric figure. Most of our houses, in which all the rooms are placed

Erik Gunnar Asplund's Pavilions for the Stockholm Exhibition of 1930. "A feeling of joy and irony animated the severe language of functional architecture," according to Zevi.

next to each other geometrically, correspond to a concept of metric spatial organization. In Wright's houses, on the other hand, the spatial organization is organic. Both in plan and in elevation they correspond to the activities of life and to the pleasures of the eye . . . What is much more important is that this awareness of internal space leads to a *spatial continuity* which embraces all the rooms. This is the principle of the free plan.[13]

Of course, Zevi admits, Le Corbusier and Mies van der Rohe used space creatively. But Le Corbusier reached the free plan indirectly by simply eliminating all internal partitions from a prism. And Mies achieved his "dancing" spaces of the Barcelona Pavilion partly under the influence of Frank Lloyd Wright's exhibition of 1910 in Berlin, only secondarily under the influence of the De Stijl movement, founded by Theo van Doesburg in Holland in 1917. Mies had, in fact, written as follows in an unpublished catalog for Wright's 1940 exhibition at the Museum of Modern Art:

This then was approximately the situation in 1910.

At this moment, so critical for us, the exhibition of the work of Frank Lloyd Wright came to Berlin. This comprehensive display and the exhaustive publication of his works enabled us to become really acquainted with the achievements of this architect. The encounter was destined to prove of great significance to the European development.

The work of this great master presented an architectural world of unexpected force, clarity of language and disconcerting richness of form. Here, finally, was a master-builder drawing upon the veritable fountainhead of architecture; who with true originality lifted his creations into the light. Here again, at long last, genuine organic architecture flowered. The more we were absorbed in the study of these creations, the greater became our admiration for his incomparable talent, the boldness of his conceptions and the independence of his thought and action. The dynamic impulse emanating from his work invigorated a whole generation. His influence was strongly felt even when it was not actually visible.[14]

Le Corbusier was less generous in recognizing Wright. As late as 1925, according to Pevsner, he claimed not to "know this architect."[15] In Zevi's view Le Corbusier did not succeed in "liberating space by breaking the box" until 1950, when he began to work on his chapel at Ronchamp. Thirty years earlier, the De Stijl group had virtually "destroyed the box," wrote Zevi, "breaking it up by intersecting planes in order to demonstrate the 'elementary forms of architecture'—line, surface, space and time."[16]

Although Theo van Doesburg founded the De Stijl group in 1917, Zevi claims that its guiding influence was Robert van't Hoff, who shortly after Wright's 1910 exhibition in Berlin, crossed the ocean to work with Wright and in 1914–15 built "two beautifully Wrightian houses" near Utrecht, Holland. Once again this was ignored by Giedion.

When first published, *Towards an Organic Architecture* was widely read by Italians, as American-inspired propaganda. About this reaction Zevi has since said the following:

I refused to enter any debate based on nationalities, because Fascism and democracy were international, and I was proud to have fought against my country when it was dominated by Fascism; such nationalistic attacks only showed up the idiocy and ignorance of the Fascists. Wright, after all, had not arrived in Europe in 1943 with the U.S. troops, but in 1910, welcomed by the European avant garde, much to the amazement of the Americans who did not appreciate his genius. Now, 30 years later, he was being reintroduced to Europe because he was decades in advance of continental architectural development. Through his help, Europe could hasten its own architectural growth and ensure the quality of its reconstruction efforts.

The principal thrust of Zevi's writings from 1943 to the present has been to act as herald for a turning away from the International Style toward a more "human" architecture, a process which he readily acknowledges occurred independently of Wright's influence. Gunnar Asplund and Alvar Aalto, as two examples, knew little about Wright and yet played a major role in creating a new tendency in European architecture, beginning around 1930. For Zevi's mind, this tendency revitalized many elements of Expressionism and incorporated them into a functionalist scheme. It was thus a reenactment of what had occurred in America at the turn of the century. And for Zevi in 1943 it represented the hope of "a new pluralistic world culture, more coherent in its many diversities." This never materialized, of course, and in the intellectual battle between Giedion and Zevi, Giedion appears to have been the victor. In retrospect Zevi has this to say about his defeat:

> What happened was exactly what I had feared. The International Style continued for more than a decade, with Giedion's book on the drawing table of every architect and architectural student. Then, in the middle of the 60s, came the beginnings of a reaction: the pseudo-Expressionism of Eero Saarinen and Paul Rudolph, the pseudo-vernacular, the pseudo-Art Nouveau and all the other pseudos that I have systematically fought. Then, predictably, at the end of the 70s came the rejection of the International Style; rhetorical proclamations about modern architecture being a "fiasco"; the apotheosis of 19th century eclecticism under the slogan of postmodernism, and the retrogressive Ecole des Beaux-Arts exhibition at the Museum of Modern Art. History is not made with "ifs." But, if you do not take the "ifs," the possible alternatives, into account, the study of history becomes mere tautology. For you end up saying, "what happened happened because it happened." I am happy to be on the losing side of those who until a few years ago exalted Giedion and the International Style and are now making an exhibitionistic revolt against them, continuing to confuse this style with modern architecture.

Notes

1. "Our analysis of the Hebrew verbs that express standing, sitting, lying, etc., teaches us that motionless and fixed being is for the Hebrews a nonentity; it does not exist for them. Only 'being' which stands in inner relation with something active and moving is a reality to them . . . Dwelling for the Hebrew is related to the person who dwells, while for the Greeks and for us it is related to the residence and the household goods." Norris Kelley Smith, *Frank Lloyd Wright, A study in Architectural Content,* American Life Foundation, Watkins Glen, N.Y., 1979, p. 53- 4.

2. Carlo Levi, *Christ Stopped at Eboli,* translated from the Italian by Frances Frenaye, Farrar, Strauss & Co., New York, 1947, p. 252-53.

3. "A Message to the International Congress of Architecture," *Metron,* v. 31–32, 1949, p. 10.

4. Bruno Zevi, *Towards an Organic Architecture,* Faber & Faber, Ltd., London, 1945, p. 67.

5. Ibid., p. 71.

6. Ibid., p. 72.

7. Ibid., p. 56.

8. *Metron,* p. 9.

9. Carlo Levi, *Christ Stopped at Eboli,* p. 243.

10. *Metron,* p. 11.

11. *Towards an Organic Architecture,* p. 61.

12. Ibid., p. 64.

13. Ibid., p. 105–6.

14. Philip Johnson, *Mies van der Rohe,* The Museum of Modern Art, New York.

15. Smith, *Frank Lloyd Wright,* p. 39. Also *Towards an Organic Architecture,* p. 115.

16. *Towards an Organic Architecture,* p. 31.

2

For modernism and history as its instrument

Upon his return to Rome in 1944, Zevi engaged in a flurry of literary and political activities that he hoped would effect a fundamental change in the traditional direction that Italian architecture has pursued for generations. In his book of 1968, *New Directions in Italian Architecture,* the critic and architect Vittorio Gregotti wrote that the trend in Italy has been one of "continuous crises . . . turning points in name only, growing out of that typical flaw of Italian culture, the search for a 'way out.' "[1] In architecture as in politics, the result has been a continually recurring and self-renewing process. It begins in outwardly strident, but basically irresolute, protest against the prevailing order, and then rapidly gives way to compromise with it and eventual absorption by it. An all but identical new rebellion is then refueled by a scattering of remaining dissidents, and the cycle begins anew. Zevi sought to put a stop to this endless replay, marked as it has been by what Gregotti called defeatist half-measures and provincialism, and to place Italy at the forefront of a modernism rooted in the European and American experience.

Towards an Organic Architecture was his initial effort toward this goal. Published in 1945, it was the first book on modern architecture to appear in Italy after the war. In 1945 Zevi also launched *Metron,* the first monthly magazine in democratic Italy committed to publishing the work of the modern movement. Soon after publishing *Towards an Organic Architecture,* Zevi began writing *Architecture as Space,* whose Italian edition appeared in 1948. He says it derived quite naturally from a question he asked himself after finishing his first book: What is the book's real meaning? His answer, of course, was that space is the ultimate protagonist of design. As he wrote in *Architecture as Space:*

> It is in space that life and culture, spiritual interest and social responsibility meet. For space is not merely a cavity, void, or "negative of solidity"; it is alive and positive . . . The facade and walls of a house, church or palace, no matter how beautiful they may be, are only the container, the box formed by the walls; *the content is the internal space.* [It] has its extension in the city, in the streets, squares, alleys and parks, in the

Cover of Metron, *February–March 1949. The magazine was launched in 1945. From top left to right: Erik Mendelsohn, Alvar Aalto, Frank Lloyd Wright, Le Corbusier, Sven Markelius, Gunnar Asplund, Walter Gropius, Ludwig Mies van der Rohe, Richard Neutra.*

playgrounds and in the gardens, wherever man has defined a *void,* and so has created an enclosed space.[2]

In the book, Zevi gives a condensed history of architecture in terms of space, discusses the different ways in which space has been approached over time, and contrasts his spatial interpretation of architectural history with others that approach the subject from political, economic, technical, aesthetic, psycho-physiological and other points of view.

The book is so widely known that it needs no further elaboration here. Interesting, however, in terms of Zevi's battle with Giedion is a review which appeared in *The Journal of Aesthetics* in 1957, in which critic Paul Zucker wrote of *Architecture as Space* in the following terms:

> Compared with it, Giedion's *Time, Space, and Architecture* [sic] represents merely a highly stimulating collection of essays, extremely useful as an introduction but without going back to basic aesthetic categories as does Zevi . . . Genuine historical knowledge and perspective make Zevi recognize the triviality and sterility of oversimplified functionalism as of all pseudo-scientific, standardized modular theories or other expressions of "modern" spatial illiteracy. They save him from such extremely superficial comparisons as Giedion's juxtaposition of Le Corbusier's curvilinear town plan with Baroque creations or of Mondrian's paintings with the two-dimensional projections of Mies van der Rohe's plans . . . One accepts also Zevi's outspoken attitude toward Le Corbusier's "superficial skimming and impressionistic judgment of various periods in the history of architecture," and his complaint that architecture today is only too often judged as a purely plastic phenomenon . . . [3]

In 1945 Zevi founded APAO (Association for Organic Architecture) as an instrument which he hoped would implement his ideas about architecture. APAO had a substantial following and influence during its five short years of existence and established branch offices in cities throughout Italy. Zevi formulated its guiding principles with an eye to avoiding the flaws apparent in Italy's dominant architectural movement of recent times, Rationalism.

Italian Rationalism, which was officially born with the formation of Group 7 in 1926, championed a new architecture in vague and cautious terms, declaring:

> The hallmark of the earlier avant garde was a contrived impetus and a vain, destructive fury, mingling good and bad elements: the hallmark of today's youth is a desire for lucidity and wisdom . . . This must be clear . . . We do not intend to break with tradition; tradition transforms itself, and takes on new aspects beneath which only a few can recognize it. The new architecture, the true architecture, should be the result of a close association between logic and rationality.[4]

Zevi's view of Italian Rationalism between the wars is best articulated in an essay he wrote in 1978 entitled, "The Italian Rationalists." As early as the winter of 1933–34, he pointed out, the uncompromising anti-Fascist critic Edoardo Persico lashed out at his Rationalist friends with the following words:

> The fact is that Italian Rationalism did not arise out of a deep need, but grew either from amateurish stands like those of the fashionable Europeanism of "Gruppo 7," or from practical pretexts lacking ethical backbone. And so, the point about their lack of style is certainly justified; their arguing only led to confused aspirations, without contact with real problems, and without any real content. The battle between "Ra-

tionalists" and "traditionalists" boiled down to an empty and inconsistent dialogue, in which the opposed parties showed the same lack of theoretical preparation and the same inability to conjure up an architecture made up of more than just sterile show ... Italian Rationalism is necessarily unable to share in the vigor of other European movements, because of its intrinsic lack of faith. And so, Europeanism of the first Rationalism is pushed, by the cold reality of practical situations into the "Roman" and the "Mediterranean," right down to the last proclamation of corporate architecture ... The history of Italian Rationalism is the story of an emotional crisis.[5]

The Rationalists, believed Zevi, were under the illusion that they could avoid a direct confrontation with Fascism and could unify two irreconcilable elements in Italian culture, the neo-classical and the avant garde. Many succumbed to the temptation of accepting architectural commissions from the Italian regime. The notable dissidents, such as Gianluigi Banfi, Ludovico Barbiano di Belgiojoso, Giancarlo De Carlo and, especially, Giuseppe Pagano, who left their drawing boards and joined the resistance movement "stand out from the general dimness of Italian Rationalism," as he puts it. Pagano, Banfi and Terragni, among others, lost their lives during the war, leaving the Italian architectural vanguard impoverished.

Although Zevi respects and admires some of the design accomplishments of Italian Rationalism—the Florence Railroad station of 1934 and the 1933 new town of Sabaudia in the Agro Pontino, as two examples—he characterizes the decade preceding World War II as dominated by the "monumentalists." He is in agreement with other scholars of modern Italian architecture in believing that "the basic mistake of the Rationalists was their failure to link up with the Futurist avant garde as their only valid precedent" but takes the argument one step further in asserting that the Rationalists misunderstood the Futurists' goals as a result of the suppression of the unpublished "Manifesto of Futurist Architecture," written as early as 1913 by Umberto Boccioni. It was not discovered until 1975. The apparent reason for the document's concealment was that it contradicted, in some ways, the views of the movement's hero, Sant'Elia, who was killed in World War I. Zevi sees it as expressing an organic, dynamic approach to architecture.

In "The Italian Rationalists" Zevi quotes Umberto Boccioni's Futurist manifesto as saying:

> The cube, the pyramid, and the rectangle, as the general line of building, must be eliminated; they freeze the architectural line. All lines must be used in any point and by any means. This automony of the parts of the building will break the uniformity ... and utility will not be sacrificed to the old and useless symmetry. Like an engine, the spaces of a building should reach peak efficiency. Because of symmetry, one gives light and space to rooms that do not need it at the expense of others that have become essential to modern living ... So the front of a house can go up and down, in and out, join and divide according to the degree of the needs of the spaces that make it up. It is the outside that must serve the inside, as in painting and sculpture. The outside is always a traditional outside, while the new outside, achieved through the triumph of the inside, will inevitably create the new architectural line ... We said that in painting we shall put the observer at the center of the painting, making him the center of the emotion rather than a simple spectator. The urban habitat is changing: we are surrounded by a spiral of architectural forces. Until yesterday, buildings ran along panoramic perspectives, house followed by house, street by street. Today, the habitat grows in all directions: from the luminous basements of the big stores,

from the multi-level tunnels of the Underground, to the giant rise of the American cloud scrapers . . . [6]

Zevi regarded this manifesto as an eye opener, showing that Futurism had incorporated Cubist and Expressionist elements and had anticipated the analytic syntax of De Stijl as well as Wright's concept of designing "from the inside to the outside."

It was according to just such principles that Zevi attempted, in fact, to formulate the principles of APAO in 1945. The organization aimed at renewing Italian architectural ties with certain aspects of German Expressionism, while maintaining its links to Cubism and De Stijl. APAO's manifesto declared:

> Organic architecture is at once a socio-technical and artistic activity directed towards creating the environment for a new democratic civilization: it is aimed at architecture for the human being, shaped to the human scale, and following the spiritual, psychological and contemporary needs of man as part of society. Organic architecture is therefore the antithesis of the monumental architecture used to create official myths.[7]

When APAO was founded in 1945, modern architecture and modern ideas about architecture were almost nonexistent in Rome; it was a vacuum waiting to be filled. While the industrial city of Milan had given birth to and nourished the Rationalists, Rome had remained an administrative center, lacking private patrons, serving as a filter rather than a goal for internal migration. In 1944 CIAM's Italian group created the first plan for the reconstruction of Milan, and the following year a Rationalist organization, the Movement for Architectural Studies, was founded in that city. The principal intent of the Milan group was to disseminate recent Italian architecture, while that of Zevi's APAO was to publicize the new post-functionalist aspects of the modern movement and fight academicism, which still prevailed in most of Italy, outside of Milan. Zevi recalls:

> The Fascist architects did not disappear with Mussolini's regime. They continued to control the schools of architecture, town planning institutes and architectural associations. Our Albert Speers were able to keep their positions. If Albert Speer, himself, had not been Armaments Minister under Hitler, he too would have been allowed to stay and play a dominant role in post-World War II German architecture. In Italy after the war, we had a Fascism without Mussolini. We expelled the monarchy with the first post-war elections, but it took a much longer time to throw out the Fascist professors and practitioners.

Not by coincidence, these were the years when Pope Pius XII asked Marcello Piacentini, formerly "Mussolini's architect," to complete the plan of the Via della Conciliazione in Rome (1948–50).

Under these circumstances, Zevi believed that the problem of the organic, as he calls it, had to take second place to the battle for modern architecture against Fascism. As he says:

> The larger political-cultural battle had to take precedence over the fight for an organic architecture. So, we had to foster the dominant functionalism, the International Style, since an organic architecture could not develop without a pre-existing functionalist tradition.

For this reason, Zevi says he was careful to avoid a clash between APAO and the Rationalist avant garde, whose members joined APAO groups in some Italian cities. Only in Milan did the Rationalists remain aloof, says Zevi:

> But the APAO worked with the Milan Rationalist group. The most important thing was to defeat Fascist monumentalism, and for that purpose all available forces for modern architecture were needed. This was the real battle of post-war Italy.

The two important victories won by APAO took place in Rome, and had no direct connection with Wright. First there was the Monument of the Ardeatine Caves (1944 – 47), a memorial for 320 civilians killed by Germans during the occupation of Rome. "The Fosse Ardeatine," explains Zevi, "had become the symbol of the Italian resistance." He recalls:

> A competition was held, the majority of the entries were quite lousy, with overblown stairs, altars, temples and the like. But the winning project, designed by four young APAO architects, resulted in the most important memorial in Italy, perhaps in Europe.

The second project in which APAO played an important role was the Rome Termini railroad station, completed in 1947. According to Zevi:

> The building had been designed under Fascism and was in place, except for the front facade. You can still see the sides, enormous brick vaults and arches, all false because the structure is reinforced concrete. An old Fascist scheme for the facade existed, a monumental marble portico, 20 meters deep and high, with double marble columns. The columns were carved, ready to be put in place. Our enemies defended the old scheme; there were all kinds of polemics. In the end, a competition was held for the Ministry of Transportation that took APAO's suggestions into consideration. The importance of the competition lay in the fact that it allowed entrants the choice of either using the existing columns or discarding them. Almost half the entries made use of the Fascist portico, but, as you can see, Rome's Termini station now has a modern facade. The building does not compare in quality with the railroad station in Florence, but it proclaimed that Fascist architecture had come to an end.

Though the building of Fascist monuments may have ceased, the influence of Fascist academicians was gaining strength. "We can therefore say," wrote Vittorio Gregotti, "that after 1948 the old academic leaders resumed control in the schools, except for the Venice Institute of Architecture."[8] In 1948, Zevi won a national competition for a chair at Venice, where he remained as a professor of architectural history until 1960. In cities, other than Venice, however, conservative academicians remained firmly entrenched, and although Fascist architecture, per se, was soon banned, formerly Fascist architects now proclaimed their allegiance to the modern movement, which, Zevi says, thus lost its ethical, revolutionary impact.

> The old cycle of Italian politics and culture had simply resumed its familiar path. The dissident minority group—the modernists—were absorbed by the old order. APAO's influence waned; it was weakened especially by obstacles put in the way of its first large housing program by the government's INA Casa, an agency for financing low-cost housing. By 1950 I disbanded the organization because I found that the APAO was satisfied with winning the battle for modern architecture and uninterested in carrying the fight further, for an organic architecture.

The Memorial to the Martyrs of the Fosse Ardeatine in Rome, of 1945, commemorates the assassination of hundreds of Italians during the Nazi occupation of the city. It was conceived by five young architects (N. Aprile, C. Calcaprina, A. Cardelli, M. Fiorentino, G. Perugini) and still remains one of the most distinguished works of the so-called Renaissance in post-war Italy.

The new Rome Railway Station (1947–51) signified the liberation of Italian architecture from the monumental rhetoric of Fascism immediately after the Second World War.

In musing today on the failure of organic architecture in Italy, Zevi says:

> One can say, 30 years later, that organic architecture failed because it did not have the needed tradition of functionalism to build upon; Italy could not reach the second stage of development without undergoing, in depth, the first. But, this is all baloney. No real organic culture has developed in the United States or in England or France, where modern architecture has been firmly established for years. Nor do I excuse the Italian architects; they are as lazy as their colleagues abroad. They took the easy way out, the International Style.

It is probably safe to say that the reasons why organic architecture failed to gain widespread acceptance lie more in the nature of institutions, how they are organized and how they view themselves, than in their architects. In short, Western democracies' large private and public organizations and corporations, architects' principal clients, appear to see themselves firmly based in Graeco-Roman traditions and culture, to which the organic movement is antithetical.

Zevi's second book, *Storia dell'Architettura Moderna,* was published the year he disbanded APAO; the following year, 1951, he became general secretary of the National Institute of Town Planning, a post he held until 1969. During the 1950s, together with Giuseppe Samonà, chairman of the Venice Institute of Architecture, he helped transform this previously traditional school into a center for modern design and open Italy's state-run university system to architects who had been ostracized during and after the Fascist period, among them Ludovico Belgiojoso, Ignazio Gardella, Franco Albini, Giancarlo De Carlo and Ernesto Rogers.

In 1955, Zevi replaced *Metron* with an expanded magazine, *L'Architettura,* and began writing his weekly column for *L'Espresso;* four years later he founded In/arch, the Italian Institute of architects.

In 1960, he won the first national competition ever held for the prestigious chair in architectural history at the University of Rome. Three years later, he began his tenure there as full professor.

The theme of Zevi's maiden lecture at the University of Rome had emerged years earlier from his *Storia dell'Architettura Moderna.* After he finished writing this book, he asked himself the same question as after completing *Towards an Organic Architecture,* namely: "What does the book really mean?" His answer was that *Storia dell'Architettura Moderna* demonstrated that the history of architecture and contemporary architecture are inextricably linked. As he says today:

> We perceive history with eyes conditioned by our own time, while history, if viewed as process, is the only scientific method for teaching design in the studio.

Zevi regards this concept, that the history of design and modern design cannot be uncoupled, as the second of his three major contributions to architectural criticism. The first was his definition of space as the fundamental aesthetic of architecture; the third would be his codification of a "modern language of architecture" in the early 1970s.

Zevi's inaugural talk in the fall of 1963, at Rome University, elaborated his second major concept before an audience of government officials and intellectuals. His thesis was that a new approach to architectural criticism and historiography was needed to make accessible to designers the lessons of modern architecture. Entitled "History as a Method of Teaching Architecture," it was published, as revised, in *The History, Theory and Criticism of Architecture* (1964). The lecture's themes sprang from his concern, based on the lessons of history about the future of design. In explaining the reasons of his worry, he says:

> Over the centuries every significant advance has been followed by regression. Typically, after a decisive leap forward by a genius, the academy rose again, first paying at least formal homage to him, then stuffing him in an archive and saying to his followers: "He was a genius and could do it. Do not try to imitate him. He will not allow it." According to legend, after the death of the giant come dwarves who, by sitting on his shoulders can see further than the giant—the genius—was able to do. In truth, the cultural dwarves hate the giant; they do not climb onto his shoulders, but remain at his feet, looking up at him with contempt and envy, and try in all possible ways to sabotage his contributions.This has happened over and over again in Italian architecture. After Brunelleschi, classicism and its academic code asserted their dominance and simply ignored Brunelleschi's new architectural idiom, because it did not fit into the traditional classical syntax.

> The same thing happened to Michelangelo. His greatest architectural achievement, the drawings for the 1529 fortifications of Florence, were stashed away in archives for four centuries, neglected. Historians and critics knew of their existence, but could not "read" them because the new "words" he invented were not incorporated into the academic architectural vocabulary, could therefore not be understood and were, consequently, regarded as merely technical achievements and unimportant. After Michelangelo came a neo-16th century revival; after Brunelleschi there had been a pseudo-Alberti period, and after Borromini architects resurrected Renaissance schemes with Baroque adjectives.

Thus, the question to which Zevi addressed his 1963 lecture was: How can we avoid a similar regression from occurring after the death of the modern masters? So long as they lived, Le Corbusier, Wright, and others had provided the architectural profession with wholesome nourishment on demand in the form of a steady stream of exemplary buildings. Now that they were dying what was to prevent their conceptual and formal messages from becoming unintelligible to designers, and lost? What was to prevent architects from reverting to revivalist styles? Zevi's answer was that the responsibility for allaying such reaction rests with critics and historians who would have to shed what he called their fear of revolutionary ideas and their academically-oriented preconceptions. For all truly creative innovations in architecture, he has always believed, are lodged in a rejection of conventionally-held precepts.

Prevailing methods of interpreting history, claimed Zevi, were as distant from modern architecture in spirit and intent as is the modern movement from the Beaux-Arts. What was needed, he contended, was a means by which history could be "read" in accordance with modern sensitivities, so that the lessons derived from it could be applied in design studios. In his lecture he therefore proposed what he regarded as a new method for teaching design which would use history. He characterized it as "a Bauhaus with historical—that is to say, scientific— consciousness." He began his talk by showing why all three prevailing systems of teaching architecture, the *bottega,* the Beaux-Arts and the Bauhaus, were outdated and inadequate.

> In the *bottega* method, employed since the Renaissance, a young man who wanted to be an architect would select a master, would go to work and learn in his *bottega,*

or office. In all the schools where you have few students and a great personality among the teachers, this method still continues. Is it good? Perhaps it *was* good, but it does not work anymore. It is typical of the *élite* school, while we have to face the problem of mass education . . .

There is another drawback in this method. To follow a master is not really a guarantee that you are going to get his process and not merely his results. We have seen people who have been for years at Taliesin or in Mies van der Rohe's school, and very often they did not get the process at all. They got the results; they became little Wrights, little Mieses. And then where are the masters, where are the great personalities today? It looks as if the new generation is not producing heroes.[9]

Of the Beaux-Arts method he said:

It is the academic system. History was taught as "styles," phenomena were reduced to rules. Design teaching was directed towards a style, and so it could easily meet history. Out of the meeting between this kind of history and this kind of design teaching the theory of architecture was formulated with its idols of proportion, symmetry, dynamic composition, rhythm and so on. The theory made the school perfectly coherent, with the perfection of a tomb. It resulted in the death of history, and the death of original creativity. I said that it resulted in them. But it would be better to say frankly that it results in them, because many of our schools still run on the Beaux-Arts system, only with less coherence.[10]

Zevi then described the Bauhaus system as a marriage between the modern movement in architecture and modern pedagogy.

Learning became an active proposition. But what about the teaching of history? As you know, Gropius threw it out of the Bauhaus curriculum. Why? With a few exceptions—and perhaps those were not available in Weimar and Dessau—the architectural historians were all more or less reactionary . . . Gropius was fully justified in rejecting it. But he made a mistake. Instead of stating that he could not have history courses because there were no good modern historians around, he constructed a funny theory according to which history, especially at the beginning, would have a negative influence on the architectural student, would influence him too much, would paralyze his creative impulse. This was the tragedy. It meant the failure not only of historical and critical teaching, but also of the possibility of finding a modern method of teaching architecture. The baby was thrown out with the bath water. So you had, on the one hand, the past left to the reactionary historians; on the other, the modern movement with no historical perspective—that is, up in the air.[11]

The gulf between the teaching of history and the teaching of design, he concluded, had not been overcome, and the effect of history courses on studio work was, consequently, minimal. Zevi had been experimenting in his own courses with teaching according to a Bauhaus system infused with history, but a history in line with modern aesthetics. What this meant for him—and continues to mean—is viewing history in terms of processes that bring a work of art to life, rather than as simply a source of models to be emulated. This, in turn, meant—and means—a change of roles for both critics and historians. Instead of sitting in judgment of the architect and evaluating his work according to established standards, the task of each becomes one of reconstructing the processes that determined the conceptions, the development and finally the completed form of an artwork. It also meant—and means— eliminating traditionally made distinctions between history, criticism and theory. For, according to Zevi, without critical involvement and a theoretical approach, the historian's work cannot

Zevi opening of the academic year 1964 in Venice with a lecture on Michelangelo.

Louis Kahn and Zevi discuss a project for Jerusalem, 1972.

reveal the dynamics of design; and devoid of a knowledge of history, criticism can only be skin deep. Similarly, a more profound understanding of process could, he believed, make the lessons of Wright, Le Corbusier or Mies more accessible to students than could even studying with the masters themselves.

To instruct according to such methods, said Zevi, required changes not only in teaching approach but also in methods of communication. He told his Rome audience:

> We are trying to do a modern history with the old instruments of writing and speaking. Words are not the means the architect uses for his work, and the challenge for us, in the next few years, will be to find a method by which historical research can be done with the architect's instruments (drawings and models). Now we know that a critical essay can be produced by painting, as in the case of the Carracci, as in the case of the majority of modern painters. Why not express architectural criticism in architectural forms instead of in words?[12]

He maintained that such a method would help to distinguish the critical from the creative elements of a design and, ultimately, allow students to make more informed choices in their own work. Zevi had employed this approach in courses at the Venice Institute, when analyzing the work of Michelangelo in preparation for the 400th anniversary of his death. Every time a student had a critical thought to express he or she was urged to illustrate it in three dimensional terms. If history could profit from using the instruments of design, then design, he reasoned, could be equally enriched through use of historical and critical tools.

In conclusion, Zevi told his audience in 1963 that:

> What the students of our schools resent more than anything else is the superficial, empirical, anti-scientific way in which their designs are criticized. How does the design critic express himself? Too often in the vaguest way: "Rather nice: A bit weak here; perhaps you could put more tension on this side. Why don't you make this part of the building more fluent?"—all that kind of baloney. We have thrown out the old, academical grammar and syntax, but having failed to replace them with new grammar and new syntaxes, open and dynamic, we find ourselves empty-handed. At this point, however, the new historical method comes to help. If history is now able to reconstruct the creative processes of the builder of a Gothic cathedral or of Brunelleschi, or Bramante or Wren, it is also able to follow, to control and to test the process of architectural creation. The method for understanding an old building and for criticizing a new one in the very process of creation is the same. If design criticism at the drafting tables is going to become scientific, it must adopt the historical method in the new active, operative sense which has been underlined. Otherwise, design critics will continue to be prima donnas expressing, with poor words, their feelings merely. The good design critic today, with the new science at his disposal, cannot but be a historian, just as the good historian is the one man who can understand and verify the inner process of a design. Design, in fact, is going to be taught in the history courses or (better) in the history laboratory; and history is going to be taught at the drafting tables. This is the challenge for all of us. We have to merge history and design courses, renewing the methods of both.
>
> If we are able to achieve this goal, we shall not only have a school as coherent as the Beaux-Arts (upside down); we shall also keep what is good in the *bottega* method of teaching, putting it at the disposal of mass education.[13]

In theory, the method would allow students to learn from Wright, Le Corbusier or Aalto better than they could have by working in their studies or listening to their lectures.

From about 1950 to 1970, Zevi's lectures, his books, his magazine and weekly columns all reflected his assumption that history was the only available tool for conveying principles of architectural design. Around 1970, a major shift occurred in his thinking. What he had seen happening internationally in architecture and in his classrooms was a proliferation of mannerist tendencies accompanied by a progressive erosion of the modern masters' salient ideas. In fact, he now says:

> Everything that has happened since the Second World War can be put under the umbrella of mannerism. British Brutalism—James Stirling and Denys Lasdun, I.M. Pei, Oscar Niemeyer, Eero Saarinen and his followers, the "whites," the "greys," the "silvers," they are all mannerist in a potentially positive sense. Some mannerists have pursued a neo-Expressionist bent, others have followed in the manner of Kahn, or Wright or Mies. Still others are very intellectual, such as the New York Five.

Zevi differentiates, as do others, between two forms of mannerism. The first consists in working in the manner of one master, the second in using, often indiscriminately, "the manners" of two or more masters. The latter, he points out, has historically produced intelligent and original work, but often resulted in the impoverishment of each of the sources used, and—as in the 16th century—has led to either a regression to academic forms or hyperbolically expressionistic ones. Invariably, he believes such mannerist tendencies have arisen in reaction to established, academic attitudes, the most recent ones pitting themselves against the International Style. And herein, he contends, lies the basic weakness of mannerism:

> The only way it can destroy classical models—either by tearing them apart or undoing them with irony—is by preserving them as emblems of sanctity to be violated. They thus need the enemy for their own sustenance; without the continuing existence of the academy, the mannerists have nothing to struggle against and eventually lose their impetus.

According to Zevi the intention of this kind of mannerism, which combines two or more styles, is, at least in part, to popularize the work of the masters by divesting them of their doctrinairism (as in the case of Le Corbusier) and in their messianic attitude (as in the case of Wright). But, unfortunately, he believes, mannerism neither popularizes nor democratizes.

> It is a highly intellectual operation and almost untransmittable. Mannerists work from results, from finished products and neglect the process from which these developed. They elaborate on forms, not on structure and formation. They annotate and destroy form in an intellectual but limited and aristocratic way. While the works of the masters are derived from the reality of life, the works of the mannerists are derived simply from those of the masters. The mannerists perceive reality only through the filter of selected and exalted images. Thus mannerists tire quickly and are sucked back into the academy, which is always lying in ambush, as happened with neo-16th centuryism, neoclassicism and contemporary neohistorical trends.

The pitfalls of mannerists who work in the manner of a single anti-classical master are fairly obvious: because their work is derivative, it produces little that is original or even inventive. Only 50, perhaps 100 architects in the world are using this form of mannerism in a significant way, says Zevi.

> Evidently, it is too difficult. Mannerism implies a highly developed historical and critical attitude, an understanding of principles rather than mere form.

Over the last decade, Zevi has become more and more preoccupied with the question: "Why are the great creative geniuses, all anti-classical, so summarily erased from architectural memory?" as he phrases it. The answer, he reasoned, was that no language had been devised that could accurately communicate their contributions. In verbal language, Zevi observed, new words, idioms and grammatical constructs are assimilated and slowly alter the way we speak and write. By contrast, he found that in architecture, critics and semiologists have regarded *langue* (in Saussure's usage, the commonly spoken and codified means of communication) as a rigid set of abstract design conventions, based on Beaux-Arts treatises, into which new *paroles* (words) are absorbed without being given their real value. Zevi thus sees architects as a strange and comic breed in the human zoo.

> One would expect that, when a creative mind has upset the codified building *langue* to a point of substituting it with a new language, the following generation would be busy in diffusing and popularizing it. What happens, instead, is that the so-called *paroles* are merely complicated and elaborated upon in abstruse, incomprehensible terms.

He contrasts this process with the development of the Italian language from Latin as one instance. As Latin became an increasingly artificial, rigid language used almost exclusively by the upper classes, a vulgar tongue—based on *exceptions* to Latin grammar and syntax— came into widespread use. In his *Divine Comedy,* Dante created a new, universally understood language, based on exceptions to Latin syntax, rather than forcing new words into an arcane language. "The process started from the people, culminated through the great poet's intervention, and went back to the people. Could not something similar happen in architecture?" asked Zevi. His answer, affirmative, of course, is contained in the book, *The Modern Language of Architecture.* It is Zevi's most recent major contribution to architectural criticism—and his most hotly debated.

Notes

1. Vittorio Gregotti, *New Directions in Italian Architecture,* George Braziller, New York, 1968, p. 7.

2. Bruno Zevi, *Architecture as Space: How to Look at Space,* translated by Milton Gendel, Horizon Press, New York, 1957, p. 242.

3. Paul Zucker, "Architecture as Space," *Journal of Aesthetics & Art Criticism,* vol. XVI, no. 2, Dec., 1957, p. 283.

4. Gregotti, p. 14.

5. Dennis Sharp (ed.), *The Rationalists, Theory and Design in the Modern Movement,* Architectural Press, London, 1978, p. 119.

6. Ibid., p. 120.

7. Gregotti, p. 43.

8. Ibid., p. 46.

9. Bruno Zevi, "History as a Method of Teaching Architecture," *The History, Theory and Criticism of Architecture,* papers from the 1964 AIA/ACSA Teacher Seminar, Marcus Whiffen (ed.), M.I.T. Press, Cambridge, Mass., 1965, pp. 12–13.

10. Ibid., p. 13.

11. Ibid., p. 13–14.

12. Ibid., p. 17–18.

13. Ibid., p. 18–19.

CHAPTER

3

The search for a
modern language of
architecture

The Modern Language of Architecture was published in Italian in 1973; its English translation appeared in 1978, a paperback version in 1981. Zevi arrived at the book's major tenets after a review and re-evaluation of modern architecture, which he undertook for the purpose of revising his 1950 *Storia dell'Architettura Moderna*. Its updated version grew to two volumes: The first, *Spazi dell'Architettura Moderna*, is a thick encyclopedia of modern architecture with thousands of illustrations; it appeared in 1973. The second, which bears the same name as the original book and is an enlarged edition of it, was published in 1975. After completing his research, Zevi asked himself, as he had done in 1945 after finishing *Towards an Organic Architecture,* and again in 1950, after completing *Storia dell'Architettura Moderna:* "What do all these facts and ideas mean?" His answer this time was that they suggested a "language." Zevi makes no claim to having invented his modern language of architecture. As he says:

> The *paroles* were there in the works invented by the masters. And they were evident also in revolutionary architectural concepts from earliest times.

Architecture had gotten along quite well without a conscious language. Why the need for one now? Zevi answers:

> Up to the 1960s, we could manage without a language because we had a father figure—among the masters of modern architecture—who fed and supported us. But in the 1950s and 1960s the fathers—Wright, Le Corbusier, Gropius, Mies van der Rohe, Mendelsohn, and a few years later, Louis Kahn—died. Moreover, some of them stopped nourishing their children long before they actually died: Mies, for example, when he began working with closed prisms and abandoned the poetics of fluid spaces championed by the De Stijl free plan; and Gropius, when he turned to teamwork in America and forgot the system of breaking blocks up into functional volumes, which had been the great achievement of the Bauhaus. Even Le Corbusier, when he took his giant step forward at Ronchamp, left teaching behind and disinherited children and grandchildren, who had to fall back on the Le Corbusier "manner" of the Lyons La Tourette monastery and Chandigarh. Now we are like orphans,

bewildered, not knowing what to do. Few of the best explore mannerism in a meaningful way; most study the early imitators of the masters, like Terragni and Schindler: a fascinating but transient escape. The majority is sceptical and cynical. All this is, indeed, rather infantile, and becomes demagogic when it defers the responsibility of a new architecture to the apocalyptic rising of a new society.

The Modern Language of Architecture is, above all, an attempt to codify—and thereby popularize and make accessible to architects and laymen alike—the singular aspects of modern architecture and planning. For without language, Zevi is convinced, these will become extinct, and the profession will succumb to a further proliferation of mannerism and finally to a revival of classicism. This process had occurred repeatedly in the past, after the deaths of Brunelleschi, Michelangelo and Borromini, and was looming again as a threat to the present. Zevi explains:

> Revolutionary concepts in architecture are all exceptions, I repeat exceptions, to the rules of classical syntax. Instead of being accepted for what they really are—legitimate alternatives to the prevailing language—and codified as such, they have throughout history been absorbed into the existing grammar as mere adjectives. As a result, the actual meaning of Michelangelo's architecture, as one example, could not be adequately communicated, became virtually incomprehensibe and reduced to trivia. His exceptions to established rules were viewed as mere seasoning, never as the meat of the matter.

It is, therefore, Zevi's belief that ideas with sufficient force to command attention and generate major change are invariably exceptions to established rules, and confute traditional ways of thinking. To underscore his point, he makes an analogy with physics:

> In Galileo's time people said the earth was flat, which is boring. When he said "the earth is round," he was not only right, but made an impact. Then when he said, "the earth, and not the sun, is moving to give us night and day," we looked and said baloney. But it was true. Only those ideas which do not seem to adhere to common sense are revolutionary; the rest are tedious. Einstein said that if we have two twins, and one moves around out in space while the other stays in one place on earth and they meet in five years, only the one who remained—let's say in Rome—will have aged five years. Space and time are coextensive. People will say—they said—"that is absolutely foolish," but it is the truth. Architects are full of common sense, and look at the results all around us.

What Zevi proposed in his *Modern Language of Architecture* is a new architectural syntax based on exceptions, or alternatives, to existing rules. The principle, he says, is similar to that employed by Arnold Schönberg when he codified a musical language, the atonal scale, out of exceptions to the established tonal mode. Instead of regarding dissonant notes as incongruities within the tonal scale, Schönberg viewed them as elements with integral validity which formed a new language of their own, independent of the prevailing one. The process by which Zevi derived an architectural language also has analogies to the creation, by Dante in *Divine Comedy,* of Italian as a legitimate language. Zevi believes that in formulating a modern language of architecture, he has, in the manner of scholars who studied the Italian poet, endowed an already existing idiom with grammar and syntax. Instead of trying to use linguistics in his search for an architectural language, Zevi sought for its principles in concepts invented by architects themselves. He explains:

Many attempts have been made to apply to architecture the methods used by verbal communication, such as those of Saussure, Chomsky, Jakobsen, Hjelmslev and others. These efforts may be interesting and useful, but they are reductive, and therefore, instead of enriching an understanding of architecture, impoverish it. An architectural language must be based on the processes peculiar to design; if we look at analogies with the process of verbal communication, we lose what is singular to the art of architecture.

Each of the seven invariables of Zevi's "language" is connected with a particular phase of modern architecture. And although no architect other than Frank Lloyd Wright has employed all seven in any single project—and even Wright used the entire sequence only at Fallingwater—Zevi believes that when taken together the invariables describe and codify the revolutionary ideas of modern architecture. Why have so few "modern" buildings adhered to the principles of this language?

It should come as no surprise that out of 100 buildings erected nowadays, 90 prove to be altogether anachronistic works that belong somewhere between the Renaissance and Beaux-Arts, while eight have some incoherent elements of modern style, and, in the best circumstances, maybe two are merely ungrammatical, that is to say, they do not speak the old language, but neither do they speak the new one. And that is not all. Even the great masters of the modern movement have sometimes produced regressive classicist works. Thus one cannot help asking, what kind of language is this, if no one, or very few people, can speak it? Let me answer with another question: How could the modern language of architecture be widely spoken without a code? For five years, I have checked these principles on the drawing tables, both in the profession and in the school of architecture in Rome. I believe that they are useful and, in any case, I do not know of any better method. I cannot understand how one can teach design, or criticize it, without some principles. You can adopt illuministic, classicist principles, or democratic principles. But, if you have no principles, pretty soon you are going to abdicate and adopt those of the prevailing power.

Zevi claims that the design concepts defined and classified by his seven invariables are hallmarks not only of modern architecture but of revolutionary architecture throughout history:

Adhering to my earlier view of historiography, one purpose of my book is to show that the vitality of today's architectural language is consistent with the task of interpreting history in a modern, almost futuristic version, so as to make it act effectively, as an incentive to creativity.

He is convinced that "all creative artists are anti-classical and therefore permanently modern," and also that "all great architects delve into the past for inspiration and modern architecture cannot be understood without knowledge of its precedents."

He meets Philip Johnson's pronouncement that "you cannot not know history" with the rejoinder: "What's new about that? All great architects not only knew history but used it." Taking Wright and Le Corbusier as examples, Zevi points out that both, though individualistic to the point of eccentricity, culled ideas from numerous historical sources. Wright was an apprentice to Louis Sullivan, a great admirer of John Root and H.H. Richardson, and an inspired student of American domestic architecture. Similarly, Le Corbusier was a disciple of European Rationalism and the puritanism of Adolf Loos. Loos, an enemy of the Vienna Secession—the Austrian counterpart of Art Nouveau as created by Victor Horta in the last decade of the 19th century—

was, again by virtue of his reaction against it, connected with Art Nouveau. Art Nouveau's principal disciple, Henry van de Velde, was, in turn, a fervent apostle of the Arts and Crafts movement, which gave birth to modern architecture in the form of Philip Webb's Red House for William Morris. Nor can Morris' contribution be understood without a familiarity of the Gothic architecture which he so admired.

> The modern language of architecture was not born suddenly in 1859 with William Morris' Red House. It does not use incomprehensible codes. Its messages are widely anticipated in Eclecticism and the Renaissance itself, as well as the epic works of the Middle Ages, the late Roman period, Greece (the real Hellenic world, not the ones defined by Beaux-Arts hermeneutics), and as far back as the paleolithic age.

Zevi's *Modern Language* is as much, or more, a statement of political as of architectural conviction in espousing what he calls "democratic, anti-Fascist architecture." The book is marred in part by his stridently ideological, polemical style of writing. Although writing in a propagandistic, ideological style is common enough among Italian critics, for most American and English audiences, it jars and fosters disbelief, no matter that the premise and the conclusions may be sound. Since the ire displayed by Zevi in his *Modern Language* is directed against what he variously calls the regressive and Fascist ideology of classicism, which he, in turn, labels a pseudo-language, it is best to understand at the start why he is so uncompromising in his opposition to classicism (and later to perhaps translate his argument into less highly charged words).

Zevi conceived his *Modern Language,* in part at least, as an answer to John Summerson's 1964 book, *The Classical Language of Architecture,* which posited some constants, though not a systematic language of classicism. Zevi described the enemy, classicism, best when discussing in *The Modern Language* Camillo Boito's essay of 1880 entitled "Architettura del Medio Evo," whose verbal darts were aimed at the High Renaissance. Zevi quotes Boito on High Renaissance architecture as follows:

> These agreeable retreats, where man seeks respite from life's fatigues (how well Horace discoursed on this subject!) should offer him all the combined pleasures of rest and tranquility; yet, with tiresome punctiliousness, those who designed them slavishly copied the exact proportions of Roman monuments, allowing for few spacious rooms, with windows that seemed to dread the surrounding nature and extremely high, dark, vaulted ceilings, thus turning delight into pompous boredom. Whoever wishes to measure the intelligence 16th century architects applied to their imitations of Roman architecture should compare Pliny's villa with one of the most praised mansions conceived by a great craftsman amidst the blessed hills of Vicenza, the Rotonda of Capra. He will see that whereas the Romans invested their houses and villas with organic unity, in the Renaissance imitations the organism was captive, indeed it vanished under a preponderant, tyrannical symbolism. . . . This was an era of rules and precepts, when architecture was reduced to mere formulas, in a series of arithmetic relationships, in contrivances of a few pre-established forms. . . . This apish irrationality soon degenerated into ranting irrationality.[1]

Boito's attack on neoclassicism was harsher yet, which is why Zevi quoted it at length in *The Modern Language:*

> Architecture did not reach back to its sources, rather it was content with second-hand erudition, it imitated the imitators. Antonio Canova thought to build a vast and rich

temple at his own expense, as indeed he did at Possagno, his birthplace. On the fifth of August 1818, he wrote to the architect Giannantonio Selva, "I considered it wise to mention it only to a few of the best architects among us and tell them of my project and how I planned to execute it, that is, to follow the model of some famous monument, without adding any other invention to it." Selva gave his approval just as the Roman architects and the San Luca Academy had already done. Soon after, Selva died, whereupon Canova sought the valued advice of Antonio Diedo, and explained that the atrium "of the church is borrowed from the Parthenon and the other parts from other ancient temples." We need not wonder that Canova was taken with such a passion for classicism that he would copy idolatrous temples in minute detail for a Christian church. Nor should it seem strange that others were of a like mind. But let us take note of Diedo's reply: "In my opinion, the plan leaves nothing to be desired. The facade is superb, but may I boldly presume to express a doubt? That is, whether it is right to reproduce the Parthenon and all its defects without altering it in any minimal part, or whether to make some small modifications whereby to purge it of those defects . . ." This purifier of the Parthenon, whose ignorance was patently abysmal, was widely acclaimed in the Veneto region as architect and author of elegant prose. Describing the Church of the Redeemer in Venice, he cried, "Here is the temple that eclipses all others, even the most exalted and marvelous." But then a worry gnawed at his viscera because the height of the nave "falls by about two feet from the harmonious mean," and commented that this must have been an oversight of the builders since it was unthinkable that Palladio "could have slept over a matter of such great moment."[2]

Zevi then reached the following conclusion from Boito's attack on classicism:

> Boito was chiding the classicists twice over for their follies, first for designing buildings like so many boxes, axial, with head-on perspectives, dreary, antifunctional and servile to the taboos of symmetry and proportion and, second, for systematically betraying the very tenets of antiquity by which they professed to be inspired. They sacrificed both the past and the present to an ideological a priori and to Beaux-Arts design dogmatism.[3]

Zevi invokes Boito once again for a passage in which he speaks of the need for an architectural language:

> The architect must feel that he has in hand a style which adapts easily and responsively to every case; which offers some means of adorning every nonsymmetrical part of a structure when this is necessary; which is free of abstract rapports; which is as rich as need be, yet modest; which can employ tall, short, thick, or thin columns, high, low, wide, or narrow windows, mullioned or three-mullioned, cornices wide and jutting or merely suggested, big, sweeping archivolts or small, arched lintels, slim pilasters and stout buttresses, arches strong and soaring or small and slender, delicate ornamentation and massive foliage; which, in short, uses a language that abounds in words and phrases, unfettered in its syntax, imaginative and precise, poetic and scientific, fitting neatly into the expression of the most diverse and difficult ideas."[4]

It is just such a language which Zevi hoped to codify. The process by which he extracted his modern language of architecture involved three steps: First, he identified the basic principles of classical architecture against which the modern movement had rebelled; then, he isolated the exceptions to the classical code which modern architecture had created, and derived from these his language of seven invariables; finally, he ranged through the history of architecture to assure himself that his invariables accurately reflected and expressed revolutionary contributions of earlier periods.

Zevi's *Modern Language of Architecture* has been met by critics and students with a host of questions, some of which will be taken up in later pages. Others will be answered, at least in part, in the following treatment of Zevi's seven invariables, which attempts to reconstruct the process by which he identified each invariable.

I. *Listing Physical and Behavioral Needs*

The first invariable opposes classicism's tendency to design according to preconceived concepts and forms, often paying scant attention to the functions a building must serve or activities it will house. Zevi described his "listing" process as follows:

> It is an honest, thoughtful lining up of functions in a free, descriptive way, without worrying about formal relationships, or the final effect. It means "no" to all conventions, habits and ready-made phrases, "no" to all aesthetic givens, such as proportion, equilibrium, balance, eurythmic and other trifles, "no" to all "orders" with or without columns. Every error, and omission made at the drafting table can be traced back, without exception, to a failure to respect this principle. Therefore it is the basic invariable of the contemporary code, the one that prevents retrogressions to the academy, old and new.

This denial of any aesthetic a priori permits more choices as opposed to classicism, which dictates sameness, order, etc.

> What appears as rational and logical in classicism, because it is based on regulated order, is, in truth, irrational, because humanly and socially foolish. All that mattered was the facade in classicism. Classical design based on orders, modules, proportion and harmony is totally arbitrary in giving mythical value to abstract ideas that repress social behavior and freedom; it results in standardizing and alienating mass production. Take for example the Palazzo Littorio in Rome. It was a symbol of Fascism, completed after the War as headquarters for the Ministry of Foreign Affairs. The bathroom ceilings are over seven meters high, the same height as those of the assembly halls. These imperial toilets are fit for fairy tale giants or Duces on five meter stilts. Instead, they are used by little men who look sadly out of place there.

The first invariable, as Zevi sees it, endows each architectural element with particular meaning and purpose. A window, for example, is intended to bring in light, and its location, size and shape should be designed accordingly. But, in classical buildings, he argues, a module is selected which controls the placement, height, width and form of openings. What is important is not how the window functions, but only how it fits into a preconceived formal scheme.

> There is simply no good reason why every opening in a building should be like every other. In fact, differentiating each according to its function—which is to bring into spaces a particular quality or intensity of light or frame specific views—has implications for exterior as well as interior spaces. For doing away with the juxtaposition and superimposition of modules, and allowing openings to be high or low, narrow or wide, canted outward or recessed, will enrich and open up the facade, permitting a building to interact with its surroundings in a manner inimical to classicism precisely because it remains unfinished in appearance. A building should be able to grow, expand or contract, like an organism, but classical buildings are conceived as perfect objects, to which nothing can be added, from which nothing can be subtracted.

Listing physical and behavioral needs was the basic design principle of the Arts and

Crafts movement and of Philip Webb's Red House for William Morris, which, in Zevi's view, marked the beginning of modern architecture.

> For Morris a building is no longer a closed image, a performance to be contemplated from the outside, an object having its own equilibrium achieved either through a priori or a posteriori synthesis. Morris totally dismissed the classical orders and notions about decoration of Vitruvius through Palladio. He put aside all past habits and thereby broadened the jurisdiction of architecture to include the entire environment of human life. For Morris, all modifications of the earth, and especially alterations of the landscape, belong to the architecture. It thus becomes a new, enlarged task whose responsibility concerns both town and country. This new vision of architecture makes almost grotesque the abstract values of "beauty," "symmetry," "rhythm," "golden proportion," "style," "balance," and "harmony." For it now becomes the responsibility of architects to understand the real life that goes on in a building. As a consequence, the rules of the academy become irrelevant, and process—open to changes and variations—gains supreme significance.

The Arts and Crafts movement, Zevi points out, looked to Medieval civilization with its varied streetscapes and building rhythms that are in tune with the requirements of everyday life, rather than to the grids and modules of classicism. In *The Modern Language,* he writes that the Arts and Crafts movement was based on:

> —an aptitude for description—a narrative, flexible design method. Modern building programs had become more and more diversified—houses, schools, factories, office blocks, railroad stations, hospitals and so forth—but their specific function was masked behind pseudo-Greek and Roman grandiosity, or behind the Renaissance orders, which imposed stern rules on axes, symmetry, proportion and central perspective . . .

> — organic unity. If every element of a building can "stand out by itself," then it is rid of the dichotomy that typifies so much classic architecture: a box with rooms inside and a colonnade to dress up the box; or, as in Haussmann's Paris, first the facade and then the structure more or less adapted to it. The Lombard style rejected Byzantine mosaics as too precious and restored the value of materials and bare walls, thus capping a trend already evident in High Middle Ages constructions. Similarly, the Arts and Crafts movement was first marked in 1859 with the erection of William Morris' mansion dubbed "Red House" because it exposed brick—for decades hypocritically concealed under stucco —to show how the honest use of materials could offer "a chance to create singularly beautiful effects."

> —free arrangement of volumes and spaces . . . The pioneers of the modern movement understood that the "picturesque" and "ancedotal" nature of the medieval language implied a profound commitment to record events in their individual substance, no longer regimenting them in majestic sequences or a priori full-and-empty balances. Taking their cue from the popular idiom, the Arts and Crafts masters and their disciples from Charles Robert Ashbee to Charles F. Annesley Voysey, worked out a vocabulary which, within a few years, completely supplanted every figurative remnant of the same Middle Ages.

An objection that immediately comes to mind with regard to the first invariable is that although the functional and behavioral requirements of buildings often change over time, buildings do not necessarily become obsolete or lose their value. Churches have been converted into community centers, factories and apartments, and, in Rome, former palaces now serve as embassies or office buildings. Zevi responds:

The Red House by Philip Webb for William Morris in Bexley Heath, Kent, 1859. It is considered the first "modern" house because it exalted natural brick, was descriptive and rejected preconceived formulas.

The Pantheon, Rome, 27 BC – 124 AD, the first architecturally conceived space, but still a closed static one, lighted only by the oculus on top.

When you fit an embassy into a former palace, as was done on the Via Veneto in Rome, you are left with an inefficient embassy, and you make holes in the cornice of the palace to utilize one more floor—something really quite indecent. If you start with a classical building you are stuck with a structure that has no room for organic change. An organic building would have been conceived for change and growth to begin with.

A second question raised by this invariable is one of economics. Are not repetitive classical forms more economical than organic ones for the developer faced with the typical problem of putting up a building with maximum square meters at minimum cost on a small urban site? Zevi answers that classicism invariably involves disrespect for the site and economic waste, and adds:

> An organic architect, even if he cannot build an organic building in an organic context, will always produce something that is organic in the interior spaces. And his solutions will be more economical. An architect should never abdicate. Masterpieces in the past often derived from almost impossible situations and conditions, as for example, San Carlino by Borromini and Adolf Loos' *Raumplan,* which originated from the conditions of the European classical urban fabric.

II. *Asymmetry and Dissonances*

The second invariable opposes classicism's insistence on consonance, symmetry and proportion and proceeds quite naturally from the listing process. For if a building is to contain spaces of varying sizes, shapes, levels and ceiling heights to accommodate different activities and human needs, it will in most cases be asymmetrical, and the relationship of its parts will lack classical harmony and proportion.

In modern times asymmetry and dissonance were basic both to Art Nouveau and the Bauhaus. Their roots go back to the Gothic period with its churches and spires of different heights and shapes, dynamic lines and twisted columns, and its crooked and winding streetscapes that followed natural patterns of terrain and permitted expansion according to need. Zevi writes:

> The composite pilasters of the cathedrals and the sharply projecting cornices of the 14th century palaces were invested with a linear dynamism, which Art Nouveau revived . . . Line is strength, said Henry van de Velde, whose restless, writhing designs were conceived in terms of *Einfuhlung,* that is, a physiopsychological function. This concept Victor Horta had already grasped in his house of the Rue de Turin (1893), Brussels. Stripping away the stone trappings with which the academics dressed their iron columns, he left them bare and extended their lines in vivid, ornamental motives.[5]

In conversation, he gives additional examples:

> In his church of Santo Spirito in Florence, Brunelleschi destroyed symmetry by placing a column in the center, where normally the apse would have been placed, thus breaking up the longitudinal axis used by early Christian churches to propel the faithful forward. In Santo Spirito, if you try to go forward, you bang your head. He made out of the middle something like a wall. Michelangelo, in his sweeping design for the fortifications of Florence (1529) very obviously defied classical concepts of symmetry and harmonious proportion. Carlo Rainaldi, in his Santa Maria in Campitelli, Rome (1657), fused two contiguous spaces, arranged along a longitudinal axis, and gave them unequal light values, thus combining dissonant dimensions and lighting effects. Borromini, for his part, used dissonance widely, as for instance in his

Sant'Agnese in the Piazza Navona, Rome (1653–57) where he placed a disproportion-
ately large cupola over a symmetrical Renaissance facade.

Of all the invariables, the second (asymmetry and dissonance) arouses in critics the
most skepticism and resistance. Among the most common questions that arise are two
which students asked Zevi after a lecture he gave not long ago in Rome. First, since
symmetrical structures would seem more economical to design, is Zevi saying that
aesthetics should outweigh economics? Second, since human beings are symmetrical,
are they not more comfortable in symmetrical than asymmetrical spaces?
   To the first question, Zevi answers:

> Symmetry is usually associated with waste. Any time you see a house consisting of
> a central core and two symmetrical lateral extensions, you can be pretty sure it is
> wasteful and silly. If the living room is in one wing, the bedrooms in the other, the
> architect wasted space by enlarging the living room to make it the same size as the
> bedrooms, while cramping the sleeping areas. And why should the ceiling heights of
> a grand living room be the same as those for the bedrooms? Little sleeping spaces with
> skyhigh ceilings are as ridiculous as a vast living area with a three meter ceiling.

When it comes to larger buildings, he points to Rockefeller Center, along with other
skyscrapers, to show that asymmetry and economic good sense are not inconsistent.
Then, when dealing with the assertion that because peoples' bodies are symmetrical
spaces should be also, Zevi says:

> The human body may be symmetrical when at rest, but not when active. Symmetry
> flies in the face of a democratic, organic architecture made for active people. The
> attraction toward symmetrical spaces is simply a neurotic attempt by an unstable
> person or, an entire society to seek security in a false sense of order, quietude, in
> short—the tomb. It shows a spasmodic need for security, fear of flexibility, relativity
> and growth. We should design in a manner that fosters emotional health, rather than
> reinforcing neurosis.

Such statements are less indicative of an intolerance for the mundane and weak
spirited in human nature, than a manifestation of an idealistic and possibly muddle-
headed wish that things were otherwise.
   In the end, Zevi's main objection to symmetry is based on political and social
conviction and evidence that rigid and authoritarian states have historically produced
symmetrical architecture.

> Symmetry is the facade of sham power trying to appear invulnerable. The public
> buildings of Fascism, Nazism and Stalinist Russia are all symmetrical . . .
>
> There are symmetrical buildings that are not rhetorical, but all rhetorical buildings—
> symbols of totalitarian power or products of sloth and cynicism—are symmetrical.
> Political absolutism imposes geometry and absolutist governments regiment the
> urban structure by establishing axes and then more axes, either parallel to each other
> or intersecting at right angles. Barracks, prisons and military installations are rigidly
> geometrical. If a building is conceived as an inanimate object, only to be looked at
> and not to be used, then symmetry is fine, because it is a perfect reflection of political
> and bureaucratic authoritarianism. But if a building must perform specific functions
> and accommodate particular contents, it cannot be symmetrical, because symmetry,
> like harmony in music, binds every element to what has gone before and what comes
> after and to what is above and below. Symmetry sacrifices the particular and individu-
> al on the altar of overall design, which is uniform, hierarchical and unalterable.[6]

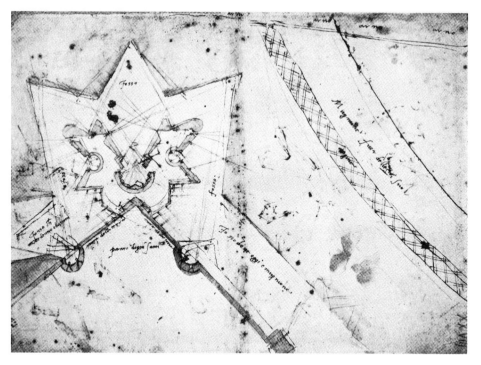

One of Michelangelo's sketches for the fortifications of Florence in 1529, an angry attack against the rules of the Renaissance.

In fact, Zevi contends that the enthusiasts of classicism distorted the arrangement of several classical monuments, because of their preoccupation with symmetry. The most striking example, he says, is the Propylaea of the Athenian Acropolis, which is asymmetrical in plan.

> Because it could not admit that such a heretical structure stood at the very entrance of classicism's chief sanctuary, the Beaux-Arts displayed the Propylaea to make it appear symmetrical. Why? Because in a moment of mental aberration the Greeks must have made a mistake, according to Beaux-Arts logic.[7]

For similar reasons, he says, the Beaux-Arts simply ignored the asymmetrical Erectheum, which served as a forerunner to Adolf Loos's multileveled *Raumplan.*

How does he account for the fact that many works of the modern masters—even Wright's—were symmetrical?

> You cannot invent a new language in a day. Wright had to fight the reigning classicism and there is nothing scandalous in the fact that he sometimes used partially symmetrical schemes. But what is more important in Wright, the rare leftovers of tradition or his revolutionary messages? The academic eye concentrates on whatever is obsolete in a genius, from Brunelleschi to Palladio. What we should look at are their original achievements.

Nor does he object to today's designers creating symmetrical buildings, so long as they have made numerous unsuccessful attempts to arrange spaces asymmetrically.

> Designing asymmetrically is not a rule, because it does not offer a solution, but defines a problem. Symmetry has one solution; asymmetry has a thousand. Therefore, symmetry is an a priori solution, while asymmetry merely pushes you to abandon your laziness, compels you to think and not apply formal, abstract solutions to social and human questions.

III. *Perspective Three-Dimensionality*

The third invariable stands in oppositon to the frontal perspective of the Renaissance, and follows quite logically from the first two: A building of asymmetric, dissonant parts is not likely, after all, to fit into a volume controlled by Renaissance perspective. This invariable is inextricably bound up with Zevi's opposition to frontal perspective.

> It assumes a privileged, antidemocratic viewpoint and it flattens space. Although perspective was introduced during the Renaissance in the name of three-dimensionality, because it was applied to central framing, it created a two-dimensional, flat, static effect. Look at any Renaissance or classical street: A fissure between building walls and a process of flat facades. Where has the three-dimensionality gone? In its place, we see flat-looking vistas, finished, boxy, self-contained packages that have no interplay with their surroundings. In theory, perspective should have provided an instrument to enhance depth, to enrich the sense of volume by the use of dramatic foreshortening. To that end, the corner view of a building should have become the driving force in order to pull the structure out of isolation and bring it into close relationship with the urban environment. Borromini did that masterfully, but where do you see it done in classicist architecture? Hypothetically, the only way to get free of perspective conditioning is to go back to perspective civilizations, usually to the Middle Ages but in Le Corbusier's case to Greece. Take Hadrian's Villa in Tivoli. With its hinged blocks swinging around and reaching out to the landscape. The idea of the "classical world" is a meaningless abstraction. Paradoxical as it may seem, so-called classical civilization was almost totally anti-classical.

Le Corbusier's Chapelle de Notre Dame du Haut, Ronchamp, 1950–53. It was a revolt against all the theories formulated before the Second World War and a search for Expressionistic eloquence. "And then he had the guts to contradict himself; he forgot the 'five principles' of modern architecture that he himself had formulated in 1921 . . . No doctrine any more, but an explosion of emotions." (Appendix p. 151)

The Rationalists, working between the two world wars, used notions developed by Cubism to eliminate frontal perspective with its vanishing points and "privileged point of view." In their search for dynamic three-dimensionality, the Cubists destroyed the building mass by decomposing closed, box-like volumes into their constituent places. They thus eliminated the classical facade and gave equivalent value to all points from which the building could be observed. By raising structures off the ground, Cubism gave importance even to their underside, and by creating transparent walls it established an interplay between interior and exterior spaces. There was however, in Zevi's view an inherent problem with this approach as pursued by Mies, Gropius, Le Corbusier and their followers:

> It enshrined geometry and stereometry—the cube, the sphere, the cylinder, the pyramid, and above all, the right angle. The result was to perpetuate the box, albeit a transparent one. A glass box is different from a stone box, but it is still a box. And Le Corbusier himself remained for a long time entangled in research based on such Renaissance ideas as proportions, golden sections and the Modulor. His Cartesian spirit led him to fight an anti-Beaux-Arts battle with Beaux-Arts weapons. Only after World War II, with the Chapelle de Notre Dame du Haut at Ronchamp, did he give up Rationalism, turning instead to a sort of informal mannerism, which though ready to offend the classical, was not prepared to destroy its code.

For Zevi it was left to Expressionism, to the work of Antoni Gaudí, Erich Mendelsohn (and others), to shake "the pillars of classical Rationalism," for while Cubism attempted to eliminate the physical object by dematerializing it, Expressionism actually broke the box while preserving its mass as an expression of energy. Mendelsohn, profoundly influenced by Einstein's theory of relativity, formulated his *Einsteinturm* (1920), as an assertively material presence without any flat surfaces or right angles. Of this Zevi remarks:

> Both its inner and outer forces are spatial. Charged with energy to the point of spasm, they press on the boulder inwards and outwards, plasticize its contours. Doors and windows are not holes cut into the walls, as in Cubism, but openings that force the energy of the interior to move outward and bring the landscape rushing into the building. Instead of decomposing the box into its constituent parts, in the manner of Rationalism, Expressionism gave to its three-dimensional masses an explosive, kinetic tension that flies in the face of Renaissance approaches.

Zevi believes that Michelangelo defied all laws of perspective, as in his Capitoline complex in Rome, whose compressed trapezoidal void inverts perspective alignment. Zevi further makes an analogy between the Baroque's relationship to the Renaissance and that of the Expressionists to the early Le Corbusier.

> Even such a hesitant artist as Bernini dissociated space into two focal points, in his ellipsoid plan for Sant'Andrea all Quirinale in Rome (1658), giving each major building element a double reference, to create an image with a sense of motion. Carrying the principle further, Borromini, in his church of San Carlo alle Quattro Fontane, created two pairs of partially overlapping ellipses joined by a curving mural band. One cannot grasp the whole from any single viewing point. Baroque brings the object closer to the observer so that he will not mistake it as something detached, something only to contemplate.

Although Zevi derides conventional perspective as a device that immobilizes the

Giovanni Lorenzo Bernini, Sant'Andrea al Quirinale, Rome, 1658–70, plan and elevation.

Michelangelo's Piazza del Campidoglio, Rome, 1538–61. The two palaces at each side in order to contain the space of the piazza, are not parallel, but open towards the city.

architectural image for the viewer he does not altogether eliminate its possible use by designers today, "so long as it is chosen out of a thousand possibilities, after the advantages of the other 999 have been examined, and not a priori."

IV. *Four-Dimensional Decomposition*

The fourth invariable takes Cubism one step further. It consists in breaking up the building box into slabs and then reassembling them in such a way that they cannot form a box. For Zevi it forms the nucleus of De Stijl's approach. De Stijl's principles, enunciated by Theo van Doesburg and deriving from Wright's work, were according to Zevi, a conscious attempt to give a grammar and syntax to modern architecture. Van Doesburg's 17 principles of architecture of 1925 postulated that space would be separated by neutral rectangular planes that could be extended indefinitely, if desired. Since internal divisions would be mobile and external walls extensible, the new architecture—as van Doesburg called it—would destroy the division between inside and outside. He also rejected symmetry and repetition of standard dwelling units. A group of houses or a city, he believed, should be as much a whole as each single house. Zevi quotes van Doesburg as having said in 1925:

> The modern architect, instead of starting with an a priori form for every new theme, tackles ex novo every new design problem. Form is a posteriori. The new architecture has abolished monotonous repetition and has destroyed the equality of a building's two halves, symmetry. Equilibrium and symmetry are quite different notions. Instead of symmetry, the new architecture suggests the well-balanced relations of unequal parts, that is of parts which are different (in position, measure, proportion, etc.) because of their functional character. The new architecture does not recognize passive components: it has defeated the hole. The window is no longer a hole in the wall. The window plays an active role. The new architecture has destroyed the wall, crossing out the dualism between inside and outside. The walls no longer act as supports. Thus, we have a new plan, an open plan, totally different from the classical one, because inside and outside spaces interpenetrate. The new architecture consists of a general space, divided into different spaces which refer to the comfort of the inhabitants. This division is made through planes which separate (inside) and planes which close (outside). The new architecture is anti-cubic, its various spaces are no longer compressed in a cube. On the contrary, the different spatial cells are developed in an eccentric way, from the center to the periphery of the cube, so that the dimensions of height, width and depth acquire a new plastic expression.[8]

Zevi recognizes the shortcomings of the De Stijl free plan, namely that it annihilates depth and has to conceal the building structure. Since this would otherwise compete with the plane, such a precept prevents living spaces from being freely molded and has obvious limitations when applied to the urban scale. He nevertheless regards De Stijl's free plan as key for modern architecture.

> Its importance is in abolishing the cubic volumes of classical approaches, which eliminates all sense of movement and time and substitutes for them a mania for proportion and a priori synthesis. The free plan, throwing off the ball and chain of perspective, is the dominating principle of the modern vision. It is valuable to city spaces as well as to interiors.

Zevi points to a 1923 exhibition of three houses designed by van Doesburg and van Esteren as a real-life application of De Stijl's principles. The buildings were, in effect, the antithesis of Le Corbusier's pure prism and resembled Wright's prairie houses in decomposing the solid cube and arranging space into separate living areas that exploded outwards from, or pivoted around, a massive central core. Despite the fact that Gropius excluded van Doesburg from the Bauhaus and attacked him bitterly, the influence of De Stijl is evident in Gropius' Bauhaus at Dessau.

Mies van der Rohe, says Zevi, is probably the outstanding exponent of De Stijl. In his German Pavilion at the Barcelona Exhibition of 1929 he eliminated closed spaces and made areas flow one into another by using the isolated slab for walls, partitions and ceilings, reflector pools, marble and glass sheets.

The fourth invariable was not a 1917 discovery of the Dutch De Stijl group, however. Among other earlier examples of its use, Zevi cites the monastery of San Filippo Neri in Rome by Borromini. The complex has a concave front that pulls in the outside world, and on its left side is a highly elaborated, angled corner that leads the eye into an adjacent, small side street. Borromini broke up an enormous city block into sections to create a sense of interior flow and a fluid relationship between building and cityscape. This exemplified, for Zevi, a superb application of the fourth invariable.

V. Cantilever, Shell and Membrane Structures

The fifth invariable follows quite naturally from those preceding it, since traditional post and beam construction would prove uneconomical and impractical, if not impossible, as support for buildings made up of variously sized and shaped spaces that reach out in numerous directions. Conventional construction tends to create box-like, rigid spaces. The fifth invariable proposes that all architectural elements, infill as well as structural supports, be revealed in the building envelope. It is an attempt to obliterate age-old boundaries between architecture and engineering.

Reading from *An American Architecture,* Zevi quotes Frank Lloyd Wright as saying:

> I knew enough of engineering to know that the outer angles of a box were not where its most economical support would be . . . No, a certain distance in each way from each corner is where the economic support of a box-building is invariably to be found. You see? Now, when you put support at those points, you have created a short cantileverage to the corners that lessens actual spans and sets the corner free or open for whatever distance you choose. The corners disappear altogether if you choose to let space come in there, or let it go out. Instead of post and beam construction, the usual box building, you have have a new sense of building construction by way of cantilever and continuity . . . in this simple change of thought lies the essential of the architectural change from box to free plan and the new reality that is *space* instead of matter. Let us go on. These unattached sidewalls become something independent, no longer enclosed walls. They are separate supporting screens, any one of which may be shortened, or extended or perforated, or occasionally eliminated . . . freedom where before imprisonment existed. You can perfect a figure of freedom with these four screens; in any case, enclosure as a box is gone . . . To go further; if this liberation works in the horizontal plane why won't it work in the vertical plane? No one has looked through the box at the sky up there at the upper angle, have they? Why not? Because a box always has a cornice at the top . . . Now you catch no sense of enclosure whatever at any angle, top or sides . . . Space may now go out or come in where life is being lived, space as a component of it.[9]

It is elementary reasoning to place the supports a certain distance from the corners, says Zevi.

Erich Mendelsohn's Einstein Tower, Potsdam, 1920–21. The masterpiece of European Expressionist architecture has been re-evaluated since the crisis of the International Style. "A turgid boulder, without any flat surface or right angles, it celebrates the material object that seems to build itself in time, as if rising out of the ground and exploding into air . . . Doors and windows are not holes cut into the wall, but openings forced through by a dual stress, by a mighty drive of the landscape which strives to rush into the building and by equal impetus of the architectural cavity which moves furiously to find its way through into the landscape." (Appendix p. 187)

Even a child can understand it. But how many architects can? Look around you. Resistance comes not from the material's mass, but from its form; the strength of materials comes not from their mass but from their form. Enormous transatlantic liners can float on water, while city buildings are made inordinately heavy just to stand on the ground. In the building field, science is still in an antediluvian slumber.

Examples of unconventional structural systems in modern architecture are everywhere: the underground automobile showroom in Turin by Riccardo Morandi; air-transportable geodesic domes and lightweight houses by R. Buckminister Fuller; Eduardo Torroja's Madrid Racecourse vaults; Felix Candela's hyperbolic parabaloids; Frei Otto's transparent tensile structures, to mention just a few.

The concept of cantilever, shell and membrane structure goes back to the Gothic period, if not earlier, Zevi points out. In 12th and 13th century French cathedrals from Notre Dame to Amiens, weights and stresses were concentrated onto isolated supports which held luminous openwork and thin screens. The continuous bearing wall disappeared.

For today's architects, Zevi further advocates use of electronic computers to solve technological problems. The computer, of course, allows architects to quickly and accurately compare a vast array of alternate solutions, and he says that its use can also make the design process more democratic.

> The client will be able to follow the development of his house step by step. He will "see" it and "live" in it before it is built. He will be able to make choices and change the house.

VI. *Space in Time*

Zevi's sixth invariable is his counterpart to classicism's static interior spaces. It is a process that transfers De Stijl's decomposition of the box (the fourth invariable) to the inside of the building.

> It creates an open design that is constantly in process, invested with time consciousness, and unfinished. What is the difference between the fourth and the sixth invariable? In Frank Lloyd Wright's work you see both, in Peter Eisenman's the sixth is absent. He breaks up the box, but fails to invest spaces with space-time consciousness.

Zevi's concept of space in time derives from Einstein's theory of space-time, which holds that time, as a concept, cannot be abstracted from that of space, that time and space are coextensive. Zevi looks to Einstein when he says:

> So far, our concept of space has been associated with the box. It turns out, however, that the storage possibilities that make up the box-space are independent of the thickness of the walls of the box. Cannot this thickness be reduced to zero, without the "space" being lost as a result? The naturalness of such a limiting process is obvious, and now there remains for our thought the space without the box, a self-evident thing, yet it appears to be so unreal if we forget the origin of this concept.

The concept also stems directly from Zevi's notion of architecture as space, space that is truly lived in, ready to act and be acted on. He opposes this to classicist space.

> Classicist spaces are devoid of all sense of movement through time. They are intended to be contemplated in fear rather than lived in. The Biblical concept of life implies movement and change; the Graeco-Roman concept involves static space. The Christian church struck a dubious balance between the two. There was multi-directional

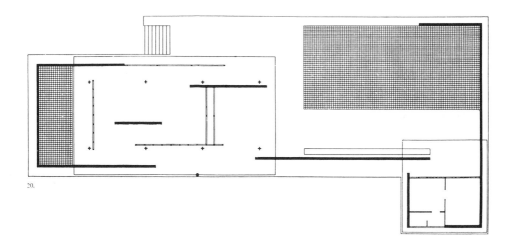

20.

Ludwig Mies van der Rohe's pavilion at the Barcelona Exhibition of 1929 with fluid spaces created with vertical and horizontal slabs. It was the main achievement of the De Stijl philosophy.

Riccardo Morandi's underground automobile hall, Turin, 1959. In a manner different from Nervi, Morandi was a most innovative engineer. His structures are based on pre-stressed concrete.

movement in the plan of Pope Sixtus's Rome and in the layout of Baroque cities. Then came the neoclassical freeze.

He tries to illustrate the concept in fairly simple, concrete terms.

> Does it make sense to have the same kind of floor surface in the hallway, the living room, the bathroom, the study and bedroom of a house? Should kinetic experience be the same in rooms with such different functions? Where could such an inane rule have come from? Certainly not the so-called classical period, which reveals a remarkable sense of movement at times. The Athenian Acropolis, for instance, is built on irregular, rocky terrain, which its architects respected. Paradoxical as it may seem, so-called classical civilization was almost totally anticlassical.

> It took centuries and centuries for man to recognize the positive, creative meaning of space, because, from pre-history to the Pantheon, "voids" were looked upon with mistrust and fear. Then it took centuries more to free space from static conceptions, and in fact the whole architectural itinerary may be interpreted as a clash between dynamic conceptions (Late-Roman, Middle Ages, Brunelleschi, Michelangelo, Borromini, etc.) and revivals of static conceptions (Renaissance, neoclassic, Beaux-Arts, etc.). Static space is typical of authoritarian regimes: Fascism and Stalinism. Dynamic space is emblematic of community and democracy. Only during one period was space annihilated in architecture and did time prevail: this was in the catacombs, miles and miles of underground streets with no landing places and arrivals. In this peculiar epoch, dominated by a metaphysical philosophy, by the idea that real life was to come after death, time-architecture corrodes space-architecture (the monumental, static, spectacular, classical city of Rome) at its very foundations. But soon, as Norris Kelly Smith has shown in *Frank Lloyd Wright, A Study in Architectural Content,* when Christianity leaves the underground and its Hebrew origin, we have a compromise between time and space, biblical and Greek approaches, with continuous academic temptations to privileged space. Sant'Ivo alla Sapienza's spiral by Borromini turns upside down the visual configuration of the cupola; it goes up instead of down. However, the Guggenheim Museum's spiral does the same in a human, functional sense, not merely on a symbolic level.

How can time be introduced into space? One way was pointed out by Louis Kahn, who distinguished between spaces to move through and spaces to be in. But, he did not go far enough Zevi writes in *The Modern Language:*

> Even the arrival spaces—living room, study or bedroom—should not be totally static. They must foster human communication, intellectual tension, or waking after sleep. Life is always full of happenings. The dynamism of living needs to be expressed, not reduced to zero. A room is entered, crossed and left and all this movement should be considered and provided for in design. What is the free plan, the principle of flexibility, moving partitions and fluidity from space to space? It is another way of expressing space in time and time in space.[10]

As examples of space in time, he singles out Le Corbusier's Villa Savoye, where the volume is slashed through from ground level to roof garden by a ramp, visible throughout the house. Zevi calls it architecture to walk through. A more sophisticated example of the same principle can be seen in Aalto's dormitory at the Massachusetts Institute of Technology, and then again in Wright's Guggenheim Museum in New York City, which is all passageway and ramp.

VII. *Reintegration of Building, City and Landscape*
The seventh, and final, invariable counters classicism's tendency to create isolated

Francesco Borromini's Sant'Ivo alla Sapienza, Rome, 1642–60. An unsurpassed genius of the Baroque, Borromini manipulated spaces and masses in the most daring ways, and eliminated the traditional cupola of Roman churches.

objects in space. It consists in making whole and coherent a design which was first of all reduced to a mere description of functions and contents, to what Roland Barthes calls the zero degree, and then decomposed in terms of both volume and space. The seventh invariable reintegrates not only the individual building, but also links it visually and conceptually to neighboring structures, the urban fabric and surrounding territory, be it man-made or natural. Zevi writes:

> Our aim is horizontal and vertical reintegration, with passages in any direction, not squared off at right angles but curving, oblique and inclined. This principle goes well beyond the single object and integrally links the building to the city. When the volume has been broken up into planes and reassembled in four-dimensional fashion, the traditional facade disappears, together with the distinction between interior and exterior spaces and between architecture and town planning. The fusion of city and building leads to "urbatecture." No more building blocks alternating with empty blocks for streets and plazas. Once the old weave is unraveled, the landscape can be reintegrated. And when the traditional dichotomy of city and countryside is abolished, urbatecture can spread into whole territories, while nature penetrates the metropolitan fabric. Thus continuity will be established between city and region, instead of overcrowded, polluted, chaotic, and homicidal urban communities on the one hand and desolate, uncultivated countryside on the other.[11]

Returning to more immediate problems of urban design, Zevi's approach mirrors prevalent planning theories of today:

> Why should buildings be remote and separate, functionally as well as visually from each other and the surrounding landscape? Why should a school building not serve also as a social center, local administrative offices? Why does it have to be physically remote from factories, professional studios and residences? And is it right to separate residential from recreational and commerical uses? Should we not rather bring closer together work, play and home. And why not integrate man-made structures with their natural settings? The theatre of Dionysius in Athens, for example, is a natural cave with the city and surrounding landscape acting as a backdrop. Like many actual Greek buildings it defied the precepts later imposed by the classicizers, who had eyes but could not see. True, you move physically in a classicized building, but in it man feels out of place and expendable. Those spaces were designed for motionless statues; they are formal as tombs.[12]

Zevi thus echoes current criticism of the International Style, but unlike most of its opponents he has always regarded it as an adulteration of modernism.

> For the invariables are concerned with the formative process (not with form), with the unfinished, with an architecture that can grow and change, an architecture that is not isolated but can communicate with external reality and even soil its hands with kitsch. Nobody wants "beautiful" consolatory objects anymore. Art has stepped down from its pedestal to meet life halfway and assimilate the aesthetic valences of the ugly and the cast off.

In explaining in practical terms how the seven invariables have and should be used, Zevi says:

> They must be followed in order. You can skip all invariables except the first, Mackintosh did that with poetic results. Then you can skip the last, the last two, three or even last four, keeping only the first three invariables. But what you cannot do is skip over one invariable and pretend to apply those that follow it. Aalto, for example,

Frank Lloyd Wright's Fallingwater at Bear Run, Penn., 1936–38, according to Zevi, "is a masterpiece, a dream of the future and it contains all the most advanced ideas of modern architecture."

omitted the fourth invariable and then pretended to apply the seventh; that cannot be done. You cannot reintegrate what you have not decomposed. Aalto's, therefore, is not a real reintegration, but rather an a priori integration of a Baroque (M.I.T.) or classical (Enso Building, Helsinki) nature.

Although each of the seven invariables marks a particular phase of modern architecture. Zevi believes that only Frank Lloyd Wright employed all seven, and that his is therefore the only fully "modern" architecture. It was, in fact, from Wright's work that Zevi ultimately derived his seven invariables of the modern language of architecture. Zevi's last work, *The Modern Language of Architecture,* in effect, comes back full circle to his first, *Towards an Organic Architecture,* and its thesis that Wright's architecture served as both fount and culmination of the modern revolution in design. And so Zevi concludes his *Modern Language* with the words:

> From the beginning of our century, Frank Lloyd Wright—profitting from a rationalist experience that matured in the United States 30 years ahead of Europe—became the prophet and genius of the organic trend. He extolled the horizontal, the ground line, unfinished materials sometimes crude and telluric, and the house anchored in the soil as a factor of a reintegrated landscape. From the language of his master, Louis Sullivan, he removed every classical residue, such as isolated volumes, waxed surfaces, sharp contours, crystal purity, abstract geometrics. In the Roberts House (1908) in River Forest, Illinois, Wright built a living room two stories high. Forty years later, for the Guggenheim Museum in New York, he designed a giant heliocoidal ramp to serve as both a stairway-corridor and street-structure.

> Compared with present-day architecture, including the most daring works, the high spots of organic poetics—Wright's Fallingwater (1936) in Bear Run, Pennsylvania; the Johnson Building in Racine, Wisconsin; and Taliesin West, Arizona—belong to the future. They incorporate all the invariables of the modern code: listing, dissonances, antiperspective three-dimensionality that discounts Cubist doctrines; four-dimensional decomposition, with Wright as the father of their supreme example; space in time; and reintegration of building, city and landscape. Fifty years before anyone else, Wright foresaw that the automobile would destroy the traditional antimony between urban nuclei and the countryside. In his Broadacre project, he proposed urbanizing the entire region, providing for fulcrums of powerful density vertebrated by mile-high skyscrapers that hark to the future.

> . . . With Wright, a new architectural language was born. However exasperatingly slow its assimilation may be, it has put its stamp on all contemporary research and trends.[13]

Notes

1. Bruno Zevi, *The Modern Language of Architecture,* University of Washington Press, Seattle and London, 1978.
2. Ibid., p. 125.
3. Ibid., p. 126.
4. Ibid., p. 128.
5. Ibid., p. 144.
6. Ibid., p. 17–18.
7. Ibid., p. 18.
8. Zevi, *Poetica dell'architettura neoplastica,* Einaudi, Turin, 1974, pp. 110–113.
9. *Modern Language,* p. 39.
10. Ibid., p. 52.
11. Ibid., p. 57.
12. Ibid., p. 59.
13. Ibid., p. 210–14.

CHAPTER

4

On architecture and
criticism today

From his early student days, Bruno Zevi has had a special interest in the United States. He has carefully watched and consistently published American architecture in *L'Archittetura* and written about it in *L'Espresso* and other publications. He is considered the leading European interpreter of the tradition of Richardson, Sullivan and Wright, and believes the architecture of their country still remains the decisive influence on design throughout the world. What, then, are his thoughts about current directions in design and architectural criticism, especially in America? Zevi's primary response addresses the functions of criticism:

George Steiner wrote in *Language and Silence:* "The critic has special responsibilities toward the art of his own age. He must ask not only whether it represents a technical advance or refinement, and whether it adds a twist of style or plays adroitly on the nerve of the moment, but what it contributes to or detracts from the dwindled reserves of moral intelligence. What is the measure of man this work proposes? It is not a question which is easily formulated, or which can be put with unfailing tact. But our time is not of the ordinary. It labours under the stress of inhumanity, experienced on a scale of singular magnitude and horror; and the possibility of ruin is not far off. There are luxuries of detachment one should like to afford, but cannot. . . ." I believe that the various currents of contemporary American architecture should be judged according to this criterion. What is the "measure of man" proposed by, let us say, the work of Philip Johnson, the "New York Five," Robert Venturi, Charles Moore, Cesar Pelli, Gunnar Birkerts, etc? How much does it suffer from "detachment," that is, to what degree is it evasive, sceptical, cynical or fake? Steiner is right in saying that this question cannot be put with unfailing tact. However, I will try to answer it with precision. Cesar Pelli, Gunnar Birkerts, Kevin Roche and what has been called the "high technology" people, I believe, are within the itinerary of the modern movement. Some of their work is excellent. At times they veer toward the monumental, which I do not like but, the "measure of man" that their work proposes and its relation to institutions, is, on the whole, positive.

The so-called New York Five architects deserve appreciation, even if their influence—in terms of the "measure of man"—is often negative. They work on architectural linguistics and they share a love of isolated volumes, which means they discard the seventh invariable, reintegration of the building and its context. Sometimes, especially with Eisenman, the preoccupation with the genesis of form is so strong and sophis-

John Johansen's Mummers Theater, Oklahoma City, 1971, projects its parts into the surrounding urban space while being penetrated by it.

ticated that even the first invariable gets lost. They are mannerists in the positive sense of the term; their language is a comment on the masters' language. Since I believe in organic architecture, I find their mannerism a bit sterile, and wish they would give more weight to the lessons of Wright. They risk, otherwise, being mannerists who comment not on the masters, but on the first generation of mannerists (Terragni, Schindler). But I like Richard Meier's work, and I am interested also in the designs of Hejduk. True, they are elitists, but that is not a crime, society also needs an intellectual aristocracy as an antidote for vulgarity.

Zevi's rather catholic tolerance for, and interest in, the critical and ironic dimensions latent in American populist architecture are borne out by his criticisms of Venturi, Moore and Halprin.

Robert Venturi has greatly contributed to a better and more generous understanding of the American scene. He has done for architecture what the pop artists did for painting. Very often, though, I do not like his architecture because it is paradoxical. Even less do I like it when it is neoclassic. However, I would not be surprised if in the future Venturi made more creative design contributions.

Charles Moore is a very good architect who, at a certain moment, got annoyed with good design and decided that cartoon architecture had more sense of humor. I hope that he will soon see this amusement as something boring and come home from his vacation.

I am very much interested in the scale, wit and humor of Lawrence Halprin's work. And I do not think he is torn between boring moralism and escapist humor. The "measure of man" he proposes can be full of brilliance and irony.

He is equally tolerant of the older generation of East Coast mannerists when he states:

The best mannerists are Paul Rudolph and I.M. Pei, because their mannerism is extroverted as much as Peter Eisenman's is introverted. I am very interested in the work of John Johansen. In fact, in my book, *Spaces of Modern Architecture,* two photos appear on the cover: Philip Webb's Red House, with which the modern movement began, and Johansen's Mummer's Theatre in Oklahoma. The Oklahoma theatre is an example of "urbatecture," of a structure perforated by the town and expanding into it. I know that this theatre has many weaknesses and I discussed them with Johansen: "What about the interior spaces, John?" "You are right, Bruno. They are boxy; the walls of my boxes should be made of rubber, so that they could stretch as needed." What is important, however is that what happens at Fallingwater between building and landscape, happens also at the Mummer's Theatre between building and townscape, and that's something.

On the other hand, he remains quite adamant in his opposition to the architecture of Philip Johnson:

As for Philip Johnson, I do not believe there is any hope. By now, it is too late. Maybe he will produce some more able buildings, if and when he becomes persuaded that postmodernism or "neo-stylism" is not fashionable anymore. But he will always feel that architecture is nothing but a joke, for better or worse. In politics, in life, in architecture, the "measure of man" that Philip proposes will always be evasive and rather cynical. Bramante, the inventor of 16th century classicism, was the first to betray the classical rules he had formulated as a doctrine. Le Corbusier betrayed Purism from the Chapelle de Notre Dame in Ronchamp on. Mies betrayed the De Stijl syntax of the Barcelona Pavilion of 1929. Philip betrayed the International Style, and it was not even his invention, when he found out with the Seagram Building that it had become classical. His fault, in my opinion, is not that he betrayed the International Style—that was a positive step which allowed him to produce half a dozen good buildings—but to have stopped, at a certain moment, to continue forward. He decided, instead, to go back to stylism, neoclassicism, Palladianism, Gothicism.

At this point Zevi goes on to make a very revealing comparison between the younger Saarinen, Wright and the current postmodernists:

> Like Johnson, Eero Saarinen also abandoned the International Style, looking for new ways of expression—Structuralism, Expressionism, vernacular and so on. But, his was an eclecticism of high level and significant achievement, with a few failures, like the American Embassy in London. Eero's doubts and oscillations never prompted him to treason. He was undoubtedly the best of the pluralists: this is why it is worthwhile criticizing him. He worked with great professional dignity, but lacking a principle or a method— one might say an ideology—he never achieved the kind of consistent, rich, true variety that Frank Lloyd Wright did. Wright proved that consistency of principle does not deny variety. Consistency lies not in results but in principles and methods. Pluralism, on the contrary, stimulates an eclectic approach, and it is a good alibi or compensation for the lack of essential consistency of the majority of today's architects. Eero was searching all the time; he liked searching so much that he seemed to be almost afraid of finding anything definite. From a didactic point of view, his influence was negative. He gave the impression that an architect could do anything, follow any idiosyncrasies whatever, but actually Eero never disregarded the principles of the modern movement; he was only unable to select from among them.

> Contrary to Saarinen, the postmodernists feel that if one can be an eclectic within the modern movement, then it is also legitimate to be an eclectic without any limitations at all. The Lincoln Center state theater by Philip Johnson was already an example of what has been called "the vanguard of the crayfish," that is the vanguard of those who go backwards. I quarreled with Eero Saarinen because of his eclecticism, but I respected him. What is the use of quarreling with Philip? It is almost impossible, because he does not believe in anything but jokes. Let us hope that sometime in the future he will play some good jokes again.

> The fashionable, self-destructive tendency today is to attribute to the modern movement the worst qualities and characteristics—all the crimes, sins and faults— of our society, so that one can feel quite safe in confirming its crisis and death. Then, in order not to appear too reactionary, one leaps to the postmodern and takes delight in it. Postmodernism frees us from an oppressive father complex and from the frustration of an unaccomplished task. There is a challenge in the modern movement, whose importance lies primarily in social involvement and a new concept of continuous space, which was born out of modern functional necessities, psychological concerns and concern for efficiency in production techniques. By refusing to accept these challenges, the postmodernist, in psychoanalytic terms, kills the father but remains guiltless and, therefore, happy, free of all rules, principles, order of any kind. It is total refusal. His is an infantile act of denial and desecration. Wouldn't it be more mature to reconquer and enrich the dissipated values of modern design?

Finally the subject of postmodernism's most volatile polemicist has promoted Zevi to make the following rather elaborate analysis:

> In the introduction of his brilliant, much advertised booklet, *The Language of Post-Modern Architecture,* Charles Jencks writes: "An architect must master several styles and codes of communication and vary these to suit the particular culture for which he is designing." And we learn with amazement that the author's approach "excludes the interiors of buildings with all those signs of comfort and habitation and daily life

which are so important in giving meaning to architecture." Since he assumes that an architect should go back to 19th century eclecticism and employ all the styles he likes and he excludes from consideration interior spaces, it becomes just too easy for him to vituperate against modern architecture. It is all so banal. Interiors are the content of a building, the spaces in which people live, the original purpose of architectural design: if you dismiss them as secondary, only the box remains. The modern movement arose to combat the Esperanto of academic architecture with its boxes decorated in classical, Greek, Roman, Gothic, Egyptian and Baroque trimmings. These containers were altogether indifferent to the content, but supposedly fit "to suit the particular culture," as Jencks puts it, for which they were designed. If one is interested only in the exterior of a building, instead of its functions and human needs, then one is not postmodern but premodern. And this, of course, fully justifies being eclectic. Mind you, in the 19th century, eclecticism may have performed a positive function, for it desecrated both neoclassicism and the neogothic. By playing with all styles, it took authority away from each of them. Especially in the United States, it was the expression of a vital civilization, the paleoindustrial one, made up of vigorous, self-made, progressive people. The eclecticism of the postmodernists, which is a product as much of the critics as of architects, is an expression of bored, self-indulgent, frustrated people.

Another of Jencks' arguments is that rationalism, behavioralism and pragmatism are the philosophies of modern architecture, which Jencks calls the "son of Enlightenment." Actually, neoclassicism was the expression of the Enlightenment. How can the modern movement which opposed neoclassicism be condemned as a product of the Enlightenment? To be sure, he uses the formula "classical modern architecture," but it is a contradiction in terms, because whatever is classical cannot be modern, and vice versa. It is certainly tempting to dwell only on the classical aspects of contemporary architecture, that is on examples where it ceases to be modern, and then criticize its "univalent form" and "univalent content." For instance, Jencks attacks Mies van der Rohe for his Lakeshore Drive apartments, the Seagram Building and the Illinois Institute of Technology, that is to say for his American work which became more and more classical. But Jencks makes no mention of the Barcelona Pavilion or the Tugendhat house. Similarly, he blames the Chicago Civic Center because "you would not recognize the civic importance of this building, nor the various political functions that occur within." But why does he say nothing about Boston City Hall, which is not a "glass and steel box" and refuses to fetishize technology and building materials or to adopt "universal grammar and universal contempt for place and function?" And is it not rather grotesque that the only building of Wright mentioned by Jencks is the Marin County Civic Center at San Rafael, whose completed design was not even Wright's?

In his earlier *Modern Movements of Architecture* of 1973, Jencks wrote somewhat despairingly of "Camp," quoting Susan Sontag as writing, "Camp is the consistently aesthetic experience of the world. It incarnates a victory of 'style over content,' 'aesthetics over morality,' 'irony over tragedy.' " To me, this is a good description of postmodernism. In the book of 1973, Jencks calls Camp amoral and destructive of the public domain. Yet six years later, he writes a eulogy to the self-same phenomenon in the form of his *Language of Post-Modern Architecture,* and he ends this book with an endorsement of Antoni Gaudí, which seems rather superfluous since Gaudí's genius has been recognized for at least 30 years. But such an apology is significant because it shows that modern architecture is far from dead, and that in its patrimony, in Gaudí as well as in Wright and Le Corbusier, there are vital incentives for the future.

As far as the future of American architecture is concerned Zevi sees "vital incentives for the future," but not in the places where they are customarily sought.

You must remember that there is more to American architecture than you see in the work of prima donnas; there are many *minor architects* who are freely developing the more valuable ideas of the modern movement. Unfortunately, their work is not published by the magazines. For some reason, the magazines prefer to display the caprices of prima donnas, labeling them with complicated ideologies, and ignoring the profession at large. They should know that the prima donnas are dominated by the fear of becoming "second donnas," that is of getting old, and will use any expedient to appear permanently young, even that of betraying their own integrity and that of the modern movement. What the magazines publish and write about is immediately reflected in the architectural schools, though fortunately not in the profession.

The fact is that architectural critics, as much as architects, get bored, fed up, start looking for curiosities and idiosyncrasies and inventing ideologies to justify them, thereby discarding their duty to evaluate the "measure of man," that a work proposes. But idiosyncrasies and curiosities do not wear well; they become lifeless and frustrating.

With few exceptions, the design trends which cause Zevi annoyance, even anguish, have been developed from European sources by American architects clustered on the East Coast. He has a novel, if idiosyncratic, suggestion for rerouting ideas coming into the U.S., so that the port of entry be shifted to the West Coast and ideas be disseminated from the west, eastward, rather than the other way around.

Instead of being imported at New York, and then being filtered from there to the rest of the continent in a pseudo-sophisticated version, European architecture should land in California, Washington and Oregon, mix with the West's architecture, and then make its way back East. I say this for two reasons: First, being sifted through the East, the European messages become more and more academic. Every "neo" becomes more neo: every principle becomes a precept and is passed, as such, to the rest of the country. During the two centuries of American history, the eastern architects have often tended to be more European than the Europeans, that is, they tried to crystalize the European messages. Some of them—McKim, Mead and White, for instance— even pretended to bring the Italian Renaissance back to Rome ! Of course, as a European, I like pro-Europeans, but not when they are inclined to accept the worst that Europe produces and strengthen it with their own contributions. American history shows that it is tremendously difficult in the East to be an independent architect with your own personality, resistant to all Europe's fashions. It takes the energy of a Richardson or a Furness. That is one reason why shifting the route by which European ideas reach America to the West Coast would be good also for eastern architects.

Another reason is that western architects have never been able to export their culture eastward. Perhaps it is because "going West" still means to be happy, and when you are happy, or busy with looking happy, you do not care too much about what happens in other regions. We all know the great personalities of western architecture: Maybeck, the brothers Greene, Gill, Schindler, Wurster and so on. We know what spreading the style of the Bay Region could have meant. But no such thing ever took place, not even when western architects, like Bill Wurster and Charles Moore, directed prestigious schools of architecture on the East Coast. No national architectural magazine ever came out of the West. *Art and Architecture* was a product of California, but never gained the influence or weight of *Architectural Record* or *Progressive Architecture.* What is worse, every time you have an important exhibition in the West, it is dominated by Eastern architects and the local culture is suffocated. This happened first in the Middle West, in Chicago, then in Los Angeles and Seattle. When I lectured in Seattle, in 1976, I proposed changing *L'Architettura,* the magazine I have edited for 25 years, into a new publication based both in Rome and the Seattle-Los Angeles-Portland area; everybody thought it was a good idea, but I have not heard about it since from my friends on the West Coast. The West is now less nationally influential from a design point of view than it was 20 years ago, and will continue to lose ground if nothing is done. Time is short: Why do they not stop being so happy?

Zevi's stance toward current architectural trends arouses a flurry of questions. To begin with, the postmodernism which he decries arose in large part, so it is argued, from a broadly based popular reaction against what we call modern architecture. Peter Blake, for instance, in his book *Form Follows Fiasco: Why Modern Architecture Hasn't Worked,* claims that modern architecture is grounded in the aesthetics of abstract art, and is as alien and little understood by the public at large as modern art. To this Zevi retorts:

> Peter Blake has it backwards. Abstract art derived from architecture, an art which was never figurative. In fact, abstract artists always spoke of "architectural values" and very often produced architectural ideas and models. Think of Mondrian and Malevich. True, Cubist architecture depended on painting, which was an excellent thing, but it prevented Cubism from having a creative consciousness of spatial values. Organic architecture does not, and never did, depend on the visual arts.

To illustrate the public's seeming aversion to modern architecture, Charles Jencks and others point to the fact that over the years Le Corbusier's Pessac Housing (1925–28) has been transformed by its residents into a conventional-looking development adorned with pitched roofs, porches and the like. Does Archie Bunker hate modernism?

> When the social program is wrong, superposed, vernacular forms aren't going to make it right. When housing doesn't work, it is because the program, location, density, connection to town services, community feeling—some combination of these things—is wrong. Remember that J.J.P. Oud's housing in Holland is still wonderful. So is the Karl Marx Hof in Vienna and the Stuttgart housing of 1927. There are plenty of other examples: May's housing in Frankfurt, the German Siedlungen built before Hitler and so on.

It has often been said that traditional forms are valued not so much for their intrinsic worth, but as a sign of continuity between generations and a connection with the past. One criticism of modern architecture is that it provides no such continuity and connection, and is therefore viewed by many as barren, arid, alien. As far as Zevi is concerned this is little but a weak renunciation of the remaining creative potential of the present.

> Okay, one can select to live in an old house, truly old, not fake old. But, I believe that the desire to create a new house, if it is your own and personalized, is equal to and perhaps greater than the desire for continuity. There is a great joy in inventing something new. I think that all courageous people want a new house. The others may feel well in a house personalized by somebody else. But let us be frank. If you believe that all modern houses are "barren, arid, alien," just because they are new, our discussion comes to an end. You have given up on culture, you are fed up and you are going to pass over to the other side of the fence, to postmodernism and classicism, fake antique. You will stop caring about creative architecture. It is so easy to assume a skeptical attitude; it is even fashionable today. But there will always be a minority

of people who refuse to abdicate—and they will be the only happy people— even if they have to fight and suffer a lot.

I do not agree that most people do not like modern architecture. There were simple, ordinary people, businessmen, not intellectuals, who allowed Wright to build hundreds of houses at a time when all aristocratic and sophisticated people would not consider a modern house. I believe that if you interview people at random they will tell you that they like Botticelli and Raphael more than Paul Klee and Kandinsky, Mozart more than Schönberg. But it would be absurd today to produce music as Mozart composed it, or to paint like Botticelli or Raphael. It is the critic's duty to fill the gap between the avant garde and public opinion. The critics are there to explain and persuade people to fight their passive habits. Why should architecture be understood without explanation, when not only science, painting and music, but also fashion is communicated and sometimes imposed by a big propaganda apparatus? How many cases do we know of past artists who were not understood by their contemporaries because the critics were not there to explain, but are now accepted by ordinary people? Of course, if the critics, the intellectuals, no longer believe in modern architecture, everything breaks down. One can say "the hell with modern culture," make jokes, be evasive, but then what? Where does it lead?

About the argument that architects should seek to support, rather than change, accepted social order, Zevi believes:

The historic bases of agreement and of social order are different in different ages; often they are contradictory. The Medieval bases were opposite to those of the Romans; the Renaissance bases were the reverse of Medieval ones. Therefore, we have to find *our* bases of agreement and social order. The hiatus, the schism, that resulted from the Industrial Revolution cannot be obliterated simply through harking backwards in architecture. I believe the modern movement has shown maturity in defending the old city and preserving it. But cities are not static, and modern signs are going to transform even old townscapes. This is good, if done with clear dissonances; wrong if done with imitations.

Finally, I may like the "bases of agreement" of the Middle Ages, but certainly not its social order. In general I do not like the term order; it smells of dictatorship.

Freedom implies a certain amount of disorder. The approach to architecture to which I subscribe is like democracy itself. It includes mess, disorder, tolerance of the unfinished, of conflict. It is in a constant process of change, which implies inconsistencies, adjustments, uneasiness. Though I prefer the mess of democracy to the order and efficiency of totalitarianism, I am not indulgent toward the mess implicit in the slogan "anything goes"—that is why I am against postmodernism. I want a democratic order, a democratic process, even in planning.

How does he suggest putting into effect such democratic a process? In Western democratic countries, government-sponsored building activity, what little remains of it, is hamstrung by ossified bureaucracies that move with glacial speed. By tying everything up with red tape, they also discourage creative initiatives on the part of the private sector. Meanwhile, large speculative developers can usually move quickly, but being motivated mostly by profit, often do irreparable damage to cities and towns. As antidote Zevi recommends perseverance on the part of architects:

An architect should never abdicate. Even if you know ahead of time that you can win only one battle in a hundred, never stop struggling. Besides, who can tell what is the right balance between freedom and order? It changes all the time, but I am inclined to believe that what we think of as the messes of private enterprise, Texan cities for example, are not as terrible in their disorder as American cities with a lot of zoning regulations.

I subscribe to the statement by Wright that culture has a definite role in dispelling the Gospel of Mediocrity. Even if it did not have any influence for a certain period, it would be the duty of the intellectuals to preserve and develop culture for future generations. This is exactly what the monasteries did with the documents of antiquity, when nobody seemed to be interested in them. This is what education is all about.

This may be a highly elitist position, especially for a lifelong Socialist but I do not know of any civilization which has not been promoted by a minority—religious, political, cultural, or what have you. Every democracy has been fostered and defended by a more or less restricted elite. The same is true of art. If you eliminate the avant garde, the minority, you have an immobile situation, which is absurd. One may select not to belong to the intellectual minority—the elite—but it is going to exist anyway. While everybody is ready to recognize the legitimacy of the elite in science, the intellectual populists—who belong to the elite— often like to deny their own actual function in society and mythologize "the people." I am happy and proud to admit that I belong to the elite; I want to promote new ideas and ideals, to enlarge the area of freedom even if I am not invited to do so. I think that the existential crisis of youth today comes from a quest for quality, that is for art.

To Zevi, this entails a responsibility to battle for his beliefs. It does not mean imposing them on others, either in the West or in developing nations, in a dictatorial way, since his overriding aim is to vouchsafe a climate of political freedom and democracy. He shares with the early modernists an unshakable conviction that architecture can be a powerful force in the service of good as well as of evil, and like them still holds that for every problem there is a workable solution. He believes that design issues can be resolved through organic architecture, that it is flexible and inclusive enough to meet the often conflicting demands of economics, zoning, energy, technics and art, and that it can unscramble the seeming conundrums of urban design. He regards urban design and architecture not as separate disciplines, but rather as being continuous and indivisible, one issuing from and reflecting the other. For Zevi, the ultimate sin is to flee from a position of commitment to the future into defeatism and the easy refuge of cynicism, skepticism, solipsism. He explains:

I have no intention of imposing democracy or organic architecture. But I know that unless you *fight* for democracy and for organic architecture, sooner or later you are going to have the real impositions of Fascism and classicism. The difference between me and many American architectural critics is that I lived under Fascism. I experienced it, and I know the difference between even the best Fascism and the worst democracy. To preach the Gospel of Quality against the Gospel of Mediocrity is not to impose, but to offer larger and larger areas of freedom. Promoting an idea is not the same as imposing or dictating it.

Modern architecture is certainly an invention of the West, an excellent one. Because if architecture is really modern, it is open, flexible, anti-dogmatic. It can be modified for the Third World. The so-called imperialism of modern architecture is only a slogan. It is classical architecture that has been imperialistic, the classic modern glass and steel boxes of SOM transferred from Park Avenue to the desert. But here, too, we have to avoid demagoguery. The Third World wants industrialization, and industrialization has its costs and risks, as it has had in the West. I refuse the burden of history; I want the joy of history, which means a forward-looking historical consciousness. I believe that the role of history is to stimulate a more and more courageous stance toward the future, and that is being modern. Certainly there is an imperialistic (that is, anti-democratic) factor in the Western democracies and especially in America. We have to fight it, without throwing the baby out with the tub's dirty water. Think more about the Western world.

Architectural critics should assume their responsibilities first of all in terms of the society in which they live, and only then worry about exporting or not exporting their solutions. It seems to me that even if the Third World cannot accept Western solutions, the West should not therefore give up its own solutions, if they are sound for its society. Really, all these worries for the Third World sound to me evasive, escapist and demagogic. Bad architecture is bad for the West. Let us do good, organic architecture for the West first, then worry about showing the Third World how to use it for themselves.

As for the energy question, you can convert any Wright building to solar energy. Not so the Seagram Building. Organic architecture that is designed for changing individual needs is most apt to take care of energy problems. In fact, it is my hope that energy problems will bring a rediscovery of organic architecture. Wright built no all glass buildings; his structures, some of which burrow in the earth, are designed to complement rather than fight the forces of nature in scientifically conceived ways.

American culture is basically anti-urban, even if American politics has built the greatest metropolises in the world. There is a mythology—and even a bit of mysticism —in Broadacre City. But between that utopia and the one embodied in Wright's Illinois Mile High skyscraper project, you have the entire range of choices for future habitats— diffusion and concentration. It includes the past, in a modern version, and the future. What is wrong with that?

It is my contention that there is no real difference between architecture and urban planning but that if we concentrate our attention on architecture it will make the signs of today's crisis more evident. Let me explain: History tells me that in all ages urban concepts have coincided with architecture capable of giving it a third dimension. One doesn't really know which comes first. In an age of Greek architecture made up of "pure volumes under light" as Le Corbusier used to say, cities will be made up of isolated volumes. If continuity is the aim of town planning, then architecture must offer a continuum, as in the small streets and piazzas of Siena or Venice. In the same way, Medieval architecture cannot be used for a star-like city of the Renaissance, nor Renaissance architecture for a Baroque town based on a continuity totally different from the Medieval one. Therefore, to speak of town planning without checking all the time its coincidence with architecture is useless. One could say, "Tell me the kind of architecture you want and I will give you a city plan," or vice versa. One who believes in such architecture as the "grand ensembles" of Paris will produce a type of city consonant with this kind of architecture. On the other hand, an "architecture of escape" goes with an evasive plan. Pop architecture calls for pop planning, and the other way around.

What does he think, then, of the current tendency of architects to emulate popular or vernacular forms, and their emphasis on symbolism and contextualism?

I love *authentic* vernacular architecture, because it spontaneously embodies the seven invariables of modern architecture. The real vernacular, in its forms, asymmetries, dissonances, anti-perspective volumes, decompositions, structural play and so on, derives from listing elementary human needs, without any a priori or a posteriori synthesis. I hate pseudo-vernacular architecture simply because it starts with a priori romantic forms, and not with contents and functions. And therefore it is quite often symmetrical, consonant, has three-dimensional perspective and doesn't fit into its surroundings.

It is simply impossible to imitate vernacular. You can try to copy the Parthenon, the Pantheon or St. Peter's, but not the minor, prosaic architecture of a Medieval town or of a farm in the countryside. Look at what was done in Florence after the Second World War. The important monuments—including the bridge at Santa Trinita—were restored or even rebuilt, but when they tried to imitate the vernacular architecture of the Lungarni, it was a total failure. It cannot be done, that is all.

In order to achieve again the spontaneity of the vernacular, you have to be a genius or, at least, a great architect. The pseudo-vernacular of mediocre architects is both ridiculous and disgusting. It is fake from many miles' distance.

Symbolism is always compensation for what is not there. That is why it applies so well to metaphysical abstractions. Charles Jencks writes that "The architect must overcode his buildings, using a redundancy of popular signs and metaphors if his work is to communicate as intended and survive the transformation of fast-changing codes." This is nonsense. You need such a "redundancy" of symbols only when you have nothing to say. If you have something to communicate, as all real designers have proved, the authenticity and ambiguity of the message will survive the "transformation of fast-changing codes." It is a great mistake to apply mechanically the assumptions of semiology, as derived from verbal communication, to the domain of non-verbal communication. These assumptions are subject to question today even in verbal language, and to force them into architecture and design is a desperate undertaking: it is not enough to be witty to get away with it.

To contextualism, I say yes and no. In any situation, as bad as it can be, the architect can insert inventive ideas. New buildings should fit into the environment, but on their own merit and terms, thereby changing the environment, making it richer and better. An architect never works in a void, but contextualism is too often used as an alibi for laziness and abdication. The idea that new buildings must harmonize with old can be foolish and lead to compromises, laziness and falsity. The environment is never static, and dissonances are what make its transformations alive and true. I am sure that Wright could have designed a wonderful modern building for the Piazza Navona in Rome; he designed a very appropriate one on the Grand Canal in Venice.

In his *Modern Language of Architecture,* Zevi wrote that modern architects were impelled by a "passion for the new that drove them to excavate buried erudition and bring it back to life. They spoke in terms of today and reread the past with modern eyes." But this is not, he believes, what is impelling history-oriented architects today.

> The search into the past today does not derive from a happy and proud consciousness of modern architecture or from a desire to find modern signs in the past. It derives from frustration, from a lack of faith in what we are doing today. Le Corbusier studied the classical forms much more carefully than do architects today. What study of the past have Aldo Rossi, Leon Krier and company done in comparison to Le Corbusier? Le Corbusier could learn from the past because he saw it with modern eyes, while students today can only copy, or "quote" the past; they don't really know anything about it. They play with the past, instead of really studying it. They lack a sense of real caring about it. Quotations from the past have always been compensatory. The case of the Renaissance is typical. I don't believe that meaningful ways of designing can originate from obsolete quotations. From studying processes, perhaps. The young today are heading toward classicism.

In his most recent book, Zevi opposes classicism in architecture, largely on political and social grounds, claiming that it goes hand in hand with totalitarianism. This notion raises a host of questions. For example: Does he mean to imply that Jefferson's use of neoclassical forms was evidence of totalitarianism? Is the erection of neoclassical buildings in the U.S. throughout its history somehow an indictment of the nation? How does he explain the fact that neoclassicism was the principal mode of architectural expression in all Western countries— democratic and totalitarian— during the 1930s? He speaks of classicism as though it were an immutable concept unsusceptible to change. Has it not been revised over time to meet changing historical exigencies? Does he really believe that architecture can influence social and political behavior? He answers these and some related questions while talking rather generally about the relationship of architecture and politics.

> The effect of architecture on politics and society is not a question of quantity, little or much. The fact is that if democratic institutions are enveloped in monumental, undemocratic boxes, they will appear and work less democratically. Therefore, architecture can work to promote democracy. In fact, during Fascism in Italy, the struggle for modern architecture coincided with the struggle for democracy.

> The modern movement was born to fight Fascism of a sort; its origins with William Morris and the Arts and Crafts movement were definitely anti-totalitarian. Later on, Fascist elements corrupted the modern movement.

> The International Style tried to impose a dictatorship, and this is why I have opposed many aspects of it since the very beginning of my work in history and criticism. I believed, and still believe, in a democratic, organic architecture, represented not only by the genius of Frank Lloyd Wright, but also by some exponents of the Expressionist and neo-Expressionist movements, such as Erich Mendelsohn, Hugo Häring, Hans Scharoun, Rudolph Schindler, Alvar Aalto.

> Unfortunately, there is no sure separation between Fascist and anti-Fascist architecture. The same designer can be democratic in one building and anti-democratic in another. Mies van der Rohe was democratic in the German Pavilion at Barcelona of 1929 and downright authoritarian in the Seagram Building. Aalto was democratic throughout, with one exception, the Enso-Gutzeit Building at Helsinki. Le Corbusier was a bit Fascist in the Greek-like plan for Chandigarh. Brasilia is a dictatorial city, in spite of the fact that Lucio Costa and Oscar Niemeyer always stood against dictatorship. But I do not remember a single anti-democratic building by Frank Lloyd Wright.

> Just try to create a movement for democratic, modern architecture in the Soviet Union today: they will simply put you in jail, or in a Gulag, because they understand what lies behind your efforts. Only in a democratic society like the United States can you joke or play with classicism and postmodernism.

> Only when freedom is at stake do you discover what architecture means for political and social institutions. All American architects should have on their desks books about art written by the Nazi propagandists. Then they would stop playing the skeptic. You ask me whether an architect can be apolitical. My answer is no.

> All classicism is not authoritarian, but all authoritarian architecture is classical, including communist architecture. You are not a Fascist if you copy totalitarian architecture, but it certainly makes you a cynic, which is a step toward authoritarianism. Jefferson humanized classical forms, made them familiar instead of imperial. But I still think he made a mistake. He should have selected not Roman and Renaissance forms but the free forms of the civilian buildings of the Middle Ages. They would have embodied much better the ideas of the American institutions. Once adopted, the classical forms spread throughout America, and not their Jeffersonian version. American institutions in their classical masks remain rather alien on the landscape.

> But look at America, mostly its architecture is everything but classicist. It is marked

by the neo-Gothic, neo-Romanesque, the Chicago School, the landscaping ideas of Olmsted. The classical courthouses with their cupolas, even Washington, D.C., with its neo's are just a facade—all fake, a stage setting. When Paris was built it was not a copy like America. It was the real thing. Washington, by contrast, is openly fake. It says, "I am fake," and quite a few Americans regard it as fake.

Of course classicism changes all the time. After having classicized the Graeco-Roman, it classicized the Gothic, then Romanesque, the Egyptian, and finally the modern—producing the International Style. Classicism has changed also in degree. Palladian classicism is much more human than other forms of classicism. As in music, the rules have many exceptions, the consonances contain many dissonances. Mannerists, like Palladio, offended classicism, but remain linked to it by their very opposition; without classicism, mannerism could not survive. Modernism is different. As Schönberg said, the modern event consists in the discovery that dissonance is emancipated: it no longer depends on its contrary— consonance.

How does Zevi explain the enormous recent popularity and influence, especially on younger designer, of such neo-academicists as Aldo Rossi, Leon Krier and others?

If critics continue saying Rossi's influence is enormous, it will be enormous. Who invented Aldo Rossi? It was the critics. His buildings hardly exist. As for the students, it is so much easier for them to copy academic models than to think. Louis Kahn's impact on them was similar. Same for the New York Five. Wright, on the other hand, cannot be copied, because it is too difficult. I find these fashions laughable; let's not exaggerate their importance, nor underestimate their danger. The Academy is always waiting behind the door.

The young, because of frustration, often turn reactionary. And why are they frustrated? Because they are told by critics that the modern movement is a failure, shown an exhibition on the Beaux-Arts by the Museum of Modern Art and read in the press that we need a classical revival—postmodernism.

Critics are funny people. They sell a perverse product, they create a market for it, and then they blame students for stimulating what they themselves have created. The influence of the architectural press is enormous, especially on students.

Indeed, I feel that criticism is responsible for much of the confusion in architecture today. Critics accept every phenomenon—and its contrary; they don't seem to believe in anything, but just explain all kinds of aesthetic trends and in the most sophisticated way talk about ideologies that they claim back every architectural idiosyncrasy. Every bit of nonsense becomes highly important, because they dress it in a tremendous amount of intellectual virtuosity.

Let me give you a few examples. The New York Five were undoubtedly a significant aspect of contemporary mannerism, but Colin Rowe and Kenneth Frampton gave them such a halo that for a while all architectural students felt it their duty to imitate them. Eclecticism is a reaction to the ridigity of the International Style, but Charles Jencks, with his theory of postmodernism, has encouraged—perhaps contrary to his own intentions—a most chaotic and meaningless anarchy. Arthur Drexler, of The Museum of Modern Art, really felt, in all likelihood, that after four decades of ostracism it was time to reconsider the Beaux-Arts. But his exhibition became an alibi for a crazy Beaux-Arts revival. And when Philip Johnson designed the AT&T Building with Palladian forms—you knew some critic would come along and applaud, or at least explain there was some grandiose philosophical motive behind this grotesque atrocity.

You may object: If architects are confused, then critics become confused. But that assumes that criticism is mere tautology. In my opinion, the critic who is ready to accept and "explain" every passing fashion—no matter how downright silly it is—is not a real critic. Being passive is destructive in criticism as in history. Criticism should have the courage to say "no"; the main task of the critic should be to preserve the basic values that fashion, for commercial reasons, tried to destroy. The modern movement has produced many values worth preserving, and it is up to the critic to see that they are not lost. Instead we find the majority of critics proclaiming that the modern movement is a fiasco, that it is dead, or that architecture itself is dead. Such necrophilic inclinations are laughable, but they influence architectural students, reducing the joy they find in their chosen work, frustrating their better impulses.

Every critic should feel it his duty to state clearly what he believes in and what he stands for—and against. I am quite ready to do this and do not worry if my beliefs are viewed as "oversimplified," "rather naive," or "overstated," as has been the case. I am against totalitarianism in politics, ethics, and of course, architecture. When I say totalitarianism— or Fascism—I do not only mean Mussolini, Hitler and Stalin, but all kinds of absolutes, the absolutes of the Enlightenment, of Marxism. All fixed rules, order, precepts, tendencies toward monumentalism are expressions of power that tend to oppress the individual, to deny what is different, to exclude the exceptions. Therefore, totalitarianism— or Fascism—is a rather complicated disease which infiltrates everywhere and which we have to fight within ourselves every day.

I purposely overstate my point, and in the present epidemic of tautology overstatement may be inelegant. But is is necessary. At least it gives you something to disagree with at a time when most critics neither agree nor disagree, but simply "explain." The critic's responsibility is to keep alive the revolutionary values, the ones George Steiner talks about when he says the critic must ask, "what is the measure of man this work proposes?"

If modern architecture was indeed a revolution, would it not inevitably follow the path of all artistic and political revolutions throughout history, namely revisionism and counterrevolution? Is Zevi not calling for something like Trotsky's "permanent revolution?" Is he not, in fact, something of a Trotsky in the camp of modern architecture?

The critic's responsibility is to contain and limit revisionism and keep alive the revolutionary values. I believe in creativity and if you want to call that permanent revolution, I have no objection. I am the Trotsky of art and architecture? I am honored!

Others see the consistency with which Zevi has defended the modern movement, and especially organic architecture, for over 30 years as a stubborn, perhaps naive, refusal to change with the times. His response is that he would readily rally to the defense of a worthwhile new trend or discovery if there were one. He sees recent trends in architecture and criticism as revealing little that is, in fact, new.

Take the rediscovery of history: For 30 years I have been saying that the main challenge lies not in formulating a history of modern architecture but in framing a modern history of architecture. It is no coincidence that while Jencks's book is titled *The Language of Postmodern Architecture,* mine is called, *The Modern Language of Architecture,* not The Language of Modern Architecture. The fact that history is being rediscovered pleases me, except that most of those who talk about it do not know enough about history, or they would not be defending historicism.

Nor does Zevi regard as novel the realization that the International Style is impersonal, anonymous, cold and so on. He has been criticizing modern architecture, especially the masters, on just such grounds for decades.

I have rarely criticized buildings by lesser architects because every step forward they take needs to be encouraged. But where the masters are concerned, I think, or thought—they are all dead now—that every mistake should be denounced. As a result, I lost the friendship of Mies, Gropius, Aalto and many others, but this is the price one must pay as a critic.

Finally, Zevi sees nothing essentially new in the idea that design should be "impure," ambiguous and contradictory.

Venturi's first book was excellent in its diagnosis, but not in its conclusions. Wright, for one, was never "pure," and it is not necessary to go outside of the modern movement to find "impurity." Contemporary mannerism existed long before Venturi discovered it; look at Terragni and Schindler as two examples. The mistake is to think that an architect can mix architectural idioms at random. If you combine Aalto and Palladio, Gropius and Bernini, Mies and Brunelleschi, the result is not Mannerism but simply pastiche.

He readily admits that in fundamental ways his thinking has not changed during the last decades, regards the fact as worthy of neither praise nor blame, and explains it as an outcome of (1) his experience under Fascism, (2) his Jewishness and (3) his disdain for risk-free conformity:

I grew up under the Fascist regime and fought it from the age of 17. When I decided to become an architect and critic, I had to ask myself: what is intrinsically Fascist in architecture? The Fascist sickness was far older than Mussolini, classical authoritarian vandalism was evident in Rome much earlier. Look at the Victor Emmanuel Monument in the Piazza Venezia. It is an obscenity. So, my answer evolved into a "no" to Greece and old Rome, so exalted by the Fascists; "no" to the Renaissance and its compensatory grandeur; "no" to the Baroque, a Catholic affair; and obviously "no" to the eclecticism of the 19th century.

When I learned from Theodor Adorno that from Voltaire you could jump directly to Hitler, I became opposed to the Enlightenment and all absolutes, dogmas and principles that do not admit diversity.

By exclusion, my answer was "yes" to the civil architecture of the Middle Ages. At that time, when I was 17 or 18, I did not know that Medievalism had been the premise of the modern movement. I selected it because it seemed the only non-style of Italian architectural history, a flexible varied language capable of representing the most diverse communities in the most diverse natural and man-made surroundings. It was, for me, the only valid precedent for a democratic architecture.

The modern movement is not based on a single language; between the expressive systems of Wright and Le Corbusier, for instance, the differences are enormous, the potential for variety endless. All the strains of modern architecture have in common, however, a revolt against classicism; when that is lacking you get such contemporary classical monuments as the Seagram Building.

During the last decade, architectural criticism has been unable to establish a clear separation between the truly modern and the pseudo or classical modern. As a result, critics have ended by attacking modern architecture as a whole. The inevitable results are neo-academicism and postmodern, eclecticism, a return to conventional rules and classicism. And classicism, whether pseudo-modern or stylistic, is conservative and stands for the *status quo* or rather the *status quo ante.* That is why I fought the International Style from the start and why I continue battling today's fashionable trends.

Monument to Victor Emmanuel by Giuseppe Sacconi, Rome, 1885–1911. Its gigantic rhetorical, academic mass still remains an unbearable, offensive intrusion at the city's center.

In principle, the problems of architecture and dangers of its major trends are not very different today from what they were 30 years ago, and so my approach in attacking them has not undergone basic change either.

Because I am Jewish, I belong to the "diverse," which has nothing to do with whether I am an observant Jew, liberal, orthodox or reformed. Since the Holocaust, I consider myself orthodox as a matter of principle. As such, I must oppose the Enlightenment and its neoclassical architecture, because it spurns the diverse. Throughout the millenia, from the neoplatonism of Maimonides to the Existentialism of Martin Buber, Jewish philosophy has absorbed a variety of philosophies without changing its own. Similarly, the modern movement can absorb new elements without betraying itself. I also believe that Einstein, Freud and Schönberg form a triangle on which a modern way of thinking and living, a modern culture of living, can be built. The architecture for this culture is that of Wright, a Biblical figure even if not Jewish.

Finally, I appreciate changes when they are big and risky, costly, expensive in human terms: Schönberg's shift in music from tonality to dodecaphony; Einstein's deviation from restricted theory to the notion of relativity; the dramatic discovery of the unconscious by Freud; Wright's evolution from Prairie houses to Taliesin, from Expressionism to the 1932 House on the Mesa, from Fallingwater to the Johnson Wax Building. Big changes do not deny consistency. Conformist changes, on the other hand, like those now occuring, require no risks, no conviction. They are indulgences of mediocre people, who believe in nothing and care about less. It is so boring to hear the sophisticated explanations of those who change their minds with every season.

APPENDIX

I

Essays and Articles

AN OPINION ON ARCHITECTURE

Zevi wrote An Opinion on Architecture *in 1941 and published it in booklet form while at the Harvard Graduate School of Design. The manifesto's criticism of architectural education and practise has a surprisingly contemporary ring. The tract also makes abundantly clear that Zevi's distaste for compromise and insistence upon upholding principle, on developing an architectural criticism based on historical method, on taking a stand as a critic, as well as his distaste for "mere style" and passing fashion had strong and early roots.*

Cambridge, Massachusetts, 1941

Why Are We Writing This Paper?

To answer such questions as:

1. Is Modern Architecture a matter of personal preference or a matter of historical necessity? Are there basic principles by which it can be defended?

2. We maintain that *Modern Architecture* is the only architecture that has a positive function in contemporary society. Do architects today express this function *in their buildings?*

3. We maintain that *Modern Architecture* must be directed by a social consciousness. Do the men we consider the masters of Modern Architecture, Le Corbusier, Gropius, Wright, etc., exhibit this social consciousness *in their living?*

4. Does the content of our training and the life in our school recognize architecture as a social activity?

We speak of the modern and of the Beaux-Arts approach to architecture. Is there any great difference?

5. Nazi Germany and Fascist Italy banned Modern Architecture accusing it of having an international approach to social problems. How do the modern architects react to

such an accusation? Do they consider it a tribute? In other words, if Modern Architecture is an expression of a new society, how is it fighting Fascism?

We are treating the problem of the position of the architect in modern society from two points of view: the educational and the professional.

The several sections which form this paper, although dealing with aspects of the same conception, do not necessarily have direct continuity.

Our method is confined to an objective analysis of our work and the work that has been done in the past decade.

To those who accuse us of breaking the unity of the modern movement in architecture, we answer: We identify ourselves with the modern movement and its tradition. Self-criticism is not a sign of weakness: on the contrary it shows the vitality of a movement. It means a continuous search for clarity and it is a basis of democratic thought.

Our Generation Is Behind Our Fathers

Our fathers' generation produced Le Corbusier, Gropius, Mendelsohn, Mies van der Rohe, J. J. P. Oud, Wright. They were followed by the younger architects Aalto, Neutra, Breuer, the Swedish, Dutch and Swiss groups. *On the horizon of our generation there are too few good followers.*

But more than individual personalities, the last generation produced a certain common background of ideas for modern architecture all over Europe. *We have not assimilated the principles of the pioneers.*

Poverty of personalities, absence of a standard, confusion in principles are the characteristics of our time. Very often we take modern architecture for granted—its historical necessity is not explained. (By historical necessity of a movement we mean the ability of that movement to meet with clarifying theories the phenomena of social development.) In other words, Modern Architecture faces the danger of becoming a style that we like better than others, but that has no particular reason to be defended.

Criticism of the School

We find the training in our school to be:

a. unclear from a social point of view:

Our school is isolated from outside life. In consequence, out of 120 weeks (three and a half years) of training in design, we devote only seven weeks to housing, the main architectural problem of our time. Another consequence of this isolation is that our school reflects little of the social organization of contemporary society; our life in the school is not fundamentally different from that of any Beaux-Arts school.

We too often have a settled attitude towards modern architecture. As a consequence, the school faces the danger of becoming a workshop of mannerism, or a playhouse of individualistic preference.

b. unclear from an aesthetic point of view:

Cause: The conscious (or unconscious?) drive towards originality. Instead of having a conception of architecture based on common ideas, able to answer the new collective needs of society—to find something new (not something good) has largely become our aim.

Consequence: Very often we are not able to grasp, behind the politeness of the jury report, what is really thought of our work. The impersonal attitude of the teacher, and the mystery of the jury meeting are two keys, as we shall later point out, to this situation of aesthetic confusion.

As far as aesthetic tools are concerned, is there the great difference we have always taken for granted between our system and the Beaux-Arts? Have we substituted for the "art for art's sake" of the "rendered project," the "art for art's sake" of the abstract model?

c. inadequate from an engineering point of view.

d. inadequate from the point of view of construction (materials and methods). We find insufficient relation between construction courses and design courses.

e. insufficient from a professional point of view (knowledge of costs, building manufacture, land values, estimates, specifications, etc.) The mystery in which the professional activities of our teachers are shrouded contributes to ignorance of these problems.

f. inadequate in knowledge of landscaping, regional planning, furniture design.

Private enterprise has practically come to an end in continental Europe and Russia. In the United States centralized authority is developing in housing and in manufacture.

To such facts of modern society, modern architecture answers with the theory of the end of the isolated building, the theory of coordination of regional planning, town planning, and community groups.

At the same time, modern architecture proclaims the end of the architect's exploitation of his own originality; and, more than this, it proclaims the end of architecture as pure abstract creation and as a result of divine inspiration in a garret of Paris or Berlin. This means it proclaims the end of the Beaux-Arts approach to design.

The result of the Beaux-Arts system is the differentiation between plan, structure, and elevation. This is differentiation between the social, the structural, and the aesthetic point of view. As far as the profession is concerned, the result has been, and still is, the division of engineers, practical architects, and architects of facades. As a consequence of this differentiation, we have a self-sufficient plan, on which we can put any elevation we like. This is the problem of individual preference for a style.

The Modern Movement advocates the principle of indissoluble synthesis between plan, construction, and elevation.

We call to the young architects of the United States to hold to that principle of unity which justifies our affirmation of modern architecture as a matter, not of preference, but of historical necessity.

We accuse as betrayers of the Modern Movement anyone who tries, for any reason (good or bad from a moral point of view), to break this principle of unity. We shall hold responsible for breaking this unity, either those who forget the social ideas and the structural clarity of modern architecture, exhibiting only a superficial appearance of modernism, or those who accept the social and structural points of view, but ignore their expression. Such attitudes of compromise are fatal to the growth of the modern movement. They retard a positive formation of public opinion about modern architecture.

Granted there are always sacrifices made in design among problems of orientation, structure, circulation, materials, techniques, etc., the result is not compromise, it is *balance.* Balance is the perfection of the whole. Compromise is a conscious disregard of an achieved clarity.

In Europe Le Corbusier designed the Palace of the League of Nations completely in the spirit of the modern approach to architecture. We hold that, by sacrificing his own interest and renouncing the opportunity to win first prize, he did more for propaganda of modern architecture than an executed building with compromise could have.

We appeal to modern architects on the issue of integrity. We believe that one cannot serve the principles of modern architecture, and, at the same time, serve the irrational preference of those who do not know the problems of architecture.

To hold a passive attitude towards society is not to serve it. Architecture must interpret actively and creatively the needs of society.

We believe that any movement is shaped by a minority; but what we preach is leadership, not an elite. This leadership is formed by those architects who, without compromise, as technicians of coordination and design, best meet the needs of the majority. Their buildings will not be the architect's buildings, but the people's buildings. These architects must be ready with clarity of principles to defend their work. We need propaganda.

The Problem Of Propaganda

The problem of many architects is how to persuade people of the historical necessity of modern architecture. The so-called *realists* say "after all, architecture is a matter not of words, but of buildings." We agree that words can never express or demonstrate any kind of architecture. We repeat that the historical necessity of the modern movement lies in its power to answer with clarifying theories the phenomena of society's development.

Modern architecture was one of the first demonstrations, in an intellectual and . practical field, that a new civilization had arisen. If this civilization were clear in people's minds, then the architecture which expresses it in architectural forms would need no explanation in words. If the characteristics of the industrial age were clear, we would have needed no Gropius to state the relation between design and industry. The fact is that, in intellectual history, synthesis always precedes analysis. The age of poetry always precedes the age of philosophy. Art is not arrived at by analysis, only explained by analysis. Architecture did not wait until everyone had become aware of this new civilization to create its synthesis; but was part of the origin and development of this civilization, and announced it in architectural terms. Gropius, speaking of the relation between design and industry, did not give an architectural explanation, but only tried to point out that modern architecture, consciously recognizing, reflecting, and expressing this characteristic of the new civilization, had historical necessity.

The task of any conscious pioneer is to be at the same time creator and critic. This was the merit of Le Corbusier and Gropius in Europe. On the contrary, the "realists" who, to our effort to clarify the principles of modern architecture, answer "we need buildings, not writings," make no contribution to the consciousness of the modern architect's place in society. In actuality, they are not realistic at all—without ideas we cannot control the passing waves of ephemeral preferences. They limit themselves to a negative attitude which substitutes a daily changing psychology for the historic method which we advocate. Their only philosophy of criticism is that of the "amusing and interesting." They protect themselves under the guise of absolute individualism— an individualism lacking coherence or continuity. They don't propose to the public any other justification for their architecture than that "they like it." It is this lack of moral responsibility which shows the decadence of our generation in relation to the generation of Gropius, Le Corbusier, Wright, etc.

The Future: collaboration

Modern architecture had to face four main problems, products of our age.

1. The problem of new types of buildings, always more and more specialized (hospitals, airdromes, schools, factories and their variations).

2. Daily and striking development in the engineering sciences and in scientific processes of construction.

3. An astonishing increase of new materials and of specialized industrial products.

4. As a result of these points, the problem of organizing new kinds of specialized workers.

The tasks of the modern architect are almost staggering. New social, economic, and structural problems have been added to the problem of correlating them, which is the problem of design. The practice of architecture did not change, as a result of these new tasks. The modern architects that we see about us are continuing the methods and life of the architects of the 19th century. They are still isolated. Each one must be something of an engineer, of a sociologist, of an economist, of a builder—which is like saying a bad engineer, sociologist, economist, builder, and often a bad architect.

When, in order to be an architect, one must be a genius, the profession, as such, is obsolete. Architects in the past had mainly unspecialized problems for their buildings. Now, every building is a matter of thorough knowledge of materials, structure, site, and, above all, of the life of the people who are going to use it; a life which every day becomes more complex.

We see only one solution for the future of architecture as an expressive and social activity: *collective work* among architects, engineers, contractors, and the working class. In other words, collective work among all the branches connected with the building industry.

Our appeal to our colleagues in the architectural schools and to modern architects in the United States, is for this new collaboration, in a democratic sense, in which the architect has the task of pointing out constantly to his specialized collaborators that the whole purpose of this collaboration is directed toward the unity of architecture. We want interrelation between spatial intuition, mathematical intuition, and structural intuition. We want the slogan "Form Follows Function" (Sullivan) finally to become a reality. We want a working class with recognized technical rights; men specialized in their fields, not slaves of the *specifications* of the architect who does not know.

We are asked: "What then, is the architect's special contribution to this collaboration? Is he still necessary?"

Architecture is not the sum of a plan, a structure, and elevations, no matter how good they are. Architecture is *coordination, balance, unity,* and *synthesis* of all the aspects of a building. Specialized men, no matter how many, are insufficient. A coordinator is necessary: therefore, *the architect is necessary.*

This conception of a new collective life, and this vision of the architect as a worker in design, among workers, is not a dream of the future. We do not think that a new society, with basic economic and social changes, has to come into being before such a collective life is possible in architecture. Architects, as social men, should be concerned with politics; but, apart from that, the system of work we propose is possible now.

Architecture conceived on a collective basis will resolve the difficulties of the profession, and, at the same time, the difficulties of our school.

For instance in our school, we hear complaints about an inadequate training in engineering and construction. We hear complaints about the insufficient time given to housing problems. We could say of almost every problem, that we face its conclusion in the charette, before having arrived at a satisfactory meaning of the design.

Some of the criticisms we hear are weak, because they are always concerned with "what" we should learn, not with "how" we should learn. We shall speak later of some proposals for the school, but let us make it clear once again that, although more engineering training would be useful, we will never be engineers. We will never be able to calculate a suspended bridge, and still we say that a suspended bridge is an architectural problem.

We hold that modern architecture is a synthesis of plan, structure, and their expression; and that its complex realization can only be achieved on a *collective* basis.

What Was Done

The collective method of work which we urge is not an abstract proposal that has suddenly occurred to us. It evolves from the very structure of contemporary society, and is a direct solution to problems that modern architecture has faced, though not solved.

The fact of increasing specialization of building types, and increasing difficulty in solving their social and structural requirements, is being met, in many instances, with a new kind of specialized architect (architects of residences, architects of hospitals, schools, factories, office blocks, etc.). We think that a specialized architect loses all reason for existence, because, as we tried to point out, one of the main objects of architecture is to achieve a proper relationship between the building type and the community as a whole.

We already have some examples of good collaboration between architects and engineers:

The Tecton group —from the point of view of coherence of conception.

Albert Kahn and the Rockefeller Center group —from the point of view of work organization.

Other groups in America, Switzerland, Sweden, etc., could be quoted.

We have individual examples of collaboration between architects and engineers: Le Corbusier and Pierre Jeanneret is the very best example of such collaboration. In their designs and buildings, we recognize the best results of the combination of structural and spatial intuitions. The presence of these two kinds of creative minds is apparent, not through a study of working drawings, but through the very organization of the architectural expression. Their buildings are no longer a skin without body, nor a body without skin. At last a living being!

As an example of the collaboration between architects and industry, the ideas and the work of Walter Gropius are of basic importance for any concrete collective movement in the field of building organization. Alvar Aalto, Marcel Breuer, and Richard Néutra have carried out important work along this line.

The Present Picture: the pioneers today

LE CORBUSIER: has done no work for five years. During the architectural reaction in France, he preferred to renounce work rather than compromise.

J.J.P. OUD: has done no work for over five years.

MIES VAN DER ROHE: this great architect is an example of a man with absolute disregard for the conception of the architect as a social entity. He is mainly interested in types of building dependent upon a particular financial and intellectual elite.

ERICH MENDELSOHN: continues his strong tradition always on an individual basis.

ALVAR AALTO: an architect of the younger generation who shows perfect comprehension of the different factors of the modern approach to architecture.

THE ARCHITECTS OF SWEDEN: continue to maintain their high standard of work, which is closely integrated with the social conditions of their country.

FRANK LLOYD WRIGHT: this obscure genius has a deep interest in social problems, but, in their solution, he is overshadowed by his own personality. We regard him, as he probably will be regarded by history, as a genius able to free himself from the conventions of the outside world, but never able to free himself from himself.

WALTER GROPIUS: he is the only architect from Europe, who was able to carry on the tradition of what the *Forum* called the International Style; which probably means the tradition of modern architecture, which, being good architecture, is international.

His work in this country, in partnership with Marcel Breuer, is of basic importance in the present stage of architecture in the United States. For their first building (Gropius' own house, the Ford House in Lincoln, and the Haggerty house in Cohasset) we have, from an analytical point of view, nothing but admiration. Their latest work is of the same high quality, and our only complaint is that it is done on a strictly individual basis, and not in the light of a school or a movement.

The Philosophic, Historic and Social Problem: some points

1. The problem of personality

In speaking of Frank Lloyd Wright, we said that there is a domination of his personality in his solution of social problems. In so doing, we advocated the principle of collective work as the only one which can solve the architectural problem, but, of course, we do not mean to deny the value of personality. Collaboration and collective work does not mean anonymity, but a meeting of personalities in mutual understanding. It means: no more individual separation in momentary preferences, but, on the contrary, liberation from those preferences through a consciousness of an arising civilization.

2. The architect as a social man

The architect is a social man, but he is not a passive agent of society. By this we mean that the architect is concerned with the needs of society (economic, technical, intellectual). He is not called upon to judge those needs, but to answer them. He is concerned with "how," not with the "what." His duty, as technician of coordination, is to determine the expression in design of those needs. In this determination, he must not compromise in the gratification of irrational (false) and traditional (stylistic) desires, no matter who has them.

3. It seems there has been concern over the phrase International Style. If by style architecture is meant, and the fight over terms is between international and national, then we state that modern architecture is international. It springs from scientific and industrial development, which was an international fact. It was the aim of the pioneers to meet the collective development of society, which is international. It arose with the consciousness of new discoveries in the visual field, which was an international phenomenon. In fact, any architecture is regional, and, more than regional, is individual within its own specialized functions. But, in its aims, and its approach, and its spirit, modern architecture is international. It is for these reasons that the struggle for modern architecture is similar to the fight for a new civilization. In this sense, modern architecture is *fighting Fascism.*

4. The meaning of groups

In the common psychological approach we are accustomed to speak of the individual in the abstract, and then to jump to humanity as a whole. In fact, history does not evolve in terms of these abstractions. It evolves in terms of men related to men in religions, in classes and in political creeds.

In architecture, history does not work with the architect as an individual, nor with architects as a whole. It works with associations of men concerned with, and united by, common principles and a common fight. Our call for collective work in modern architecture is on this basis.

5. Social Consciousness: in content and in form

We sometimes hear: "I wouldn't have built the Frank house. I am not concerned with the houses of millionaires," or: "we must have housing projects which will get built, that is all." These statements do not concern the architectural problem as such. They concern the "what" are the needs of society, not "how" we are going to coordinate these needs in architectural design. In other words, the architectural problem, as such, is not the building problem in its quantitative content. Architectural criticism is based on quality; for example, the Frank and the Savoye house have about the same quantitative content, but there is a difference in quality. One is the expression of a client; the other is the expression of a civilization of definite and common principles, springing from (not applied to) a special problem. The Frank house, with its cosiness and individualistic extravagance, has no relation to the Cohasset or Lincoln houses. The Savoye is a special house that fits a conception of a world; there is a perfect continuity between the Poissy house and the Pavillon Suisse of the University of Paris.

6. The genius

We must recognize the existence of the genius as a philosophical necessity. Outside and above collective work and group movements, there has been in the past, and there will be in the future the man of self-sufficiency in analytical and comprehensive work: the man of synthesis and creation. We call for collaboration but a Leonardo could work alone.

7. A warning—Russia

It was not the communist party but the modern architects themselves who killed modern architecture in Russia. We are not concerned here with the mistakes the party made later, on its own. But it should be remembered that in the first phase, foreign architects were given great possibilities.

Concerned only with the affirmation of their own individual characteristics, and often extravagant, ignorant of the possibilities and conditions of building in Russia, uninterested in any kind of new meaning that architecture could have in a new society, modern architects answered the Communist call for a modern architecture with the arrogant attitude of super-men. It was not the people's architecture, but architects' architecture; an architecture of Paris or Berlin at the service of an intellectual elite.

Conclusion

Dean Hudnut:

Our purpose is to change the mild course of modern fashion architecture into a struggle for a revolution in the architectural world. Because of you, Harvard University has one of the best architectural schools in the world. Students from five continents testify to this fact.

We ask you to establish a review with *definite principles of criticism.* The commercial reviews based on a Gallup system of architectural criticism lead nowhere but to the confusion of public opinion. We want a small review of the *Focus* type, of perhaps no more than four issues a year, but with clarity of leadership. This review should be the center of a movement in architecture with the purpose of making the people of the United States aware of modern architecture, which is now known and understood only by a small group. Together with this review, this movement, through conferences and propaganda, should state the principles on which modern design is conceived, and, through a cold criticism of their work, should stimulate architects in the United States.

The main aim of this movement and of this review should be *collaboration:* its possibility, its experiments.

Collaboration is the credo and the faith of architecture today.

John B. Bayley   Frank C. Treseder
Robert Hays Rosenberg   Arthur Koon Hing Cheang
Bruno Zevi   Wm. Joseph
John Taylor Moore Jr.   Dahong Wang
Warren H. Radford   T. J. Willo

The Educational Program

We believe the following problems are faced in many architectural schools, and therefore have an appropriate place in this paper. At Harvard, much has been done to solve these problems. A progressive dean and faculty have gone far, in spite of the restrictions imposed by a large university.

1. The Program

Schools should have a direct tie-up with actual practice. They must collaborate with local and national organizations. Schools should be workshops for experimentation—experimentation that the architect in practice does not ordinarily have the time or the means to accomplish.

Working with local housing commissions, students can assist with the preliminary ground work of inventory and analysis that precedes every housing project. They can give invaluable assistance and, at the same time, gain first hand experience. They can work with local, regional, and national planning boards in the same way.

Schools can collaborate with groups experimenting in prefabrication, standardization, new materials, and building techniques.

To accomplish this, the school must be flexible. The student must be able to follow a problem to its logical end, wherever it will lead him, however long it takes. He therefore should be encouraged to write his own program with the advice of the faculty and he should be free to set his own schedule.

2. Jury Meetings

Jury meetings should be open to the students.

3. Office Conferences

We agree with Professor Gropius that the teacher must be a practicing architect. The problems he faces in actual practice can be presented to the students at conferences each month. He can discuss his relations with his client, with the contractor, with his collaborators; he can discuss office practice, actual plans, specifications, costs and materials. This will give the students an integrated conception of the problems of professional practice.

4. The Profession—the Contractor

There is need of a working agreement between the schools, the practicing architect, and the contractor. If the schools are focal points of research and experimentation, they can offer a real service to the profession. This too will provide a greater opportunity for the schools to place students in architects' offices and with contractors on the building site. This not only opens to the student a practical educational field, but enables the architect to keep in touch with the new members of his profession and will work toward a greater understanding of the collaboration we propose.

5. Furniture Design

Architecture is concerned with the human's relation to his environment. To design a room, one must be able to furnish it. Therefore, the design and construction of household articles and furniture are important. Time should be allocated to this study each year.

6. Visiting Lectures

Outside speakers in related fields are valuable and it is important that the faculty and students hold discussions after these lectures to clarify their own attitudes to the ideas expressed.

7. Landscape, Regional and Town Planning

Landscape students at Harvard are required to take first year architectural design. Architectural students should also be aware of landscape problems. This can best be accomplished through collaborative problems. Thus, the landscape student and the student of architecture will have an understanding of each others' problems and will have experience in collaboration. This should hold not only for the larger problems of town and regional planning but for the small house problem as well.

8. The Students

The students of all schools should discuss their common problems and experiences. This calls for conferences and a publication.

THE ITALIAN
RATIONALISTS

The Rationalists: Theory and Design in the Modern Movement, Dennis Sharp, ed., Architectural Press, London, 1978

The distinguished Italian historian and editor Bruno Zevi investigates in his specially commissioned contribution to this book the confusion over the term Rationalism in modern Italian architecture. He refers in particular to the unpublished "Manifesto of Futurist Architecture" drawn up by Boccioni but suppressed by Marinetti. The article was translated by Giorgio Verrecchia.

As far back as 1933–34 the uncompromisingly anti-fascist critic, Edoardo Persico, lashed out at the compromises and at the muddled thinking of his rationalist friends. He wrote: "The fact is that Italian Rationalism did not arise out of a deep need, but grew either from amateurish stands like those of the fashionable Europeanism of 'Gruppo 7,' or from practical pretexts lacking ethical backbone. And so, the point about their lack of style is certainly justified: their arguing only led to confused aspirations, without contact with real problems, and without any real content. The battle between 'Rationalists' and 'traditionalists' boiled down to an empty and inconsistent dialogue, in which the opposed parties showed the same lack of theoretical preparation and the same inability to conjure up an architecture made up of more than just sterile show." And went on: "Italian Rationalism is necessarily unable to share in the vigor of other European movements, because of its intrinsic lack of faith. And so, the Europeanism of the first Rationalism is pushed, by the cold reality of practical situations, into the 'Roman' and the 'Mediterranean,' right down to the last proclamation of corporate architecture . . . The history of Italian Rationalism is the story of an emotional crisis."

These rather severe judgements were explained by the thinness of the socio-cultural background. With a much later process of industrialization than in the other, more advanced, western countries, the development of 19th century engineering was rather rickety: Alessandro Antonelli, in his astounding domes in Alexandria and Turin, tried, paradoxically, to rival metal constructions with brick and mortar. Giuseppe Mengoni in his magnificent Galleria Vittorio Emmanuele in Milan of 1865, set against the luminous vaults, grey, classical buildings, dressing up the fronts with triumphal arches. There was, besides, no corresponding movement to the English Arts and Crafts.

The neo-medievalism and Art Nouveau found anaemic followers in the eclectic personalities of Raimondo D'Aronco in Udine, Ernesto Basile in Palermo, Giuseppe Sommaruga and Gaetano Moretti in Milan. Italy had missed a century of history and has to pay the consequences of her backwardness and her swaggering nationalism. Persico fully realized that, under fascist rule, it would prove impossible to regain the time lost. The new architecture, without a genuine social ideology, could not help becoming corrupted, by coming to terms with the leaders of the academic monumentalism—Gustavo Giovannoni and Marcello Piacentini.

Italian Rationalism was born, officially, in 1926, when a group of seven young architects, in a series of articles, championed a new architecture. Their statements were vague and cautious: "the new generation announces a revolution in architecture, a revolution set to organize and build—sincerity, order, logic and, above all, a great clarity—these are the real features of the new spirit." The seven had the naive conviction of being able to avoid a frontal conflict. In 1928, they organized the first exhibition of "Rational Architecture" and found MIAR (Movement Italiano per l'Architettura Razionale). The compromise did not last for more than three years. In 1931, the second exhibition, characterized by the "Table of Horrors" displaying the works of fascist academics, caused a big scandal and the demise of MIAR—and inglorious end of trying to marry dictatorship and modern architecture. The defection of three of the original seven left only Luigi Figini, Gino Pollini, Adalberto Libera and Giuseppe Terragni, while many other MIAR members succumbed to Piacentini's offer of Commissions for Rome's University complex. The collapse of MIAR was not the complete end of Rationalism. In fact, Florence Railway Station and the new town of Sabaudia in the Agro Pontino, were built after 1931. But the decade immediately preceding the Second World War was dominated by the Monumentalists. To the Rationalists was left the small peripheral area centered on the Milan Triennale and the magazine *Casabella,* edited by Giuseppe Pagano.

Before we consider the works of this period, we should mention that the basic mistake of the Rationalists was their failure to link up with the Futurist avant garde as their only valid precedent. A still little-known episode should size up for us this failure. In 1975, among the unpublished papers of Umberto Boccioni, was discovered a *Manifesto of Futurist Architecture* dating back to the end of 1913 and the beginning of 1914. Filippo Tommaso Marinetti knew of it, but kept it in the dark so as not to steal the show from the young Antonio Sant'Elia, killed in World War I. Boccioni's text is so illuminating that it deserves at least partial reproduction here:

> The cube, the pyramid and the rectangle, as the general line of building, must be eliminated: they freeze the architectural line. All lines must be used in any point and by any means. This autonomy of the parts of the building will break the uniformity . . . and utility will not be sacrificed to the old and useless symmetry. Like an engine, the spaces of a building should reach peak efficiency. Because of symmetry one gives light and space to rooms that do not need it, at the expense of others that have become

essential to modern living. . . . So, the front of a house can go up and down, in and out, join and divide according to the degree of the needs of the spaces that make it up. It is the outside that must serve the inside, as in painting and sculpture. The outside is always a traditional outside, while the new outside, achieved through the triumph of the inside, will inevitably create the new architectural line. . . . We said that in painting we shall put the observer at the center of the painting, making him the center of the emotion rather than a simple spectator. The urban habitat is changing: we are surrounded by a spiral of architectural forces. Until yesterday, buildings ran along panoramic perspectives, house followed by house, street by street. Today the habitat grows in all directions: from the luminous basements of the big stores, from the multi-level tunnels of the Underground, to the giant rise of the American cloud scrapers. . . . The future is preparing for us an endless vista of architectural skylines.

Though written in a hurry, forgetting a few grammatical rules, the text is surprising for its not only Futurist but also Cubist and Expressionist elements, anticipating the analytical syntax, later devised by De Stijl in 1917, and Wright's concept "from the inside to the outside." During his stay in Paris, Boccioni had realized that (*a*) the Futurist theory of movement was not enough to support an architectural language; (*b*) the Cubist lesson remained of basic importance, in spite of the fact that, without the Futurist dynamism, it was running the risk of getting caught in a tangle of static rules, anti-Beaux-Arts but, at the same time, showing attitudes similar to it; (*c*) Expressionism had the extraordinary ability to shape matter into gushing, explosive forms. As we know, together with Guillaume Apollinaire, Boccioni planned a joint front for the three movements, in his "Manifeste-synthèse" (*Le Figaro,* June 29, 1913), signed by Marinetti, Picasso, Boccioni, Max Jacob, Carrà, Delaunay, Matisse, Braque, Severini, Derain, Archipenko, Balla, Palazzeschi, Papini, Gleizes, Laurencin, Léger, Kandinsky, Stravinsky, Duchamp and many others. The Rationalists did not have access to Boccioni's *Manifesto of Futurist Architecture* because Marinetti had prevented its diffusion. But they could have found inspiration in much of his other writings, particularly those on "plastic dynamism." Instead, they completely ignored the Futurist precedent and its Expressionist component. They took in Le Corbusier and the Bauhaus, and, only minimally, De Stijl. In fact they emphasized the intrinsic dangers of Cubism: many of the Italian Rationalist buildings were symmetrical, box-like with little or no invention in the external and internal spaces; in short, they were leaning towards the classical. In Italy the dogmas of proportion, of regulating lines and assonance still prevailed along with the picturesque of the Mediterranean. Futurism entered the mainstream of European avant garde groups; the Rationalism of "Group 7" and of MIAR remained an often provincial sideshow.

Three figures stand out from the general dimness of Italian Rationalism: Giuseppe Terragni on the creative level; Edoardo Persico as a critic and Giuseppe Pagano, promoter and leader of the campaign moving from architecture to civil rights.

Terragni was born in Como in 1904 and died in 1943, broken by the Russian front. Persico, from Naples, died at 36 in 1936. Pagano, born in Parenzo in 1896, was a determined fascist. When he realized his mistake he joined the resistance, taking command of a partisan brigade. He was taken prisoner and tortured but managed to escape and to start many other partisan initiatives. In the end, he was murdered in

Mauthausen. As usual in Italian history, it is the best few who pay for the dull majority.

More than thirty years after his death Terragni has become the object of intensive studies by, among others, Peter Eisenman, the intellectually more able of the New York "five architects." What is the reason for this interest? The fact that he was, perhaps, the first complete "mannerist" of the Modern Movement.

He started with the project for a Gas Works, shown at the Monza Biennale of 1927, influenced by Russian Constructivism. Then the Novocomum, a compact and blocky building that, with its glass corner cylinders, goes back to a solution attempted by Golosov in the Zujev Club in Moscow. In 1932 he began the construction of the Fascio House, the best-known work of Italian Rationalism. Giving up Constructivism, using a square plan and a structural cage of square moduli in the frontal part, he fitted the roof garden with the perimeter of the volume, like Le Corbusier, employing regulating lines based on the golden section. But, having started with a cubic shape, he did not cover it with surfaces without depth and did not use pilotis and "free facade". The cube was not cut by skin-deep continuous windows, but perforated and sculpted in such a way as to emphasize the concrete pillars and beams. In the facade on the square, the relationship between flat plane and structural frame was not bidimensional; the flat plane carried on round the corner, becomes volume, unbalancing the composition; the other three facades each have their own identity, characterized by the implosion of the plastic cavities. In the interior, in spite of a certain classical solemnity, we find faultless details and mouldings of confident originality. After the war, the Casa del Fascio became a Casa del Popolo fitting perfectly the new democratic shoes.

Terragni's most successful work was the nursery school Antonio Sant'Elia: planning freed from geometrical elementarism, a dominance of the horizontal, expressed functionally by partitions, either clearly defined or veiled by structural netting, linear play in the transparent overhanging projection, a symbiosis between classrooms and open spaces. It is a smiling and happy language that filters with its spontaneous quality, the programmatic strictness of the Casa de Fascio. In the Villa Bianca at Seveso, Terragni explored another tool of the time—the separated slabs of De Stijl and Mies van der Rohe, as is shown by the plan, whose flat planes do not extend beyond the corners so as to avoid becoming volume. As the building is a box-like parallelepiped, the play of the slabs cannot cut through the main construction, but departs from it in the ramp, in the balcony and, above all, in the roof terrace with the flat planes thrown towards the sky with a moving and almost metaphysical lyricism. In his last works, especially in the block of flats Giuliani-Frigerio in Como, Terragni unbalanced the volume with projections, junctions and contrasts between the ribbon windows and the deep cavities, between the casing and the structural cage.

Terragni's mannerism has its roots, first in Russian Constructivism, then in Le Corbusier, Gropius, Mies, deriving from them an original and incisive linguistic code. Starting from a study of the contents, he brought them out by using the asymmetric and dissonant features of the plan, rejecting the vision of a central perspective in order to fulfil its tridimensional dynamism, cut up the building into slabs to avoid the box, and made use of every architectural recipe in his structural game. A good proof of all this is the project for the Palazzo dei Congressi, entered for the World Exhibition that should have taken place in Rome in 1942. What is lacking in his linguistic contribution is a genuine consciousness of space-time, creativity in the field of spatial images and the ability to reintegrate the building into the continuity of land and city. In fact, the Italian Rationalists had not yet grasped the genius of Frank Lloyd Wright.

The strongest group was the one formed in Lombardy, led and inspired by Terragni, Persico and Pagano. Its best-known members were Figini and Pollini with their delightful villa-studio, in the park of Milan Triennale (1933), and then with the Olivetti Factory in Ivrea; the Office of BBPR (Gianluigi Banfi, Lodovico Barbiani di Belgiojoso, Enrico Peressutti and Ernesto Nathan Rogers) with the heliotherapic Colony in Legnano (1936); Cesare Cattaneo from Como, particularly with his villa in Cernobbio (1940); Piero Bottoni, with his town planning that was to materialize, after the war, in the QT8 district in Milan; Ignazio Gardella with the TB clinic in Alessandria, grafting Scandinavian feelings on to the Rationalist severity; Giuseppe Pagano with his Faculty of Physics in Rome (1934) and Bocconi University in Milan (1936 – 42) and also his projects for "Green Milan" (Milano verde) and the "Horizontal City." Edoardo Persico himself tried his hand at building in partnership with Marcello Nizzoli: the Gold Medal Room at the Milan Aeronautics Exhibition (1934) was an endless cavity, uprooted from any kind of context, with the rhythmic dissonance of its black and white (square section) thin bars: an abstract, Kafkian atmosphere explored further by Franco Albini in his museographical productions. As in literature, hermetism proved to be a good weapon to sabotage the vulgar Fascist monumentality.

Turin can boast of an incunabulum: the Fiat-Lingotto Works (1914 –26) by Giacomo Matté Trucco, reproduced by Le Corbusier in *Vers une Architecture.* The spiral ramp for motorcars and the testing track on the roof give a micro-urbanistic character to this structure, emphasized by the internal "road" about 1 km long. The Turin Exhibition of 1928 swings between Art Deco and Futurism, with painters like Prampolini, Depero, Fillia taking part in designing rather inferior pavilions. Pagano and Gino Levi-Montalcini carried on with Rationalism in the Palazzo Gualino, while Luigi Carlo Daneri represented the renewing force in Genoa that was to, eventually, culminate in the grandiose serpentines of Forte Quezzi (1960).

In 1933, in Florence, a group of young Tuscans led by Giovanni Michelucci, won the competition for the new railway station. Apart from the meaning acquired in the furious polemic let loose by the conservatives it remains an ageless piece of work. Opposite the apse of Santa Maria Novella a low volume of pietraforte, with its horizontal plane emphasized by the cantilevers, leans like an arcade towards the town with the glassy waterfall of the main entrance; inside, a sequence of narrow roofings of masterly design heads into the contracted space of the main gallery, underlined by the clever use of light and fittings. Balanced between Rationalism and the organic, the station merges the plastic cavities with the walkways and fits, by its very dissonance, into the urban landscape.

This creative "ease" followed Michelucci in his later work: the Borsa Merci in Pistoia (1950), grafted sober geometry onto the medieval context; the small and moving church of Collina where he attempted to rescue the anonymous language and the continuity between cottage and land in the peasant world; the Cassa di Risparmio in Florence, a sort of gallery or covered street in the town center; the church of the

Autostrada del Sole of 1961 where the Expressionistic vein pushes and modifies the crowded space of structural webs.

The whole of Michelucci's "school"—Italo Gamberini, Leonardo Ricci, Leonardo Savioli, among the rest—was at odds with the "Renaissance" leftovers of purist Rationalism, knowing their high cost in social and poetical terms. The situation in Rome was not so clear cut, heavily mortgaged as it was, to the Mussolinian academics. In 1932 the fascist Revolution Exhibition of Adalberto Libera showed a come-back, in a decorative vein, of the Futurist themes; he followed it with the compromise of the Palazzo dei Congressi for the 1942 exhibition, the villa Malaparte in Capri and, after the war, the horizontal Unité d'habitation in the Tuscolano district of Rome while Mario Ridolfi, whose imaginative flair was already evident in the Tower Restaurants project and in the post office of Piazza Bologna, channelled his craft-like skill on to Rationalist tracks.

The same applied to Giuseppe Vaccaro and Luigi Moretti, known respectively for the Youth Colony at Cesenatico and the Fencing Academy of the Foro Italico in Rome.

The south of Italy had much less to offer—in Naples, Luigi Cosenza working with Bernard Rudofsky; in Palermo, Giuseppe Samonà who, after the war, was to run the Venice school of architecture, introducing radical new trends in teaching.

The figure of Pier Luigi Nervi rises well above the national boundaries. His masterpieces are represented by the hangars of Orbetello (1936), with the extraordinary weightless trellis of the roof vault and, above all, the "cavities" (more shelter than enclosure), and the profiles, the wonderful angular plastic solutions. Reinforced concrete finds here an exceptional artistic synthesis, while, later, his daring structural inventions are often conditioned by a classical sensitivity: a new technique at the service of outdated spatial schemes. Rationalism had no chance to grow on the urban scale, where the fascist regime ruthlessly disembowelled historic centers—among the major crimes were Brescia, Via Roma in Turin, San Babila in Milan, Via della Conciliazione and Piazza Augusto Imperatore in Rome—replacing them with buildings in the rhetorical and classical manner. The towns in the Agro Pontino are either ridiculously monumental, like Littoria (today's Latina), or pseudo-vernacular, like Aprilia. Sabaudia is the only exception, whose competition was won in 1933 by Luigi Piccinato, Gino Cancellotti, Eugenio Montuori and Alfredo Scalpelli. A satellite nucleus in human scale, inspired by the centers of the Ruhr, the Russian Autostroy and Wright's ideas on the crisis of the metropolis, it became the pivot of a vast farming complex on reclaimed land. Piccinato looked back to the medieval urban organization, articulating community life in a series of separate squares, finely adjusting the visual echoes and fitting the open shape into the landscape of Lake Paola. We must not forget the contribution of Adriano Olivetti, prime mover in the setting up of the Val d'Aosta regional plan, conceived together with Figini, Pollini, Bottoni and the BBPR Studio.

The range of figurative tendencies got wider and richer with the years; Alberto Sartoris's axonometrics are typical of the 20s, while Carlo Molino's "ripples," especially in Turin's Riding Club, are characteristic of the 30s and a prelude to the post-war organic developments.

But this evolutive process stopped short in 1938, during the preparations for the

World Exhibition of 1942. Rationalism was completely outlawed. Lining up with Nazi Germany meant a grotesque orgy of false arches and false pillars, with the best—goose pimpling—symbol in the so-called "Square Colosseum," clearly visible in the EUR district of Rome, with its reinforced concrete structure dressed by fat arches of travertine. Faced with these obscenities the whole of the avant garde realized that the problem had moved from architecture to political and civil rights. All hopes of fighting fascism from the inside had gone. Those who believed in modern architecture had to leave the drawing board and join the resistance. The writer Elio Vittorini said that only in revolutions politics coincide with culture, and the Rationalist architects verified the truth of that statement with their lives. As we saw, the price had been very high, and after World War II, Italy was without most of her leaders: Terragni, Persico, Pagano, the critic Raffaello Giolli, the architect Gian Luigi Banfi of the BBPR group and Giorgio Labo, shot by the Germans in Rome.

The Italian Modern Movement started again, but cruelly mutilated. It is not by chance that the first post-war work was the Monument to the Fosse Ardeatine, celebrating the sacrifice of more than three hundred Romans, murdered in a Nazi reprisal: a moving homage to the glory of Rationalism.

WHERE IS MODERN ARCHITECTURE GOING?

GA Document 3, ADA Edita, Tokyo, Winter 1981

When Philip Johnson first proclaimed, around 1962, that "modern architecture is dead," he thought that, free from its puritan consistency, "we could have a lot of fun." It was a masochist illusion. Nobody is having fun, in spite of all attempts to kill modern architecture which stubbornly refuses to die. Piles of books, special issues of magazines and essays on the crisis of the modern movement have appeared during the last two decades. They only prove that this movement is quite alive. When you are dead, you are not in crisis. The academy is never in crisis because it is a corpse filled with absolute truths, eternal and universal principles, dogmas which can be applied in every place and on all occasions.

The Modern Movement has been in trouble since its start. Even considering only the period between the two world wars, it had troubles when: 1) it was unable to keep its two souls together, the Functionalist and the Expressionist; 2) in 1924, the Bauhaus rejected the contribution of Theo van Doesburg, that is the grammar and the syntax of "De Stijl" group; 3) in 1928, at the foundation of C.I.A.M., it had to choose between Le Corbusier and Hugo Häring; 4) in 1930, it did not understand that the Stockholm Exhibition by Erik Gunnar Asplund was an important turning point, from a tragic to a joyful vision; 5) during all this period, it did not consider the genius of Frank Lloyd Wright and the significance of those who were working on the same path, like Alvar Aalto.

For those who know something about history, such crises are not astonishing. The troubles of the Renaissance or the Baroque were more dramatic, even in 20 years' time. Art is always in crisis, and academic or vernacular suicides are the only alternatives to this impasse.

Already in 1945 it was quite clear to some of us that, unless it assimilated the organic trend, Functionalism or Rationalism, as it was called in Europe, was going to fail. The International Style was doomed, although only very few critics had the courage to state it openly. It could not grow, it was becoming a "style" in the mechanical sense of the word. F. L. Wright was there, fifty years, perhaps a century ahead of his time. He condemned the International Style with the same arguments used, in the 70s, by so many critics. With his exceptionally creative spirit, he was offering a way out of the crisis. But nobody listened to him, and nobody caught the pregnancy of his message. As a genius, he was taboo for everyone mediocre. Even now, repeating his attacks on the International Style, critics do not mention him. As happened in the past for personalities of similar stature, Brunelleschi, Michelangelo, Borromini, he was put into the heroes' archive and forgotten.

What did happen afterwards is known. We lived on myths: Le Corbusier, Mies, Kahn. Expressionism was revaluated, but not Erich Mendelsohn and Hans Scharoun. Some of the masters, Mies van der Rohe in particular, betrayed their initial inspiration and "classicized" the modern language. The Seagram Building in New York was not the last modern monument, as Philip Johnson wanted. It was a most traditional monument, as it satisfied all obsolete academic rules: symmetry, rhythm and harmony; hierarchy between main facade, sides and back; privileged view-point, that is perspective; a closed box, pure object; no creative spaces inside, total isolation from its context. Indeed, there is no great difference between Palazzo Farnese and the Seagram. They are both static and classic. Perhaps Palazzo Farnese is a bit more advanced, because of Michelangelo's few interventions. All that took place much before Venturi and Jencks.

To be sure, it was not the Modern Movement that failed, but its very opposite. The thousands of dreary towers, slabs and glassy boxes that are built around the world have nothing to do with the basic principles of the modern language. Anonymous envelopes, they do not express their specific contents and functions. They ignore the "invariable" of dissonance, which is common to all modern art, from painting to music, and are often symmetric. They ignore spatial fluency and they respect the anachronistic canon of proportion. They line up cubic rooms one after the other, and one over the other, using the same method as that of the Renaissance's "orders." It looks as if Einstein, Freud and Schönberg had never lived. These buildings do not seem to belong to the epoch of relativity, space-time, dissonance and psychoanalysis. Very old buildings with contemporary technology, they belong to some age between Bramante and Napoleon.

The assumption that the Modern Movement is responsible for ruining our environment cannot be seriously accepted. The disaster came because too many buildings simply applied modern cosmetics to obsolete organisms. Is was not that the Modern Movement was unable to create a decently articulated physical scenery. It had no chance. Not modern, but pseudo-modern architecture was built, very similar to academic architecture, only more gigantic in scale, and therefore more cancerous. It would not have made any difference if, instead of curtain wall towers and slabs, pseudo-Palladian towers of the AT&T kind, designed by the Johnson/Burgee office, had been built.

Here we come to the society-architecture relationship. There are many economic forces in society which require a type of environment unacceptable to modern planners and architects. Therefore traditional, "modern-classical" architects are asked to build, because they are ready to serve any client and any program. What can we do about it? Though we no longer have the illusion that architects can control the entire environment, we must continue to fight on two levels: preserving the past and enlivening it with dissonant insertions, like the Pompidou Centre in Paris; and building new environments as modern as possible. It is, more or less, what all creative architects have done. I trust that contemporary architects will have the same opportunities that Wright, Le Corbusier, Mendelsohn, Scharoun and Aalto had. The question is: are they catching these opportunities, or are they evading the issues? At least in a certain measure, "where is modern architecture going?" depends on architects and architectural critics. As a critic, I feel that, in the present confusion, our role is quite important. It may be negative if it is simply tautologic that is if it gives ideological superstructures to all idiocies and idiosyncrasies. It may be essential if it fights reaction and totalitarism of any color, fascist or socialist. Critics who "explain" and justify every phenomenon and every fashion should be mistrusted. They don't really believe in anything.

Let us examine the main tendencies prevailing today. They may be reduced to three: Populism, Academy and Mannerism. A fourth one exists underground, but it is doubtful that it will explode in the near future.

Populism. From the pop-architecture to advocacy planning, it is stimulating and enriches our vision. It shows that there is an aesthetic value even in the most derelict slum. The "City Beautiful" is a mythology of the past. We want a significant city, human and intense, which can derive only from the dialectics between the ugly and our actions. Just as Rauschenberg does. Populism has quite solid roots in America, because it is based on the old dream and on the will to free oneself from European styles and all that they represent in political and civic terms. But actually it is the dream of what Roland Barthes called "the Zero Degree of Writing." No dogmas, no preconceived forms, no proportions, no Vitruvius and Palladio. No grammar and no syntax, but only words with specific meaning, without verbs and adjectives, without hierarchic orders and impositions. This dream was always defeated, but always boils up again. In any case, the populist research is intelligent and fertile, from Rudofsky's "architecture without architects" to Venturi's signs and symbols. It discovers new aspects of reality. It reminds architects of the "Zero Degree" of building, of the permanent necessity of destructuring the accumulated conventions.

Since 1966 *Complexity and Contradiction* by Robert Venturi has provoked both admiration and suspicion. It has offered a very acute criticism of the International Style and an excellent understanding of Mannerism and of the American vernaculars. But, like the following books by Venturi, it was interpreted as a reaction against the Modern Movement as a whole instead of an attempt to enrich and integrate its language. If the diagnosis was almost perfect, the therapy suggested by Venturi's buildings, and particularly by those of his followers, could not persuade. A vernacular revival may be a fascinating hypothesis, but it can't work, because vernaculars cannot be imitated artificially. All great architects, including Wright, found an inspiration in the vernacular, because there they found buildings free from academic conventions, the "Zero Degree." Dialects can inject some fresh blood into a language, but they cannot substitute it. All Venturi's work could be instrumental in the development of the modern language; unfortunately, it was presented as an alternative to it.

Neo-Neoclassic or *Neo-Rationalism.* The rétro tendency can be found in every period of architectural history. Generally, it prevailed after intense creative activity, after Brunelleschi, Michelangelo, Palladio, Borromini. No wonder that it emerged once again after Wright and Le Corbusier, when architects felt somewhat like orphans. No matter how refined and sophisticated its theorization may be, the academy, with its Beaux-Arts revivals, is always fascist. One can be surprised by the fact that many Marxist architects are following this tendency, but it should be remembered that, even during the French revolution, the Greek-Roman myth, that of Athens and Sparta, was exalted by people who were to the left of Robespierre. In Italy, during Mussolini's dictatorship, the Modern Movement stood for anti-fascism against the regime's classical monumentalism. Now, on the contrary, the most reactionary architects agree with many leftists and extreme leftists. Paradoxically, the "death of architecture" is proclaimed, and classicism, the architecture of death, rises again. It stands for abdication, lack of creative power, authoritarian formalism, suicide. The buildings designed by its advocates look like cemeteries or prisons or mental asylums.

The success of this Neo-Neoclassic tendency among architectural students can be easily explained. Beaux-Arts styles can be taught and learned almost mechanically. Their codes, stiff and repetitive, satisfy lazy people. They embody the principle of death against that of pleasure, and they may correspond to the pessimism of part of the youth. Moreover, a Beaux-Arts revival sounds cultured, in so far as it always speaks about history. In fact, it is totally anti-historic. It bases its ideology not on the real monuments of Greece and Rome— quite anticlassical, indeed—but on the shamefully abstract reductions of them operated by the Ecole des Beaux-Arts. It is, by now, quite evident that the Greek language has nothing to do with the Greek canons of the Beaux-Arts which made generations of architectural students hate the Hellenic world. The same with ancient Rome. The same with Palladio, and so on. The Neoclassic or Neo-Rationalist tendency of today should be rejected on two grounds: it is Fascist and its historicism is false. Historical knowledge is essential for every architect. But, if it is true knowledge, it never leads to historicism.

The vernacular, at least in its intentions, has therefore something to contribute to the development of contemporary architectural language; its only danger lies in producing pseudo-vernacular buildings. The academic trend, instead, is destructive and self-destructive.

Modern Mannerism. Interpreting this term in the most positive sense, as it should be since so much literature has been dedicated to it, we could say that all valuable buildings erected in the last 30 years are somehow Mannerist. Which sounds quite logical. In the 16th century, Mannerism was the attempt to combine the languages of Michelangelo, Raphael and Leonardo. Now, it is the attempt to combine and strengthen the multiform heritage of Wright, Gropius, Le Corbusier, Mies, Mendelsohn, Aalto, and perhaps also that of the Arts and Crafts, of Art Nouveau and of 19th century engineering. This heritage is comprised of seven factors; a) the Zero Degree, that is the listing of contents and functions, as derived from the experience of the Arts and Crafts; b) asymmetry and dissonance, as derived from Art Nouveau and the Bauhaus; c) anti-perspective three-dimensionality, derived from Expressionism; d) four-dimensional destructuring of the box, derived from Cubism and De Stijl; e) structural inventivity inherent to the architectural process, derived from 19th century engineering; f) space in time, dynamic creativity of the cavities where people live, derived from Wright; g) continuity between building and city, city and landscape, derived from modern planning. Seven factors that can motivate hundreds, thousands of different combinations, an extraordinary patrimony which can nourish five or ten generations. Mannerism includes Neo-Expressionism, Brutalism, contextualism, metabolism, de-architecturization in fact every active tendency of American, European and Japanese architecture. It includes, or may, pop-architecture, "do-it-yourself," and also conceptual architecture. With some risk, it may include vernacular. However, it excludes neo-academic, classicist, fascist trends. Mannerism loves "complexity and contradiction," as Venturi well understood. It cannot stand the vulgar or refined simplification of a Beaux-Arts revival.

Let's be clear about the Mannerist operation. It combines and contaminates the languages of the masters, and it may add some dialect to them, some "architecture without architects." No more than that. When it pretends to combine Palladio and Raymond Hood, the Parthenon and Neutra, Borromini and the Islamic cupolas, it is not Mannerism. It is merely eclecticism of the worst kind. Grotesque sometimes, stupid as a rule.

Mannerism has two faces: the conceptual and the dynamic, the introvert and the extrovert. The New York Five represent the first face, and they deserve great respect. Theirs is a fine, deep excavation into the patrimony of the Modern Movement, a "speech over the speech" of the masters, which is valuable intellectually, didactically and creatively. There are, however, some legitimate questions about their work: why is Wright so little considered? Why is their attention concentrated on the "first Mannerists," like Terragni and Schindler, more than on the masters? Why exclude "space in time" and "continuity?" Although we never got an answer to these questions, I continue to hope that the Five and their followers will enlarge the field of their research.

The dynamic face of Mannerism includes all others. Rudolph and Stirling (forgetting his present academic bent), the Dutch architects, from van Eyck to Eitelbergher, the French, from Claude Parent to Jean Renaudie, the Italians, from Michelucci to De Carlo, the Japanese, from Tange to Kurokawa. Mannerism can be extremely creative: Safdie's Habitat '67 in Montreal, Johansen's Mummers Theatre in Oklahoma City, Kikutake's Aquapolis in Okinawa, Passarelli's polyfunctional building in Rome, just to mention a few examples, are Mannerist in a sense that overcomes the limitations of the historical term. Which is natural. What was wrong with Mannerism, four centuries ago, was the fact that it had to recognize the authority of Classicism, in order to offend and destroy it. Modern Mannerism does not need to rebuild its enemy to demolish it every day. As Schönberg said, dissonance is no more an exciting dressing of consonance. It has created a new, independent language.

Besides populism, academy and Mannerism, there is a potential, almost clandestine trend: the *organic.* Signs of it are evident here and there: from Lawrence Halprin's landscaping to John Lautner's houses. The organic is also present in the "Charter of the Machu Picchu" formulated, in December 1977, to integrate the Charter of Athens of 1933.

Consistency and morality are out of fashion today. I am sorry: my first book, in 1944, entitled *Towards an Organic Architecture,* was anti-Giedion and I still believe in it. All my other books, from *Architecture as Space* to *The Modern Language of Architecture,* insist on this optimistic aspiration, as I am still confident that, one day or another, architects will have the courage to discover Frank Lloyd Wright. True: an inorganic society does not call for organic architecture. But architecture is not the passive mirror of society, it can be a prophesy and announce a change. I am sorry: I cannot be postmodern, that is, academic or vernacular. I am post-postmodern.

To conclude. I was rather impressed by the declarations of Reyner Banham, as reported by Neil Jackson in *Building Design,* May 30, 1980. Leaving Buffalo for Santa Cruz, California, he decided to leave the architectural schools, because "they don't ever use their minds." He added that "the mood of the profession, particularly as reflected in the schools at the moment, is one of intellectual retrenchment, which is the polite phrase for total loss of nerve . . . is cautious if not actually cowardly." Commenting on the neo-academic tendency, he said that "the McKim Mead and White revival . . . is to a large extent a desperate attempt to make up for the fact that studio conversation has become desperately boring." Because "a lot of the pop stuff is not a teachable subject," one is driven back to "the old standbys . . . Generally speaking, when in doubt the profession tends to back up into classicism anyhow; that's where it comes from." Even the teaching of architectural history is losing its meaning, as it is not reflected in design courses.

I wonder why these explosive declarations did not provoke a scandal. A few months before, when I left the Rome School of Architecture for the same reasons, the polemics went on for two weeks in the first pages of newspapers and on TV. What Banham implies is that postmodern architecture is not transmittable. But modern language can be codified, because it has precise principles and methods. Of course, it does not tell the student what to do, like Beaux-Arts teaching, it does not preach styles, not even the modern style; its principles are open, flexible, experimental, pragmatic; destroying every convention, they always go back to the Zero Degree. They are viewed "as a fail-safe check list rather than a binding code," as William Moser wrote in *Dichotomy,* Fall, 1979. But they are supported, on one side, by all creative architecture of the past (always anti-classical, including Brunelleschi, Michelangelo and Palladio) and, on the other, by the tremendous mistakes of those who, in the last 30 years, betrayed the modern language.

These are many signs that architects, architectural critics and the public are getting tired of academism and postmodern escapism. Killing modern architecture is no fun anymore, if it ever was. If that is so, the end of cynicism and utopia will open up some new itineraries.

APPENDIX

II

Speeches

TOWN PLANNING AS AN INSTRUMENT OF AMERICAN FOREIGN POLICY

Paper presented at the Annual Meeting of the American Institute of Planners, February 9, 1946, Cleveland, Ohio. Journal of the American Institute of Planners, Volume XII, Jan. Feb. March, Number 1, 1946

Today I hope it will be agreeable to all of you that I do not recite the story of hundreds of destroyed European towns, of millions of homeless people, of material and spiritual starvation. The story is well-known by now, and every time we put it into words, we tend to slip into a description of frustration which is not deserved by the people of Europe, because there are still great energies there. And frustration is not to be emphasized here before Americans, and especially American townplanners, who have the opportunity, if they wish it, to help Europe. My theme therefore will be that townplanning is an instrument of American foreign policy. Everything I say will be a function of this idea.

Let us take the case of Italy. American planes, guns, tanks and armies have bombed, burst open, knocked down, destroyed hundreds of Italian cities and villages. We said we were bringing democracy. We assaulted these cities, then said: "Look, we have overthrown Fascism; we have brought freedom. Good-by." Imagine yourself to be an Italian peasant, or for that matter, a member of the country's intelligentsia. What would have been your own reaction to this kind of statement?

At this point someone will object: "Italy was an enemy country which declared war on us. We had to do what we did." But is there not an easy answer to this objection? The basic conditions of European countries are very similar, whether enemies, co-belligerents, or allies. Then, we did not fight only to destroy. Democrats of all nationalities fought for a constructive idea, for the upbuilding of democratic world community, and along with it, the only kind of physical scene in which such a world can arise and grow—a scene created by imaginative, healthy, intelligent planning of regions and towns all over the world.

What would have happened if someone in Washington had advanced this idea: As soon as our armies have liberated a town, let us see that there is a townplanner attached to the military government or to our Embassy, who will summon the local townplanners, encourage them to go to work immediately on the reconstruction of the city; a townplanner who will help the local people and will give them the information everybody is so eagerly asking for in Europe on American experience, American programs of townplanning, the facts about public housing, what you have learned about prefabrication, and so on.

Visualize the reaction of an Italian to this approach: "Okay," he might say, "the Americans have knocked down my house and my town; they had to do that. But now they are offering to help." I believe that the amount of goodwill created by such a relatively inexpensive action as this would have been very great.

Housing and city planning are the Number Two problem in every country of Europe. To help with the very first problem—food—we are able of course to send supplies. As for the second, we should have been in a position to offer and to send planners. We have been spending many millions of dollars in propaganda. As a result of my war experience, I am convinced that the planning contribution would have been the very best possible propaganda for the United States. By recruiting and advancing the necessary townplanning experts and housing missions we would have established relations and a working basis with the political leaders, the intellectual and academic groups, the technicians, the officials of the country whose bent is constructive—the good and decent common people. I submit that we lost, for lack of imagination, one great opportunity to strengthen America's authority and influence abroad.

But let us not regret the past. Townplanning has a function and an important role in our foreign policy now.

I have been working during the past two years in Italy as a member of the Information Service of the United States Embassy in Rome. Our purpose was, speaking in the vernacular, to "sell" America abroad; to show how happily and how beautifully one can live in a democracy. Each one of us there was tremendously excited about his job. Very often, in fact, so excited that he oversold America.

On various occasions I was asked to describe some of the American townplanning or to show and discuss examples of some of the most successful war-housing projects, and I would try to project over to my audience America at its best.

I remember an evening a few months ago in Rome. I was speaking of city-planning and regional planning here. I spoke, I suppose, a little too emphatically about it. At the end a little fellow in the audience got up and said very coldly: "I have been there." He had been in America, and he knew that here there are still far too many slums and far too many decayed and obsolete cities.

The tone of my critic's voice saying "I have been there" meant: "It may be that here in Europe we do not have very good townplanning. But we are poor. We have had continuous wars and much destruction; unlike America we have not 'got the goods'! But look at you in America—the richest and the most powerful nation in the world. Your land is the land of opportunity, but look how you live. The physical scene of your democracy is one of obsolescence, of decayed towns and slums; you have slums of the rich and slums of the poor. You do have modern plumbing, refrigerators, atomic bombs, and coca-cola, but don't try to sell us townplanning and housing. For your towns and your cities there is only one word: squalor."

I wish some of you had been in my spot to answer that fellow. I found myself embarrassed. I got up and said that within limits and allowing for many exceptions, I agreed with him, but that what was lacking in American townplanning was to be explained by the fact that this nation had to grow up very quickly; the expansionist tempo of American growth did not always permit of stable, settled and well-planned communities.

An American, I said, could well afford to live in a slum because he reasoned, if he were any good, next year he would make more money and go and live in a better house. Or he could move to a better town, or even move to a new region— one presumably somewhere to the west. With the exception of some few towns, all America, I said, had been on the move all the time. Because of that the country had not in the past felt very much the need and the value of good townplanning.

Now that the frontier has been reached, now that America is a stabilized nation, I said, a new culture will follow hard upon the dynamism of the past, and a new vision of life will follow and replace the emphasis upon mechanical multiplication of the means for living. I concluded that, within this new culture, the time for American townplanning was now.

That was more or less my answer to this unpleasant fellow's "I have been there." Perhaps you would have given a better one. But the point of the story is to reiterate once more that townplanning, being one of the clearest manifestations of a social culture, is instrumental—is the best instrument, in point of fact—in our task of projecting abroad our democratic way of life.

When one works on a townplan one has so many problems to deal with, the problem of pressure groups, of technics, of finance, that one is quite apt to forget sometimes the profound cultural basis and significance of this work. I can testify out of my own experience that in Europe to show a good regional or townplan of the United States is more important than tons of propaganda. Your planning therefore is important not only to the welfare of your community. It is important for the world around. It is fundamental as a proper medium to carry abroad the central idea of American culture.

Now that the United States has acknowledged itself to be one of many nations; now that the United States has realized its international responsibilities; now that we have created a political United Nations Organization, we must build up and must assume our genuine responsibilities in an international organization of townplanning. The American Institute of Planners, I am confident, will feel the necessity of living up to the new challenge that this country is facing. You can help very much, much more than some of you may realize, in this international function of America. This is not dreaming.

I have a minimum practical suggestion to make: if some of you agree with this idea of international cooperation, perhaps, during this convention, a motion will be made to the effect that your *Journal of the Institute of Planners* be sent to the Information Service libraries of our Embassies all over the world. This may seem a small but is a significant contribution, sending about 60 copies of your magazine abroad. It seems to me that it would be an excellent starting point. Your work will be made more useful, not only in the United States, but for every country.

I come now to the second aspect of what may be called, somewhat paradoxically, a foreign policy for American townplanning. I have dealt with what we can give, I want to deal now briefly with what we can get.

Believe it or not, while we are proud of American achievements, we are not the only well-civilized country in the world. There are many other countries that are doing excellent planning work. I have lived in England for one year during the war and have studied the plans for post-war reconstruction. Also, I have been in Italy and worked directly on quite a few town plans.

In France, in England, in Finland, in Sweden and many other countries, townplanners are at work. I wonder if American townplanners are acquainted with the magnificent work that the Finnish Institute of Architects is doing in the reconstruction of the cities of Finland. No magazine in this country, so far as I know, has illustrated the Finnish work. Perhaps Finland is too far, far, away. But take the example of the plan for the reconstruction of London—the Abercrombie and Forshaw plan. How many American townplanners have deeply studied this plan, surely a classic of contemporary townplanning approach? Whatever that number, it should be still larger, as there is much for all planners in this splendid work.

It is my contention that an international consciousness in townplanning and an active movement to serve it is a two-way proposition. America can help Europe, Europe can help America.

I have the impression that the post-war years in Europe will be very important in the history of modern townplanning. Under the stress of postwar reconstruction townplanners there will have often the possibility of experimenting on a large scale, of tackling on a national scale the social problems integral with townplanning; for example the problem of land, the control of population densities, the distribution of industry and so on. Out of sheer necessity Europe will have to focus attention upon the basic problems of modern living and must solve them comprehensively.

We know that our actual way of living always lags somewhat behind our progressive culture and ideals, because habits, traditions and vested interests are often opposed to the realization of new patterns. In the United States, fortunately, there is no war destruction that compels political leaders to get down to hard, urgent work on the basic problems of national, regional, and urban development. Oddly, lacking the spur of the damages of war and a striking need of far-flung reconstruction, American townplanners sometimes find greater psychological obstacles here than do their colleagues in Europe.

I have the feeling that a more widespread knowledge of what is faced in Europe, of what is being done there today, would help American city planners create a townplanning consciousness in the American people. I think hopefully therefore of better information services on townplanning abroad, not only as generally useful in a cultural sense, but as a powerful medium to be used in mobilizing American public opinion. I do not need to say that this may be an invaluable vehicle regardless of whether the ideas that you want to advance and strengthen in the States are similar to or are different from the ones that underlie the various facets of European reconstruction.

To be specific I would like to give you a few examples that have occurred to me while working on the townplanning reconstruction of Italy. Modern townplanners there are struggling to get a Ministry of Town Planning established. England has already created such a Ministry and so has France. In every country of Europe, the need is felt to have a Government department to coordinate town and regional planning activities. It is an obsolete concept to have numerous different departments to take care of location of industry, distribution of schools, planning of airports or railroads or hospitals. The very function of townplanning is harmonizing in an organic balance all the different and sometimes contradictory elements of the townplanning problem. The task of townplanning is integration of social, economic, psychological or spiritual problems. This is an integration never achieved by piecemeal unilateral approaches. Different men with broader vision of the need are required today, and a new Government department to serve new goals.

When I was at work in the townplanning bureau of the Italian Government I found that many good town plans had been blocked by the Ministry of Fine Arts. When a town plan was submitted to the Ministry of Fine Arts by a local authority, the archeologists in the Ministry would scarcely look at the town plan. They would take the report that went with it and look for any monuments whose destruction or alteration was proposed. To save one monument they would veto a whole townplan. The same sort of thing was apt to happen in the Ministry of Industry, in the Ministry of Communications, in the Ministry of Health, in the Treasury Department. Everybody defended his own little realm and disregarded the broad community needs of the situation. Our point was that townplanning was not the sum of all unilateral interests but the integration of them. The Ministry of Fine Arts should most definitely be interested in townplanning, not however only to defend, after the plan had been produced, a single monument, but so as to deal effectively from the beginning with the problems of townplanning in a monumental country. The same thing was true of the other ministries. The proposal was therefore advanced that a central committee of townplanning be created, that every ministry send as its representative a city planner, a man who knew the specific problems of the department in which he was working, but one who would have enough vision and enough understanding to be able to sacrifice, when necessary and justified, the specific technical interest of his department for the greater collective interest of the community as a whole.

I wonder if this Italian experience is valid in the United States. Do we not need a better coordination nationally, regionally, and locally of townplanning activities here? If so, the organizational examples of European practice may in time prove to be a useful instrument helpful in advancing the movement here.

There is still another example. The problem of prefabrication has been discussed at length in Italy. Everybody there has felt that the prefabricated building may constitute a real danger to the age-old inheritance of Italy. "We cannot do that"—an Italian friend of mind would say, "Italy is all ancient, historical, monumental. Every town has its own specific traditions and special character that we must value and protect against destruction. We cannot put up even ten prefabricated houses in a war-destroyed area of Florence. We cannot even build a prefabricated housing project in the outskirts of Florence. It can be done in America, but because of cultural and artistic heritage of Italian towns, we cannot attempt it here."

A week ago, in New York, I was discussing with Aalto, the Finnish architect, this type of problem. He said that Finland is producing a lot of prefabricated houses, but selling them to Sweden, to England and to Russia. He commented that they are being used sparingly in his country until the industrial production of houses can be made to satisfy a biological and psychological demand of the people for flexible design.

Do we not have that same problem in America? Is it not a problem that American planners face today? Without an efficiently established department and an appropriate administration of town and regional planning programs and standards, will not a million or more prefabricated houses proceed a distance on the road to make for this nation a large new contingent of slums? On a different scale and for different reasons the problem is the same here as in Europe. We are all for the industrialization of the building activity, but in so far as it does not kill or damage the living pattern and the specific qualities of our communities.

I would like to mention one more example: the problem of community buildings. You remember the long discussions on prewar housing in this country, whether they should have community buildings or not. The progressive architects and townplanners then fought to get across the elementary idea that a mere aggregation of houses does not form a community. You need schools, civic centers, recreational grounds, and many other things. In Europe today, where millions of people are literally without a roof over their heads, the people are asking that reconstruction be done in an organic way, that schools, libraries, community buildings be designed and built along with housing. Even for desperate people life means something more than biological survival. It means genuine community life and cultural development.

In conclusion, the point I have tried to stress is very simple. American townplanning faces today an international responsibility. Its international responsibility is closely bound up with its domestic responsibility. The work of American townplanners is essential to a twentieth century American foreign policy, in creating good will and in projecting abroad our system of government and our way of life.

I submit to you the proposition that American city planners should employ all the facilities of the United States State Department, specifically the cultural and housing attachés in our embassies, to send and circulate their publications, their designs, their ideas, abroad. Finally, I submit that every support should be given to the creation of a townplanning department in the United Nations Organization, a department which would coordinate and distribute all over the world information about the planning activities in every country.

A MESSAGE TO THE INTERNATIONAL CONGRESS OF MODERN ARCHITECTURE

Zevi's 1948 address to CIAM (International Congress of Modern Architecture) urged a change in the orientation of that organization away from the dominant influence of its Secretary General, Sigfried Giedion, who equated modern architecture with the rationalism of Le Corbusier and Gropius. By refuting Giedion's principal theses, as elaborated in Space, Time and Architecture, *Zevi attempted to show that Wright, Aalto and Asplund's organic approaches to design were at least as important to modern architecture as the rationalism of Le Corbusier and the Bauhaus.*

Published in *Metron* 31–32, 1949

We are most happy that the work of the CIAM has begun again, but we must not hide from ourselves the fact that modern architecture has lost a major battle in this post-war period partly because the world's most active and intelligent architects have not succeeded in organizing a practical and productive body within the framework of international organs. The city-planning and building center of UNESCO does not have the power and the prestige it could have had, partly for reasons for which we are not responsible, but also because we architects of today have not yet learned how to cooperate together on the political scene. We limit ourselves to working individually and to coming together in congresses which are profitable culturally but of little use for broad social achievements. And as far as the problem of representation in the CIAM is concerned, the mass of the architects from the United States are still absent.

This must not be considered as a criticism of the CIAM. It was created for other purposes and perhaps cannot change them. But the organizational problem has become so urgent in this post-war period and remains an unsolved one with which we must come to grips here in this congress or elsewhere.

The recognition of the practical limits of the CIAM bears with it the necessity of deepening its cultural substance. It is here that we come to the heart of the matter. Can these congresses organized by the CIAM accomplish today achievements of importance equal to those brought about by the first congresses? If these congresses can not have a deep politico-social influence, can they at least attain a worthy cultural level?

These questions may seem abstract. But history teaches that every organization, every movement, is bound to its origins and can evolve out of them only with great difficulty. Every movement has its leading class, its mentality, its tactics. Theoretically all can be changed—and in this case it would not be desirable—in the historical reality not except if one wants it very deeply. The CIAM, in the general feeling of modern architects, is bound to the architectural mentality of Le Corbusier, Walter Gropius, and generally with that period known as the rationalistic one. It is bound to the historical perspectives and interpretations of Sigfried Giedion. These three personalities are most important and determinant figures today, so much so that there is no foreseeable lessening of their influence, which perhaps would facilitate the development of a more appropriate and comprehensive culture. The other branch of modern architecture, that which is no longer rationalistic, the movement which is called organic, or of human architecture, or of the New Empiricism, doesn't have adequate representation in the CIAM and its cultural position has been defended by architects who entered the CIAM as proponents of the rationalist school ten years ago and have since undergone an evolution. An entire generation of young architects who have contributed to the advancement of the modern movement, and all the adherents of the Wright school, have been more or less excluded. Why? The Congress of Bergamo must face this problem. There is no modern architect living who does not recognize the great versatile ability of Le Corbusier and his followers, but many feel that his approach is only one of the aspects in the present order of things. All, and especially this writer who had the good fortune to have been his pupil at Harvard University, recognize in Gropius the most openly human and elastic personality of the modern movement; but Gropius the man and master is one thing, the Bauhaus another. Although a magnificent and fundamental experience is modern history, the Bauhaus has value now largely as an experience of the past. As for the General Secretary of the CIAM, Dr. Giedion, it is enough to say that all of us have always in mind his *Space, Time and Architecture* and that we find in it continually elements and data useful to our research. But to recognize its superior scientific qualities does not mean that we agree with its historical theses. *Space, Time and Architecture* is a splendid book, but a misleading one.

For the purposes of this article it is proper to concentrate our attention for a while on this book. The writings of Le Corbusier and Gropius are autobiographical documents, most useful for revealing the personal viewpoints of the authors on architecture but not to be confounded with objective historical interpretations. Giedion's book is different, and the historical vision of him who is the guiding light of the CIAM has an importance in any cultural appraisal of the whole organization. While it is evident that the members of the CIAM need not all swear by Giedion's theses, it is nonetheless useful to dwell a while on his book because, in analyzing it, we can derive illuminating considerations on the pre-rationalist, functionalist and post-rationalist approach.

Architecture and architectonic culture are one and the same thing. If architecture is not infused with a rich, living and stimulating critical sense, it degenerates into mere mannerism. Every artistic age has viewed and interpreted history in the measure with which it could mirror its own creative art in it. Thus a discussion of Giedion's interpretations can lead to determine where contemporary architecture stands at the moment in regard to the first age of modern architecture, to the functionalist movement, and to that present movement called here organic. If some of the criticism the writer shall make seem sharp, the very fact of concentrating our discussion on Giedion's book will suffice to demonstrate its importance.

The Need for a Historical Revision

1. The fundamental objection to be made about Giedion's book centers about its classicistic or biological conception of the history of art, according to which every historical period has three phases, these being (a) the immature infancy, (b) the splendid and active maturity, (c) the decadence. It is known that the classicistic fallacy can be found in many phases of architectural historiography and is indicated by its identification of a model work, a perfection, a maximum stylistic level with a given architectural period. Thus the 5th century Hellenic serves to identify the perfection of the Greek historical period, the French cathedrals of the 13th and 14th centuries that of the Gothic period in France, or Bramante that of the Italian Renaissance. Further, when the fallacy of the progress of arts is substituted for the classicistic one, we find a Vasari who conceived the whole history of architecture as culminating in a supreme achievement, a maximum greatness, in one personality who would never be surpassed—Michelangelo. *Après lui, le déluge.*

For Giedion, the perfection is fundamentally represented by Le Corbusier's Villa at Poissy and by the Bauhaus.

2. To identify stylistic perfection with a certain period of years or with a certain artist, even if he be a great one, implies a devaluation of the age preceding the perfect one—the so-called immature age—as well as the age that follows. In fact, in Giedion we find a somewhat incomplete history of modern architecture from 1850 to 1914, and a very brief history of it after 1933. Or rather this last part is so brief as to be practically non-existent. Let us take some precise examples.

3. In Giedion's book the contribution of the Arts and Crafts and also that of the Art Nouveau movements is given a secondary place to the contribution of the technical achievements. Between the Red House of Philip Webb and the whole Vienna Secession deep gaps are to be found, primarily because—in the name of Le Corbusier and Gropius, and more the former than the latter—the elements which were taken up and developed in the rationalistic period of 1917 to 1933 are more heavily accented than those elements which, for various reasons, rationalism had abandoned.

In a book so rich in illustrations we find not a single picture of an object from the Arts and Crafts, not one of a building by a Voysey or even a Mackintosh, not a photograph of a work of Josef Hoffman or Josef M. Olbrich. Now can we consider such a historical outlook as objective when it undervalues and labels as marginal phenomena the whole rebirth of English domestic architecture, the Glasgow School of Art, the Stoclet Palace at Brussels, and the *Ausstellungsgebäude und Hochzeitsturm* in Darmstadt?

You will all agree that Dr. Giedion is too learned a scholar to be unaware of these fundamental advances in modern architectural history. Then why does he omit them or not give them sufficient emphasis? Evidently because of the classicistic or biological fallacy, that is, of a historical appraisal which tends to hold that Le Corbusier and the Bauhaus are the perfection and that everything preceding them was not capable of attaining any perfection. But the buildings noted above, and with them many other words of the 19th century and the 1900–14 period, are definite cultural and artistic accomplishments which must be studied for their own real significance and not just as forerunners of a perfection to come later.

4. Giedion gives an enormous importance to technical progress in the development of modern architecture. Who could maintain the contrary? But he often falls into a unilateral interpretation, into the kind of old technicistic positivism typified by Choisy, Enlart, and Viollet-le-Duc. He takes much time, for example, to describe the first iron bridge over the river Severn at Coalbrookdale in 1775–79, yet he does not ask himself what importance this bridge had in the architectural culture of that eclectically-befuddled age. Now do you believe that this bridge influenced the architectural culture of its day to the same degree as the Red House built for Morris in 1859 did in its day? A moment's reflection is enough to realize that the bridge of Derby was a phenomenon quite on the periphery of architectural history, while the Red House was a fundamental contribution. But the bridge serves the technicistic, functionalistic mentality of Giedion where the house of Morris does not.

These examples could be multiplied. The works of Augustus Welby Pugin, even if in the neo-Gothic spirit, and those of Karl Friedrich Schinkel, even if in the neo-classical, had a decisive influence on the course of modern development. Yet one looks in vain for these names in that long list appended to Giedion's book.

5. Giedion also gives an enormous importance to the "isms." And this too is proper. But which "isms" are these? Only those abstract-visual ones which do form an essential component of modern culture, but not the only one. Take the case of expressionism. Giedion notes in passing that it was a transitory phenomenon and not a constituent element of modern architecture; but whoever among you lived in the Germany of 1918–22 can bear witness that such a judgement is quite superficial. To declare, as Giedion does, that futurism was a more constructive phenomenon than expressionism, sounds fallacious even to those who, like the writer, recognizes the authenticity of the art of Umberto Boccioni. The truth is that Giedion occupies himself only with visual media, with the mechanical formula of a plastic composition much more than with the moral world and the inner inspiration of artists. Expressionism is concerned with psychology, not with abstract-visual media, and treats of sorrow, of the moral fracture, and of the despair in the world, things which seem much less interesting to Giedion than grammatical instruments.

One is moved to ask what would happen if Giedion were to write a history of modern literature. Would he exclude Döblin and Kafka? And were he to write one of modern painting, would he forget Rouault and Kokoschka?

6. Artists appear to interest Giedion only when the qualities of their inspiration can be expressed in logical formulae. That perhaps would suffice for an understanding of Picasso or Mondrian, but not of all the artists. *Space, Time and Architecture* gives the impression that previous to the cubist discovery of the fourth dimension modern painting did not exist. But what about the impressionists, and Cezanne, Degas, Van Gogh, and even Munch, Delacroix and Ingres? They are the moving forces of vital cultural changes, but, not being reducible to formulae, they are forgotten or played down. This same thing is happening in architecture; we have already noted that Giedion didn't portray some of the architects of the Arts and Crafts and Art Nouveau movements; but even when he writes of Otto Wagner, Peter Behrens, Adolf Loos, of the great pre-rationalist figures in architecture who are the counterparts of the painters named above, he sees only their *functional* importance in technical progress, as it is viewed by rationalists.

7. Let us come to the post-war period. I do not know what you think of Erich Mendelsohn, but I wonder how it is possible to write a book of 601 pages on modern architecture without naming him at least once. The fact is that Mendelsohn is neither cubist, nor neo-plasticist, nor purist, nor constructivist, nor futurist. And when an artist cannot be labelled in terms of an abstract-visual "ism," even though he be great like Dante, Giedion ignores him.

The tone of this criticism, let me say again, may seem sharp and therefore I feel it incumbent upon myself, before continuing further, to reaffirm my deep and sincere admiration for the work of Giedion. I am speaking here only on some points where there is an area of disagreement and which permit of some certain conclusions. This is no book review of *Space, Time and Architecture,* where the excellent parts of the book would be accented. If Giedion's book has enjoyed a good sale in Italy I believe this is partly because of our wide mention of it. Once this has been restated, we must recognize that Giedion's book is programmatical and one-sided and that if Platz's *Die Baukunst der Neuesten Zeit* and Pevsner's *Pioneers of the Modern Movement* had not been written, the origins and the first age of modern architecture would not yet have had their biographies. One may fear that the historical outlook of Giedion is similar to that of many leaders of the CIAM and particularly of Le Corbusier, who seems sometimes to delude himself with the belief that he discovered and initiated modern architecture, not being content to remain merely that eminent figure of it which he is enthusiastically recognized to be.

In the innocent enthusiasm of the peak of the rationalist period it was possible to undervalue the contributions of modern architecture's first age and of those who did not take part in the rationalist movement. Now some decades have passed and it is time to bring about a cultural revision. If the CIAM does not wish to become a nostalgic monument to the rationalist period, if it has deep in its heart, to quote Goethe, the problem more than the truth, then it must discuss these historical themes, which, however much they may seem out of place in a professional meeting, are in reality most vital insofar as they help us to understand our origins, our predecessors, and thus our historical function. These themes must be discussed with that same passion which marked the discussions on the city-planning papers and on the formula- tion of the conclusions of technical debates in the past.

Recognition of Post-Rationalistic Architecture

We come now to the second part of the problem: having briefly dealt with pre-rationalism, let us analyze the architectural period which follows rationalism. In spite of the connections between the two problems, here we come to a more exciting field and an extremely topical one which, as it came to the fore at Bridgewater, will reappear at the Congress of Bergamo, for whatever the technical limits assigned to a discussion may be, the demands of culture will always qualify them.

8. Post-rationalism, as we said, is not to be found in Giedion's book. There the history of modern architecture is concluded with Le Corbusier; and this is quite coherent because if Le Corbusier, as Giedion implies is the perfection, all that comes after him can only be decadence.

As a matter of fact, Giedion, in view of the position taken by the MARS group and by other members of the CIAM, has played down his functionalism in this post-war period and has conceded that our field of inquiry is turning to bio-psychological problems somewhat more than to mechanical and abstract-visual ones. But it is enough to note the firm position taken by him in regard to the Swedish New Empiri-cism to realize that this evolution in Giedion's philosophy does not yet enjoy his full inner conviction.

The Exhibition Hall of Asplund at Stockholm in 1930 was a memorable event in the history of modern architecture—it signalled the overcoming of mechanistic and economic rationalism in the name of ideals that were essentially human. The architec-ture of Alvar Aalto solidified for all Europe the bases of this conquest. Through his works and his philosophy, Aalto came to be the source and inspiration for an entire generation that had absorbed the themes of Le Corbusier and the Bauhaus and that considered them, while still continuing to admire them for their intrinsic worth, to have been culturally superseded.

Just what this problem is, the humanizing of architecture, is known and document-ed. It is enough to see a building of the first Markelius as opposed to the Swedish

Pavilion at the New York World's Fair of 1939, or the pavilion by Aalto in 1937 at Paris against any building of Le Corbusier, to realize this. The sensitivity of Walter Gropius has gone through this evolution, and if you compare the plan of his Siedlung Dammerstock in Karlsruhe with that of the New Kensington housing development, you will recognize it.

Giedion himself, in a recent article in *Werk* dedicated to Aalto, has registered these differences, but, true to his temperament, accented those of technical and abstract-visual nature. It was said that Aalto follows Jean Arp rather than Mondrian; Giedion published a drawing by Ozenfant full of curves, claiming it to be concomitant with the visual approach of the Finnish architect. One must say in all frankness that these observations seem somewhat superficial. If everything is to be reduced to a substitution of pictorial trends, to a question of exterior phenomena or to a new planning aesthetic, post-rationalism would not even be worth mentioning. But actually it is a phenomenon too deeply established and widespread for the CIAM to ignore.

We do not know if the Swedish New Empiricism is a healthy movement and the forerunner of a new period of civilization. But it is certainly a fact, a definite symptom of the reaction to rationalism, a reaction not brought about light-heartedly but the result of a profound re-examination of values made by Swedish architects. The problem of progressing beyond rationalism is current in the whole world, from Scandinavia to England, from the United States to Italy and Switzerland. In Switzerland also, in the very country of Giedion, while Max Bill is carrying out his abstract-visual researches to highly exasperating ends and with an intent we find interesting but culturally sterile, Alfred Roth has built a house near Zurich whose points of contact with the Wright and Swedish schools are evident.

Post-rationalism, with its approach that we term organic, is a phenomenon that has been going on for about 20 years. It means a new and distinct chapter in modern architectural history. To fight it, to fight for example the New Empiricism in the name of the abstract-visual theories of 1910–17, means to seek to stop the course of history, to seek to yoke sons to their fathers' ways and not to permit them their own development. Personally, each of us can feel that the block recently built by Le Corbusier at Marseilles is preferable to all the works of the New Empiricism. But the CIAM as such cannot make such a judgment without causing two great consequences: (1) first of all, it would no longer control the New Empiricism, whose road is without doubt full of difficulties and danger; (2) it would isolate itself from the current problematics of architecture, withdrawing into an ivory tower of the conquered past.

9. Here the problem of Frank Lloyd Wright arises. After I had written my first book *Verso un'Architettura Organica,* I told half-seriously those who complimented me on it, "The praise is not for me, but for Giedion. All I did was translate *Space, Time and Architecture* with one modification: I transposed the chapter on F. L. Wright so that it followed the one on Le Corbusier." But this was a variation of no little importance. It changes the whole historical perspective and the development of modern architecture appears in a new light.

To speak of Fallingwater or the Johnson Building of Wright 50 pages before the description of the Bauhaus and 75 pages before the Villa Savoye and the Swiss Pavilion at the University of Paris is chronologically, scientifically and historically incomprehensible. One can understand when Giedion may see fit to ignore Asplund; it is inconceivable however, even within the framework of a tendentious historical interpretation, that he considers Wright merely as a predecessor of Le Corbusier and Gropius.

Frank Lloyd Wright has certainly been a pioneer of modern architecture. But he has also been a master of the functionalist period and one who has shown the way beyond it. To many young architects he still seems very much up-to-date today. It would be wrong to interpret the enthusiasm held by many architects for Wright's work as a form of post-war snobbery. The house that Asplund built for himself in 1937 near Stockholm showed already a reaction against the rationalistic formula with elements which Wright had been carrying further in America. The work of Aalto preceded the post-war era. In conclusion, if all Europe looks today with extreme interest to the American master, this is based on the fact that he is working with problems that Europe has been facing for more than a decade, working free of any influence whatsoever, directly as the result of the rationalist crisis. What are these problems? A hundred pages would be necessary to describe them all; I myself have written scores of pages on the psychological aspects, dimensional problems in city planning, etc. In any case I will limit myself to mentioning briefly a single point which seems the most important and in every way the most vital to architecture.

I refer to the spatial conception, the imagining, designing and building of interior spaces in both the fields of architecture and townplanning.

The discovery of perspective, while an event of great technical progress, did not necessarily or indefinitely mean an advantage of the architect in every way. The architects became used to drawing, to like drawing for its own intrinsic beauty, and to conceive of architecture in terms of two dimensions. Naturally architects were drawing before the discovery of perspective but those drawings were mere hints, more an idea of the architecture than its clear definition. The true experience of the builder was the act of building itself, and the architectural problems were not solved a priori but, as they arose, in the actual construction in space, in the reality of work itself. This reality, the exceptional importance of the architectural void and the city-space void, became evident through direct experience.

From the time when architects learned to draw with mechanical and impersonal methods, it has been only exceptional geniuses, and then only after long experience, who have been able to recapture this sensation again, this consciousness of spatial reality. In the pre-modern period, the eclecticism that flooded the second half of the 19th century witnessed the triumph of drawing over architecture; that is, the impoverishment of architecture and its corruption into two dimensions.

With the birth of the Modern Movement has come a new consciousness of architectural volumes. Cubism gave to this consciousness a quasi-scientific substratum; rationalism was the sign of its definite acceptance. It was a notable and immense advance that Giedion describes in his book in memorable words. But plastic volumes do not form the entire reality of architecture. Interior space was forgotten or at least had no predominance in the rationalist period, with some few exceptions as Mies van der Rohe.

The great contribution of Wright has been to bring up the problem again specifically in terms of interior space. To *see* the architecture before drawing it, or even sometimes rather than drawing it. It is because of this that the drawings and models of Wright are often only hints, clues to the image known only by the author.

The reconquest of a spatial consciousness is the order of the day for modern architects. From the first house of the Art Nouveau up through the whole of rationalism, plastic research prevailed over architecture. Architects made use of the plastic conquests—two, three, or four-dimensional forms that the various *isms* offered—which served to revolutionize the building plans and volumes that enclosed the spaces. With the post-rationalist, or organic, movement in Europe and the Wright school in America the basic interest has been focused on interior spaces, both in architecture and townplanning. A drawing or a model cannot represent more than a hint in this architectural approach. If one asks why this spatial conception is important, it can be answered that space does not make up a single visual category like the plane, the line, the volume or the surface, but is the site of the collective and individual social life, the very projection of it. It is thus a new psychological consciousness, as Giedion has noted, a new social consciousness which leads to a new concept of space. The artistic debate is detaching itself from means to go back to causes and results. It is a problem which is not only economic and technical, but also integrally moral and intimately religious. For this the example of Wright is of exceptional importance today, quite beyond the matters of his anarchic philosophy, his very debatable ideas, or the expressionistic and Art Nouveau elements which permeate his architecture. This is why the Amsterdam plan no longer represents what is accepted in townplanning as the perfection. But all our attention is concentrated on the problem of the urban community and on the qualities of towns; in this respect, the medieval town, the town-building of an age when cities were not built with impersonal two-dimensional plans nor with models that moved cubes and towers around indefinitely, is more closely related than any other to this trend.

These are only brief introductions to the problems which have been under long discussion in Italy. I believe, however, that they will be sufficient to give you an idea of the trends of thought now emerging in this country.

CULTURE OF THE CITY

Talk delivered to the 1961 American Institute of Architects Convention and published in the *AIA Journal,* April 1961

My gratitude to the President and friends of the AIA for the invitation to participate in this panel is so much greater because I have a few positive things to say and many questions to raise.

Such questions, I fear, will have to deal with the fundamentals of a contemporary culture of cities. I have been trying to stay away from them and to concentrate instead on specific problems. I had prepared a series of slides documenting what we are doing in Italy and in Europe, but then I realized that in the evaluation of each specific case, be it the Roehampton development in London or Vallingby near Stockholm or the most recent Italian settlements, the same old questions emerge. They concern the dimension of the modern city, the architects' role in the process which goes from city planning to city making, and the philosophy of urban renewal. Unless we reach some common views on these issues, it will be difficult even to understand one another.

Consider, for example, Brasilia. We have heard the most unconditional praise of this capital city, and also the most violent criticism. This happened because we started from different perspectives on what a city is or should be today. Again, take the case of the satellite communities on the periphery of the metropolis: is this the right way to cope with city expansion and, if not, do we have a better way? As for urban renewal, it is needed in Los Angeles and Detroit just as much as in Rome and Venice, but its meaning is totally different here and there. Sure, it is easy to agree on official platitudes such as: "In cities of historical value, the respect for the past should be balanced by the needs of contemporary society." But when we come down to how to reach such equilibrium, the divergence of opinions is very strong in Venice and in Rome, and perhaps also in Philadelphia.

This is why I consider this panel and the discussions of this convention extremely pertinent also for the future of European cities. The American contribution is needed in Europe and in the world now more than ever before. During the present period of western prosperity, it is no longer a matter of money or material help, but of ideas and methods. Perhaps another Peace Corps is needed, made up of architects and city designers.

Well, where can we start from to understand what a modern city is? Oddly enough, I started way back in 1492, just the year of the discovery of America. This is what happened: a few years ago I was reading the famous historian Jacob Burckhardt, and all of a sudden I was struck by a sentence. After visiting Ferrara, a town between Bologna and Venice, in 1860, Burckhardt wrote: "Ferrara is the first modern city in Europe." He did not give any explanation for this amazing interpretation. I looked into townplanning literature, but found very little about Ferrara. Many authors were repeating Burckhardt's sentence, but none would explain the reasons for it. Finally, I decided to devote a few years to the study of this town. Last year, on the centennial of Burckhardt's statement, I published a book about it. In a very few words, these were my three conclusions:

1. Ferrara could be defined as "the first modern city in Europe" because there was a man who in 1492 designed a master plan for its expansion. He made the city three times as large as it was during the Middle Ages and the early Renaissance. It was, in a way, an open plan, because the territory urbanized in 1492 has never been completely developed even today. This approach was certainly new, in basic contrast both with the pragmatic attitude of the Middle Ages, when planning and building were almost synchronous activities, and with the Renaissance habit of inventing abstract, ideal, and static cities.

2. Such an extensive plan could not be implemented throughout by a predetermined third dimension. The planner of Ferrara could not build the whole town; he had to have some confidence in its natural growth, and leave something for future architects to do. But he was an architect himself, and knew that a plan is meaningful only when

it gets a third dimension, that is, only if architects make it true. And here was his genius. He was able to identify the few key structures of the new town that would guarantee for four centuries and a half the urban pattern. Mind you, these focal points were not monumental plazas or princely roads, but sometimes very small buildings at the corners of secondary streets which, even when isolated, would suggest the image of the city. A flexible image, so that it worked, yet a precise one, so that it could not be betrayed.

3. Lastly, this man, Biagio Rossetti, spent about ten years developing the new section of Ferrara, but then he spent about 20 years in renewing the old city. At the end of his life, in 1516, he had integrated the old city with its addition, thus creating a new modern organism.

There it is again. Ferrara was a modern city because it grew coherently in relation to the same basic problems of any organic culture of cities: the measure of the city, the passage from its plan to its architecture, the approach to urban renewal. The answers are naturally different, but the main questions remain, perhaps, the same in 1492 as in 1961.

Let us then tackle the first of these three questions: the measure or dimension of the city. I may be wrong, but I have the impression that our urban culture went to pieces because architects were unable to see that a city could have a form even without having a dimension. They are not to blame: the notion of form had somehow been dependent on the notion of measure throughout history; and therefore, town planners tried to impose on the modern city a dimension which, however, big, was always too small and deceiving. All of the 19th century culture, which continued deep into the first half of our century, suffers from this psychosis about the size of this city. It is indeed surprising: just at the time when modern technology was destroying the mechanical justification and the social function of an urban measure, its determination became the ideal and purpose of town planners.

You will remember that *The Art of Building Cities* by Camillo Sitte was published in 1889. The garden city idea, by Ebenezer Howard, became the offical doctrine of townplanning a few years later. Thus, the utopia of an industrial autonomous community found its historical mirror in the idealistic interpretation of the agricultural autonomous community of the Middle Ages.

A similar approach was applied to the metropolis. Looking at the successive town plans designed for London, Paris and Rome in the last 100 years, one has the impression that the chief concern of the planners was to impose a dimension on the city. The old walls were destroyed; they tried to build new ones—never mind if they consisted of green belts instead of brick and stone.

The theoretical ideal became the self-sufficient settlement in a self-contained city form. Now this kind of vision may continue to work for small towns, but it looks anachronistic not only for the super-metropolis, but also for the metropolis between one and two million inhabitants. We see in Europe that people resent the artificiality of this kind of overgrown villages added to cities, because they cannot offer the benefits of the old town, and deprive them of the advantages of the metropolis. Moreover, a city with its high buildings at the center, lowering down to the periphery until it merges with the country, is a sort of pyramidal structure of an oligarchic society. It cannot embody a democratic society with our contemporary technological instruments.

I think that we should recognize, sad as it may seem, that our modern city has no more a dimension, or at least we do not know how to measure it.

Once we have recognized this fundamental character of the modern city, we can interpret it in two opposite ways. We can repeat that the city is doomed and disappearing, because the suburban sprawl nullifies the difference between town and country and amalgamates the whole territory. There is, however, another hypothesis: The city is still there, strong and alive, maintaining its social and cultural functions, but it is looking for a new urban form which has nothing to do with the old one, because the new urban form is dynamic, sizeless and continuous.

It may be hard to discover and express the connotations of this new urban form which is so different from the ones of the past. Perhaps we could apply to it a designation used in contemporary painting: a-formal. However, we should not be afraid or impatient. A painting by Jackson Pollock has a logical and severe composition, even if it has nothing to do with the laws of academic composition. Schönberg's music is firmly organized, even if, when compared to the musical tradition, it sounds chaotic and arbitrary. The same is probably true of the modern city: It has a structure, a new and powerful form which we have up to now sacrificed to a 19th century ideal which is dying, once and for all, with Brasilia. It is the challenge of contemporary city designers to uncover this kind of a-formal structure and let it free to grow.

So my first question is: how can we identify this new sizeless urban form, so essentially different from the traditional, static city that we all know by now as obsolete and bleak?

This question brings us into the core of the second problem: the relationship between city planning and city making. The architects are, in this phase, the real protagonists of the city. But this does not make the situation much easier. In fact, modern architecture, in spite of its great achievements, seems to have fallen into a state of confusion and eclecticism. Without some agreement on architectural language, is it possible to redesign a coherent urban scene?

When we look at the history of Western civilization, we see that architecture either preceded or was simultaneous with town design. That is to say, all space-conceptions in towns reflected and translated in bigger space-conceptions which had been embodied in some building. I do not assume this to be a divine law, but it is a datum worth considering. Medieval town space is identical with medieval architectural space; the pattern of Ferrara is the same as the pattern of its buildings; this is true for Fontana's scheme for Rome and for Haussmann's Paris. A perfect convergence of planning and architectural thinking is to be found in Wright, or Le Corbusier, or Gropius, or Mies; that is, in the urban theories formulated between the two world wars. Does this convergence of research and criteria still exist today? And, if it does, which are the buildings that express a space-conception capable of being magnified in city scale? Is it the Seagram Building or the Guggenheim Museum? Idlewild or Ronchamp?

So far as we can see, the International Style ideal of isolated, pure, transparent prisms in space has been, if not denied, at least complemented by a tendency towards expressionistic plasticity and by a sort of neo-Baroque inclination for visual continuity through undulating serpentines. I do not think such plurality of expression is necessarily negative. In the process of disclosing a new city form, richness of architectural language may be interpreted as a happy event. I have a liking for the architects who, when planning or redesigning a city, leave some problems unanswered, trust the natural growth, refuse to be dictators up to the window curtains and the flower pots. This liberal attitude seems congenial with a democratic approach, but to what extent can it work? One can visualize a sizeless and formless city of the future, just as beautiful as a Pollock or a Schönberg composition, made true and vital by a various, audacious, personal architecture that, again taking from painting, we could denominate "action-architecture." But, in order to achieve such a challenging purpose, architects must be able to seize the present great opportunity to remold our cities, they should think in bigger terms, they should reorganize the profession so that it becomes the driving and promoting power of the entire building industry.

And here I am afraid that too many of our colleagues, at the very moment when we can win and become the leaders of the building industry, retreat, give up, are tired, for I do not know what neurotic reasons. They seem to be content to continue to be a minority report. They stop at Mondrian and Arp, or are bemused with stylistic details, vernacular evasions, neo-Art Nouveau, neo-historicism, filligree and other architectural delights. You know that I have hailed architecture's emancipation from the doctrinaire of the 30s. But such freedom was won to meet new and bigger tasks, to extend architectural research in city scale, and not to indulge introversion and individual idiosyncrasies. Urban design is not an architectural cosmetic. Within the different sectors of the new a-formal city we should have a coherent sound and eloquent architecture to produce a vital third dimension. Let us remember that the degree of resistance of the third dimension is the barometer of the vitality of an urban pattern. Sixtus' scheme for Rome is three-dimensionally so strong that not even Mussolini could destroy it, although he tried. But the small streets of the Borghi leading to St. Peter's were not so strong, and the crime was committed.

My second question, therefore, is: What kind of interaction is there of different architectural tendencies in today's city making?

The third and last question, urban renewal, is perhaps only a consequence of the first two. But it has difficulties of its own. I hesitate to offer any conclusions based on a quick look at present-day American cities. But since my arrival in California, I have toured the major large scale renewal projects in Los Angeles, San Francisco, Chicago, Detroit, Pittsburgh and Washington. Perhaps a subjective impression from a friendly outsider may be of some use. I was certainly impressed by the brave effort made to deal with housing, urban expressways, industrial and commercial developments. However, it was not always clear to me whether these projects, taken together in their aggregate, will make the future city, will establish the framework of a new urban society.

If cities are to survive as cultural instruments, they must be more than a collection of public works projects. Houses or expressways may be produced on assembly line methods perhaps, cities are not. And where is the coordination between residential communities and motorways, business districts and recreational centers—in other words, where does urban design come into the picture? The architectural profession is evidently conscious of the new role it is called upon to fulfill in the national task of redesigning urban America. Indeed, the very significance of the architectural profession is at stake. In the process of city making, there is no second, or third, or fourth place that architects can occupy: either they come in first, or they are going to be the last. Either they promote, or they become the passive reflection of a disintegrated city life. Organic relationships between public works projects, organic relationship between these projects and the building industry at large; this is what urban design amounts to, this is where urban design becomes public policy. Either architects can show a way toward an integrated urban policy, or architecture is lost.

Never before was architectural design so dependent on urban design. The scope of urban renewal cannot be limited to housing, office triangles, shopping centers. When it is, architecture itself is not going to be very good. For instance, in many American cities, urban renewal, so far as I could see, means demolishing, with bulldozer technique, an urban section in order to rebuild it according to contemporary criteria. Often, at the end of a carpet of old houses, we see a series of tall buildings, in the shape of towers or elongated prisms. Such contrast of dimension, structure and character is sometimes successful, as it attains a surrealistic beauty. But can isolated towers or slabs constitute the entire semantics of urban renewal and offer a consistent method for redesigning urban America? Do they not sometimes lacerate the structure and the texture of the city, depriving it, together with the slums, of some of its historical and social assets? A city atmosphere means interchange, movement, continuity, and the architecture for it cannot always be so violently discontinuous.

This is true especially of city sections reserved for pedestrians. There, we should have a type of architecture consonant not only in scale but also in quality to the pedestrian's tempo. In fact, too many pedestrian's centers in Europe look artificial and unconvincing because they do not have an architectural form of their own.

But urban renewal becomes a much more difficult operation when it is applied to monumental towns. In Italy, I happen to be Secretary General of the Italian Institute of Architecture, and university professor of architectural history. It is more than enough to give me a case of split personality about urban renewal. Historians would not change a stone of the past, some architects would like to clear everything up, planners change their opinion all too often. In the meantime, Palermo has become socially degraded to the point that only the *Report* by Danilo Dolci, perhaps the best living Italian who recently visited this country, succeeded in depicting. Venice is going to pieces, and its new town plan just approved does not offer any long-range solution. Milan, yes, is totally renewed, with the result that it is perhaps the ugliest city in Europe, a city where the Duomo and St. Ambrogio are the only buildings which look out of place and tune. In the next five years the historical center of Rome is going to be renewed, and the question is, once again: how to do it?

I think that this problem too concerns all of us. In spite of the differences between American and European towns, a philosophy flexible enough to be applied to American cities quite probably might work also for Europe.

These, Mr. Chairman and friends, are my main questions regarding the city's size, its new third dimension and urban renewal. They are questions of an economic, social and aesthetic nature at the same time, because the notion of anti-social beauty is just a contradiction in terms. I could stop with these questions, but I ask of you two more minutes to stress a point about which I feel very strongly, and which concerns international cooperation on planning policy, city design and urban renewal.

To be frank, can we expect a definite answer to these questions, from this panel or this convention? It is doubtful: we are no longer looking for formulas, for theories valid everywhere and nowhere. We believe in experiences and mutual collaboration, and this is an urgent problem about which perhaps we can do something right here and now.

As you know, there are many international bodies and organizations that are supposed to take care of exchange of information. But, for some reason or another, they do not seem to work. First of all, many of them collect facts and figures from official sources, general facts and apologetic figures; they never touch the real core of the matter, the specific city problems. Secondly, these official organizations either do not follow any clear philosophy concerning our urban future, or they follow two or three different philosophies at the same time. On one side, they have an abstract, illuministic approach: they imply that there are certain universal values in urban civilization, which should work from Brazil to China because they are good for everybody. When you come down to find out what these universal values are, you discover that they are vague common denominators of no interest to anyone. Sometimes, they take the opposite approach: they try to adhere to what they call the specific cultural pattern of every nation, they find that everything that exists has some reason for existing, even the slums if they are picturesque enough. This is a paternalistic attitude, almost a colonial approach, and it works just as badly as illuministic abstractions. Finally, the major fault with all these international organizations is that they are paralyzed by the principle of non-intervention.

I submit to you that a totally different type of international cooperation on city design should be organized. Something coming directly from the profession, anti-bureaucratic, quick to intervene in every part of the world, around a drawing board, with pencils in hand. Towns are to be redesigned, and in this task every country needs the support of others, and can contribute. A timely, friendly and competent intervention from outside can remove many difficulties that arise within a single nation.

However, whether you will consider this suggestion or not, I want you to know that whatever you do in redesigning urban America has a great impact on Europe. When the plan for Fort Worth was published, there was in Italy a sincere enthusiasm: we felt that something had been done for Texas which was instrumental and meaningful also for us. The same can be said of the Golden Gateway Redevelopment in San Francisco, of your experiences in Detroit, in Pittsburgh, and in many other cities, of the admirable campaign on urban renewal that some of your architectural magazines are conducting. The same is true especially of Philadelphia, a city which, for the work being done in the University, in the planning commission and in the redevelopment authority, might be considered one of the world's major centers for city design today.

Fifteen years ago, I had the honor to speak at the Convention of The American Institute of Planners which was held in Cleveland. This was in 1946. The title of my address was: "Town Planning as an Instrument of an American Foreign Policy." I meant what it implied. Unfortunately, during the last 15 years, this instrument was little used, and American foreign policy was not always brilliant and successful. Something, however, is changing now, here as in the whole world. Expectation is in the air, and I feel once again that the architects' contribution can be determining. Town making will perhaps be the final battleground between the East and the West.

In an affluent society, the quantitative competition is going to become less and less important. The final battle will be fought on quality, and here city designers and architects will bear the greatest responsibility.

This is all, at least for the time being. I am one of the many European disciples of Lewis Mumford. I am here to pose questions to the master and learn from all of you. Thank you.

THE MODERN DIMENSION OF LANDSCAPE ARCHITECTURE

International Federation of Landscape Architects Convention, 1962

As an architectural historian, I feel somewhat uneasy speaking about landscape architecture. In our universities, we teach nothing on the history of landscape. This is perhaps already a symptom of a basic scientific "dimension"— old and modern, at the same time—which is lacking in this field: I mean the historical dimension. Until we will have a satisfactory history of landscape, until such history will be integrated with the urban and architectural history, it will be rather difficult to outline a consistent landscape policy, because a policy is founded on a certain set of ideas, and ideas are either historically justified or abstract and gratuitous. It is my impression that the philosophy of landscape architecture is too often based on dated illuministic principles, on romantic "lags" and wishful thinking, and this is why in many countries, in Italy at least, it does not work.

A historical consciousness about landscape is badly needed. The research done by agricultural historians can be of great help for us. You are all familiar with the famous book by Marc Block, published in 1930, *Les caractères originaux de l'histoire rurale française,* which started a new method, one might say a new vision on this subject. A few months ago, Emilio Sereni published a *Storia del paesaggio agrario italiano,* from the Greek colonization to contemporary times, conceived with the same criteria. The economic and sociological motives of the transformation of landscape across the ages are rather clear. The figurative and visual results can be traced, at least partially, because we still have examples of well preserved Greek, Roman, Feudal, Renaissance and Baroque landscapes. More than that, mosaics, paintings, old maps, descriptions by agricultural historians—from Diodoro Siculo who wrote about the landscape of Turi, a Greek colony founded in 446 BC to Leon Battista Alberti, indeed one could say from the Bible on—they all offer a rich and essential documentation. But the insertion of this history in the architectural history is still lacking, and it is of capital importance for our culture and for a new, modern standard of education.

I submit to you that, without the landscape ingredient, urban and architectural history is either incomplete or more difficult to understand. Consider the case of the Italian villas from the 15th to the 18th century. Everybody knows that the Tuscan villa is structurally different from the Venetian villa, but too many architectural students are unaware of the change in agricultural systems and thus in the landscapes which were the direct cause of the difference in forms. In the 17th and 18th centuries we find grandiose villas which have a character of their own and cannot be assimilated to the ones of the preceeding epochs: here, again, the disintegration of rural life is the motive of these "architectural compensations."

To conclude on this first point, I trust that you will all agree that the time has come to enlarge the scope of architectural history in order to include the history of landscape. This broadening of our historical horizons seems, in point of fact, quite logical. From an architectural history conceived as a sequence of masterpieces and artist-heroes, we have moved on to an approach which also considers vital the minor structures of the past, the houses of the common people, the regional vernaculars and idioms. Then we made a second step, toward town planning: Today the history of urban life constitutes the preliminary chapter of architectural history. The last step of this process is in front of us: its purpose is to integrate townplanning, landscape and architecture into an organic history of human environment.

A layman could ask why is it that only now, in the second half of the 20th century, the urge for such integrated vision of the territorial development is being clearly felt. We all know the reason: the separation between town and country is disappearing, the old fortifications have been torn down, the new defences of green belts either do not work or are instruments of the planned articulation of a land totally urbanized. For better or worse, we do not even know today where cities end and landscapes begin. A most interesting international congress on the relationship between town and country was held at Stresa at the beginning of this year. Its very theme was significant: "The city region," which means the endless city, the urban structure without boundaries, without measure. A reality, which has been under our eyes for quite a few decades, but which is being culturally recognized only now, because during the first half of our century the philosophy of planning has been largely conditioned by the illusion of reproducing with modern technology the old urban order, instead of building a new one.

Given this physical and cultural process, the distinction between regional and town design, between landscape architecture and architecture becomes more and more empirical. An architect, who is not a town planner, or at least who has not a townplanning consciousness, is not an architect at all, because single buildings, in the productive scale of the 20th century, are like mouldings of a collective work of art, which is the -scape: land- , sea-, sky-scape. I do not advocate the hara-kiri of IFIA; on the contrary, I am helping to organize a stronger section of the federation in Italy. But, while we recognize the need for specializations, we should not forget that specialization is one of the causes of the physical and spiritual disintegration in which we live.

The battle for the preservation of landscapes is being lost all over the world, because it is a "sectorial," defensive battle, largely fought in the name of romantic values, of "natural beauties," and of a vague sociological thesis—to which quite a few sociologists are not ready to subscribe—which postulates the benefits of nature and assumes, that in the country there are fewer neurotics than in the towns. To win their battle, landscape architects should acquire an aggressive approach, should formulate a modern, dynamic dimension for landscape architecture, based no longer on a generic naturalistic philosophy, but on a courageous plan of action. Towns are winning against landscapes, because they have such aggressive attitudes, while landscapes offer only a passive, pathetic resistance. Can this situation be reversed? It depends not so much on laws, which are seldom respected and can be changed, but on power of vision, on the creative power of landscape architects. Either they lead, or they are going to be left on the margins of modern civilization. Leading means, that they must produce a new image of the territory, capable of persuading, of fascinating town planners, architects and public opinion. This is the challenge; there are no other alternatives. As individuals, landscape architects may survive by becoming draftsmen or specification writers in the field of "natural materials" in architectural or planning offices. Their profession, however, if they do not lead, cannot survive.

At this point, instead of trying to outline a new policy for landscape architecture—which, I suppose, is the very purpose of this congress and should be formulated after long discussions—I will submit to you five questions which, I feel, need an urgent answer if, landscape architecture is to play a leading role in our culture. They are a historian's questions, and some of them may sound a little too intellectual to the professionals. However, I firmly believe that, at least in this preliminary session of our work, we should concentrate on fundamentals, trying to inject a new vital impetus in this field.

Here are the five questions:

1. Throughout the ages there is a definite relationship between the agricultural landscape and the pictorial landscape. When civilization is degraded, say at the end of the Roman Empire, during the High Middle Ages or in the Catholic countries during the Counter-Reformation, the physical landscape is wild, and the pictorial landscape is wildly romantic or expressionist. On the contrary, during the periods of integrated culture, we find so many analogies between the agricultural and the pictorial landscapes that we do not know, whether it is the former that influences the latter, or vice versa. The "landscape into art" process coincides with the "art into landscape" process, as in some decades of the Italian Renaissance. Well, where are we today in this relationship? Considering the present situation in painting, the various currents of abstract expressionism or the so-called "informal art," what is their effect on our landscape vision? One keeps reading that landscape painting is dead, that today there are only few townscape painters and not very significant ones, because the young artists are too busy with their soul— or mind-scapes. But are we sure, that in these paintings some hidden abstract landscapes cannot be found, which, if uncovered and understood, could offer a modern dimension to landscape architecture? If painting does not affect landscape anymore, either something is wrong with landscape architecture, or we should conclude, that the centuries-long relationship between agricultural and pictorial landscapes is broken. But, in this case, another question arises: why did this happen?

2. Too many books and essays on landscape architecture are concerned mainly with gardens. Is this right, or does it demonstrate that the philosophy of landscape architecture has to be brought up to date? The transition from city design to townplanning took place a long time ago: the same cannot be stated of the transition from the architecture of gardens to the architecture of landscapes. One could evade the problem saying that it is a matter of scale, of quantity, not of quality. But we know that differences in dimension and scale bare heavy consequences in criteria and methods.

Do you feel that the time has come to establish a distinction (at least on the teaching level) between garden design and landscape design?

3. One may interpret garden design as a microcosm of landscape design. In this case, the question arises: where are we in garden design? I am afraid that the record is not very satisfactory in this field. Too often, gardens are unrelated to architecture and try to be a "compensation" of it. The UNESCO building in Paris can be mentioned as an example: its beautiful Japanese garden is superimposed on the walls without coherence, without any stable glue. For years, I have followed with intense interest the development of a great artist in your field: Roberto Burle-Marx, but I must confess that recently I felt somewhat puzzled. For a long period, Burle-Marx has expressed himself along an "informal" line: his gardens were dramatically in contrast with the architecture of Oscar Niemeyer and his friends, a box-like architecture even when undulated. Lately, however, Burle-Marx has designed gardens which seem to accept this lack of relationship; they do not even protest against a hostile architecture, they are independent of it; they are painting, beautiful paintings done with greenery and exotic plants. I see a pessimistic symptom in this development, almost a renunciation. But this is not all. There was a magnificent opportunity to expand, to blow Burle-Marx's garden design up to a city, to a landscape scale: it was Brasilia. But you know that Burle-Marx, the most significant artist of Brasil, was ostracized from Brasilia. This paradoxical fact, this scandal should be analyzed here because it shows a crisis in town-planning, in landscape architecture and in architecture. It is the declaration of a cultural failure: Burle-Marx's landscapes could not fit with Lucio Costa's town plan and with Oscar Niemeyer's architecture. Why? Is it the fault of the 19th century, classicist character of Lucio Costa's plan, or of the pseudo-modern monumental architecture of Oscar Niemeyer, or finally of the intrinsic impossibility to apply Burle-Marx's garden or park design to a landscape scale?

4. A territory no more clearly divided between town and country, and totally urbanized, is a rather new phenomenon in history; no wonder that town planners look surprised and confused. The very instrument of the town plan is obsolete; we speak a lot about "open" plans, but a plan is either closed and static, or is not a plan, but simply a program. At the Stresa Congress, which I mentioned before, English, French, German and Italian planners recognized courageously the characters of the new city, the "city region" as they called it, but when they had to identify the methods by which to control its growth, they looked rather bewildered. Perhaps the modern city cannot be planned, because it is continuous, dynamic, without dimension and measure, without form. Perhaps we can give an orientation to each one of the various chapters of the urban continuum, giving up the idea of controlling its total development. Perhaps we can plan the whole of it, if we are able to acquire a different attitude towards planning, a phenomenological attitude, free at last from the preconceived ideologies, which dominated in the first half of the century. It is indeed rather paradoxical that while planning is finally being accepted by governments and regimes of the most different types, town planners do not quite know how to plan. They find that the instruments at their disposal were shaped with the old city in mind, a city which had a definite size, which was pretty well separated from the country and whose dynamism was slow enough to allow a forecast of the urban growth. A big question

mark looms in front of townplanning today. We have an action-painting, say Pollock; a dissonant, apparently chaotic and arbitrary music, say Schönberg. We need an action-town, a dissonant town, great and glorious as a Pollock painting and Schönberg symphony. The 19th century ideal of the imperial city is dying, once and for all, with Brasilia. But a new adventure is starting; the city region, the "informal" or action-city, where townscape and landscape blend together. This modern urban amalgam cannot be creatively expressed only by town planners, because the landscape is also at stake. And here is the splendid chance for landscape architects. To create the new landscape, they must invent also the new city, they must embody the functions that painters had in the past. With the present suburban sprawl, building is already in the landscape. The question is how to translate this phenomenon in something not passively accepted, but freely acknowledged and aesthetically represented. Are landscape architects big enough to give such a lead to town planners?

5. The problem of the visual continuum concerns landscape and townscape, but also architecture, which has to offer the third dimension to the new image of the territory. Do we have today an action-architecture capable of reflecting and of promoting the urban continuum? Too many of our buildings look isolated, autonomous, proudly detached, without connection one to another; and it is clear that our cities and landscapes are shapeless also because their building ingredients do not form a coherent speech. The language of modern architecture, as it developed in 1920–30, is a classical language, made up of pure, self-sufficient volumes in space. It cannot help in creating the new continuous urban landscape; in point of fact, it is in definite opposition to its image. We know that rationalistic architecture, the International Style, has passed through a fatal crisis: Ronchamp was the explosive effect of it. But out of a crisis or the wearing out of a language two results can emerge: the mere corruption of the grammar and the syntax of the old language, or the creation of a new one. A new architectural language, however, cannot be created by architects alone, because it must be in tune with the town-landscape. Another cultural burden is therefore on the shoulders of landscape architects. My last question is: which architectural trend, of the present Mannerist variety, seems best fit for the town landscape of tomorrow?

This is all. Reading the program of this Congress, I felt that five preliminary questions by a historian could not mislead your work. All the practical aspects of landscape architecture will be examined in the forthcoming sessions. In this opening discussion, we should deal with fundamentals and tackle the philosophical problems concerning an integrated vision of our civilized environment.

Our culture is in a state of crisis. Someone must lead out of it. Will it be the town planner or the architect? Perhaps landscape architects will do this leading, if they are able to rise above their professional routine giving a modern dimension to their art.

ARCHITECTURE 1967: PROGRESS OR REGRESSION?

Man and His World/Terre des Hommes, The Noranda Lectures/Expo 67,
University of Toronto Press, Toronto, 1968. Reprinted by permission.

It is quite evident that I would not be discussing such a controversial subject as
"Architecture 1967: Progress or Regression?" were it not for a fortuitous but significant coincidence. The year 1967 is not only the Canadian Centennial, a very happy
event, but also the third centenary of a tragic episode in architectural history. In 1667
Francesco Borromini, perhaps the greatest architect of the Baroque period, committed suicide. Why? we ask ourselves. Was he neurotic, sexually frustrated, unhappily
married? Actually he killed himself because he felt and knew that everything he had
been struggling to accomplish during his life was doomed to failure.

The question, "Progress or Regression?" is rather an annoying one. As an architect
and town planner, I myself feel irritated by it. We can dismiss it in an optimistic way:
what about the Montreal Expo? How stimulating, attractive, and exciting! Surely
architecture is progressing. Alternatively, we can assume an evasive attitude: who
cares? Perhaps architecture is regressing, but today the real problem is not architecture. It is planning. We conceive our task in quite different ways: on an urban or
regional scale. Indeed, architectural tendencies themselves are not very important.

Certainly, as an architect and a town planner, I can dismiss the whole question—
but not as a historian and an architectural critic. As a historian, I cannot forget that
this year is the third centenary of Borromini's suicide. It is my duty to recur to this
dramatic event of the 17th century.

Borromini built the most daring buildings of his age. He completely revolutionized
the Renaissance concept of space, based on perspective and elementary geometrical
forms. He did not work on geometry, as the majority of architects did and still do,
but on space; not on the building box, but on its content, on the cavities. Manipulating
his spaces with extraordinary inventiveness, compressing or expanding them, ac-
celerating or delaying their tempo and speed, orchestrating their depth and density
with an unheard-of use of light as an architectural instrument, he offered the world
a new vision of architecture, a message which destroyed existing conventional codes.

Borromini also gave a new significance to the relationship between interior and
exterior space, that is, between the building and the city. While the Renaissance palace
or church was conceived as something isolated and autonomous from the town, as
an object detached from the urban continuum, Borromini wanted his buildings to
belong to it, to be an energetic coagulum, sometimes centrifugal but as a rule centripe-
tal, of a street or of a piazza. For this reason he used undulating walls, a dialectic of
convex and concave forms, which meant an unceasing give and take with the urban
voids. The walls were no longer a mere separation between the inside and the outside,
but a diaphragm which could be moulded freely and originally. Finally, he gave a
different interpretation to the connection between the building and the sky, in fact
transforming once and forever the skyscape of Rome.

In almost all of Borromini's buildings you can see an active, aggressive approach
to the city's pattern: for example, the gigantic order of the Palace of Propaganda Fide

tears to pieces the rhythmic sequence of a very narrow street; the Church of Sant'Agnese in Agone breaks the classical static continuity of Piazza Navona; the little church
of San Carlino alle Quattro Fontane, with a tremendous plastic violence unbalances
the equilibrium of the most delicate cross roads of Sistine Rome. But his genius is
particularly explosive in the church of Sant'Ivo alla Sapienza. Near the Pantheon,
Borromini challenged the whole series of Roman cupolas. Instead of designing one
more monumental, heavy cupola, a cupola going downward, he invented the most
dynamic spiral in architectural history; not a Gothic arrow, but a form which twists
its way into the sky, binding it to the cityscape.

Borromini's personality can be recognized on any scale, even the smallest. Look at
the iron gable of the Convent of the Filippini, or at the altars of San Giovanni in
Laterano, or at the balustrade of San Carlino's cloister. The Renaissance and even the
Mannerist lexicon does not exist anymore. Here is a new vocabulary, a new grammar,
a new and unique architectural syntax.

Throughout his life, Borromini was fought by Bernini, who overcame him simply
because he had an enormous talent for compromise. Borromini was a revolutionary
artist who got rid of the very notion of "proportion." On the contrary, Bernini worked
in a theatrical, scenographic manner, always trying to find a balance between Baroque
and Classicism. Borromini was defeated; his suicide ratified his failure. But soon after,
Bernini, too, was defeated. In the second half of the 17th century a tendency emerged
which the art historians call the "neo-cinquecentismo," the "neo-16th century." It
was a classical revival. Thus the question "Progress or Regression?" has to be posed,
because often in the history of architecture we go back. Borromini had opened a path
so rich and splendid that one or two generations at least could have worked on it. But
nobody really followed him.

It is rather difficult for an architect to realize that history is a process and not a
progress. The regression which followed Borromini's death, however, is not an isolated case. It had happened more than a century before with Michelangelo. In 1529
Michelangelo designed the fortifications of Florence. He was then at the climax of his
architectural inventiveness. The programme was merely a functional one, free from
all academic rules which architects were supposed to apply in traditional buildings
like palaces or churches. The purpose here was practical; he could do whatever he
pleased from a visual point of view. And Michelangelo designed spaces, volumes, and
structures in such an incredible way that even today, if an architect were to produce
similar projects, he would be considered revolutionary. First, look at his interior
spaces: no rectangles, no squares, no simple geometrical forms, but magnetic fluency
of formless cavities. Neither Wright nor Le Corbusier ever conceived such daring
shapes. Then look at the outside: the very idea of a compact volume, of a mass, of
planes arranged at right angles, is denied. The walls as solid elements do not exist
anymore. They are almost flexible membranes, changing their depth all the time
according to their specific structural function. In fact, these walls are the meeting line
between the inner spaces wanting to push outwards, and the country pressing inward.
Long before the modern science of construction, centuries before the theory of elastici-
ty, Michelangelo, with his prophetic mind, understood that the strength of a structure
does not depend on the quantity but on the form of the materials.

But Michelangelo's drawings were set aside for four centuries. Nobody stole them, but it was as if they had been lost or burnt. Nobody looked at them. Nobody cared. Nobody was able to recognize the extraordinary message implicit in them. It took four centuries before architectural critics were able to grasp their value.

Therefore, when one thinks of architectural history, one cannot be too optimistic. The image of "the dwarfs on the shoulders of giants" (which says that a man who comes after a giant, even if his size is very small, sees further than the giant because he rests on the giant's shoulders) is a myth, a wishful interpretation of history. So far as architecture is concerned, the dwarfs, that is, the mediocre architects, do not climb on the shoulders of the giants at all. In fact, they hate the genius, they have an inferiority complex toward him, and they want to forget about him. They are looking ahead, and, if they can, they slay the genius.

After Michelangelo we had Mannerism and then the Baroque. Compromise and escape up to the most theatrical conventionalism. After Borromini, we had a few architects like Guarini, who tried to embody the "new system" of Galileo, giving it an architectural expression, especially through the organic play between structure and light. But then architecture became more and more rigid and went back to the Renaissance rules, to the old three-dimensional building box, which both Michelangelo and Borromini had crushed. The Louvre episode is rather symptomatic. Bernini, as everyone knows, was called to Paris to design the Louvre. He was a conservative architect in comparison with Borromini, and his design was particularly conservative. However, it was not accepted. Bernini left Paris, and the Louvre was built as a symbol of the architecture of bureaucracy, the triumph of anonymity.

Chronology sometimes is meaningful. Borromini committed suicide in 1667. The year before, in 1666, l'Académie de Peinture was founded in Paris, and then became the Academy of Beaux-Arts with its Roman outpost, Villa Medici, the very center of the classical reaction that took place during the following years.

I trust that by now I have sufficiently justified my title: "Architecture 1967: Progress or Regression?" Let us consider a giant of our age, Frank Lloyd Wright. Think of his most famous building Fallingwater, the Kaufmann House at Bear Run, near Pittsburgh, Pennsylvania. Everybody can see that Wright was a magnificent reformer on all levels of architecture. He really upset all the usual codes, creating a new language that was capable of infinite and immeasurable messages. But how did the profession, the average architects, react to his immense contribution? They were afraid. They did not try, as one would have expected, to popularize, to diffuse his messages; they ignored him. True, the majority of architects in the United States would admit that he was a genius. But to say of an architect that he is a genius means to damn him, at least from a professional point of view.

They said, for instance, that Frank Lloyd Wright was a self-centered artist. In other words, that he did not care about his clients, that all of his works were only "monuments to himself." This nonsense was reiterated for years and years by both architects and art historians. It is enough to look at the series of houses he built, from those in the first decade of the century up to the last ones, to see that this criticism is simply lunatic. The variety of these houses is almost inconceivable: they are all different in their spatial articulation, in their volumes, in their materials, in the relationship they create between the building and its environment, be it countryside or cityscape. In every house, he created a new image originating with the particular personality of the client, shaping and promoting it, not passively projecting it into architecture. "For every house, a different style," Wright used to say. But it was not a matter of styles. He had principles so consistent and deep regarding the content, that forms would derive from them spontaneously. He never started with a preconceived form. His method applied not to form but to formation. He could be extremely various without ever being eclectic. He could feed his inspiration with a limitless quantity of stimuli without being incoherent. Indeed, Wright's language is so powerful and rich that architects could develop it for at least a century.

On the contrary, architects today refuse to understand Wright's synthesis. They take a single element from it, and they formulate a unilateral theory. For instance, Wright used local vernaculars because he wanted his buildings to belong to the site; this, for him, was simply a starting point, an incentive. But today we have the theory of "anonymous architecture" or of "architecture without architects." He left the design process always open so that it could grow until the very end. Thus the theory came about of an "architecture without a project," resulting from mere chance, from an aggregation of accidents. He took very poor and prosaic elements, like a tent in the desert, and transformed them into works of art. So the theory of what we may call "pop architecture" was born.

His idea of spatial continuity has been the most dismissed. Look at one of his last works: the famous Guggenheim Museum in New York. It was completed after his death, and therefore many details, especially concerning the light, do not follow the original design. But the motivating impulse is quite clear. He did not want the museum to be something isolated and detached from the city context, where people entered with an awesome feeling, as into a church. He wanted to bring the works of art to the public, almost into the street. And this is why he chose a popular form, which belonged to common experience, a multi-storied parking. The street continues into the spiral, and then the spiral ends in the street, with a full symbiosis between interior and exterior space. This spiral recalls Borromini's spiral of Sant'Ivo alla Sapienza, but there is a big difference between the two. Borromini's spiral works up to a point, Wright's opens up, and has a centrifugal impetus toward the city. To underline this continuity between the building and the town, Wright invented a system of lighting changing at every hour of the day and at every season. He thought of a balance between natural and artificial light, a simple ingenious device. This was altered after his death along with many other details: the whole idea of a museum being part of the street scene was repulsive, almost offensive for the academic mind of a museum director.

I believe that what is happening today, after Wright's death, is very similar to what happened after Michelangelo's or Borromini's death. The magnificent heritage is being dilapidated and torn to pieces. Why is this happening? Obviously there are many reasons, but perhaps the most important is that the leaders of the modern movement of the 20s and the 30s, at a certain moment, gave up. They got fed up with themselves. Too many architects get fed up with themselves.

Consider one of the better known masters of the modern movement, Walter Gropius. In his renowned Bauhaus building of 1927 at Dessau, he showed a design principle able to overcome the perspective vision of the Renaissance and the Beaux-Arts tradition. He articulated the volumes so that, to understand them, an observer should move all the time. This is not a building with a main facade, and then sides, and finally a back. It is a dynamic object which brought into architecture what is improperly called, especially by Sigfried Giedion, the "fourth" dimension, that is time. More than that, you can read the functions of the building by looking at it from the outside. The exterior derives from and expresses, or even exposes, the inside functions. You can see immediately that one block is the students' dormitory, that another is made of classrooms and corridors, that the glass box is the laboratory whose activities can be followed from outside. This was Gropius in the 20s and the 30s.

But now take the American Embassy in Athens, a classical and symmetrical building, vaguely reminiscent of a Greek temple, a static object, a facade that conceals everything that goes on behind its walls. The old classicist architecture in reinforced concrete instead of stone. Who would ascribe to Gropius such a conventional and reactionary building? But he designed it recently, denying all the Bauhaus principles.

Ludwig Mies van der Rohe is another great master of the modern movement. Around 1920 he designed splendid skyscrapers, completely transparent and fluent. In his masterpiece of 1929, the German pavilion at the Barcelona Exhibition, he created a dance of spaces. The whole organism, with its free planes springing up in every direction, established such an intimate continuity between the inside and the outside that one was not aware of where the inside ended and the outside began.

After he arrived in the United States, Mies slowly regressed. In his apartment buildings in Chicago he went back to the steel cage, a beautiful steel cage, but still a cage. What is worse, he built the Seagram Building in New York. Architecture critics have exalted this work enthusiastically, defining it as an exceptional piece of architecture. Perhaps it is so, but it is on a cultural path which is looking backward, not ahead. This building is rigidly symmetrical; it is a box and remains such even if it is a beautiful one. Contrary to the Chicago examples, here you have a solid main facade, sides, and back, a traditional concept which defeats the space-time vision of the Barcelona pavilion. Inside there are no spaces, by which I mean creative cavities, but simply static boxes of void.

Let us consider Alvar Aalto, the Finnish architect who appeared to be the most stimulating personality in the 40s and, in part, also in the 50s. His pavilion at the New York Exhibition of 1939 was a masterpiece because its space was dynamic, originally manipulated, energetically compressed by the immense undulating wall impending over the visitors. Later on, in Cambridge, Massachusetts, he built the dormitories for the Massachusetts Institute of Technology. Near the neo-classical complex of this Institute, he created a powerful serpentine form which, in a way, reminds us of Borromini's works.

But then, all of a sudden, Aalto built the Enso-Gutzeit Offices in Helsinki. None of us, neither historian nor architect, looking at a building of this kind, could ever suspect that it was designed by the same man. It is boxy and monumental, the same old enclosure, without spaces and without representation of functions. A clamorous negation of everything that Aalto had done before.

Apart from Frank Lloyd Wright, there is another exception in this sad, regressing panorama. It concerns Le Corbusier, a vital creative mind right up to his death. He was an artist of tremendous courage, who was not afraid to be on the losing side, and to recognize it in architectural terms. He had been, between the two world wars, the leader of the Rationalist movement, what is called in the United States the International Style. After the Second World War, however, he had to acknowledge that the very idea of saving humanity through reason was a fatal illusion. And then he had the guts to contradict himself; he forgot the "five principles" of modern architecture that he himself had formulated in 1921, and he erected the Chapel in Ronchamp, which does not have pilotis, continuous windows, free facades, roof gardens, but shows a new kind of "informal" architecture where the light becomes again an essential instrument in qualifying space. An architecture of gesture, where the psychological impact prevails over all rational data. No doctrine any more, but an explosion of emotions.

Of course, Le Corbusier was an exception to the general rule of regression. A few years ago it looked as if Louis Kahn might be another exception, because he had built a most interesting structure, the Richards Medical Laboratories in Philadelphia. In a state of crisis and confusion, everybody looked at Louis Kahn as a possible salvation, even though he was not a young man. But recently his work in India and on various other projects has been rather disappointing. He used Roman arches, Palladian schemes: he seemed almost to be abdicating.

The same phenomenon can be seen in any type of architecture today. Consider the skyscraper. During the 30s, architects used to give it a dynamic impulse. In New York, the Rockefeller Center embodied space-time values on an urban scale—simultaneity and interaction of visions. But the recent skyscrapers built on Park Avenue or in downtown New York are static boxes, prisons, all more or less equal except for the curtain walls. Sometimes sophisticated, more often tedious, they are all insignificant. Architecture stops being a human art, and becomes a commercial mass-medium — classical, of course.

If we go back to the classical, three-dimensional vision of the Renaissance, we might as well go back farther still, back to the caves. Edward Stone can build a museum in New York using pseudo-Venetian forms badly derived from the Ducal Palace. An architect can do whatever he wants in an atmosphere of indifference and cynicism. He can even build a scandal, the biggest scandal of recent years—the Lincoln Center in New York. No historian, two thousand years from now, looking at the ruins of the Lincoln Center (we hope that by then it will be in ruins) will ever imagine that it was built years after the Bauhaus, the Chapel in Ronchamp, Fallingwater and the Guggenheim Museum. Nobody will believe it. People will analyze the archives but they will conclude that the documents are false. The Lincoln Center, they will argue, may belong to the end of the 18th century, or perhaps it may even be an offspring of the Columbian Exhibition of 1893, when Sullivan's school was wiped out by a classical reaction. But nobody will ever believe that the Lincoln Center was built or even conceived in our age. It is not conceivable.

This is not to say that these buildings are not often technologically perfect. Probably some of them were designed and calculated with the computer. But the computer gives only certain answers, and to use it one has to formulate questions that the computer can answer. This is just what is happening, and not only in New York: architects are only asking questions that the computer can answer. In other words, they get the answers before getting the questions. The fact is that the computer can answer very few questions concerning the biological, psychological, sociological, and aesthetic aspects of the architectural problem. This is true of the Lincoln Center just as of the new capital of Brazil. Everyone knows Brasilia: it is a classical, rhetorical, and monumental city, disguised in pseudo-modern forms. Look at the Parliament set-up. On one side the Low House of Representatives, on the other side the Low Senate. In the middle, two towers symbolizing the two powers, but actually used by a unique and most powerful power, the bureaucracy. It is clear that the bureaucrats from the top of the towers could look down on the political class and spit on them. Anyone who had "read" architecture could have foreseen what was going to happen. Bureaucracy was dominating. So it was easy for the generals to close down Brasilia and kill the parliamentary life of the country.

This reminds me of an incident. After I had selected for this lecture the theme "Architecture 1967: Progress or Regression?" I received a letter from Montreal. They asked me to change the subject or at least the title of my lecture in order to speak of town planning instead of architecture. They thought that it would be a more stimulating subject. My answer was a kind "no." I told them that there was no real difference between architecture and town planning, but that by concentrating on architecture, the signs of today's crisis would be more evident. It is my belief, based on some historical knowledge, that in all ages urban concepts are coherent with architectural concepts. There cannot be a town plan without an architectural style capable of giving a third dimension to it. One does not really know which comes first. In an age of Greek architecture made up of "pure volumes under light," as Le Corbusier used to say, cities will be made up of isolated volumes. Greek architecture cannot be used in a medieval town, which is based on continuity and not on isolated volumes. If continuity is the aim of town planning, then architecture must offer a continuum, as in the small streets and piazzas of Siena or Venice. In the same way, medieval architecture cannot be used for a star-like city of the Renaissance, nor Renaissance architecture for a Baroque town based on a continuity totally different from the medieval one, but still rejecting isolated volumes.

Therefore, to speak of town planning without checking all the time its coincidence with architecture is useless. One could say, "Tell me the kind of architecture you want and I will give you a city plan," or vice versa. One who believes in a kind of architecture such as the *grande ensembles* of Paris will produce a type of city consonant with this kind of architecture. On the other hand, an "architecture of escape" goes with an evasive plan. Pop architecture calls for pop planning, and the other way around.

At this point we must consider with more attention what the situation is today. We have a classical reaction similar to the ones which followed Michelangelo and Borromini. At the same time, we have a reaction against this reaction. Utopias multiply: the architectural magazines are filled with utopian designs. It is quite natural. If reality is the Lincoln Center, the only hope rests in flight from reality. So utopias are born. They may consist of the designs by the British Archigram group or of the endless house by Frederick Kiesler, an invitation to go back to the cave, to the primitive, to a kind of architecture which is sculpted from the inside and in which formless spaces are extolled by mysterious lights. Against classicism, of course, we have anti-classicism even in its most arbitrary versions.

There is another theory which we have to discuss, because to some extent it attempts to mediate between the two opposing tendencies of today, that is between classicism and utopia. It is called architectural pluralism. It states that our world is too complicated, too various, too contradictory to be expressed in one coherent style. Only a dictatorship can express itself with one style. A democracy can be managed only with many tendencies and contradictory elements.

In speaking of Frank Lloyd Wright, we noted that consistency of principles does not deny variety. The consistency is not in the results, but in the method. Pluralism, on the contrary, stimulates an eclectic approach, and it is a good alibi or compensation for the lack of consistency of the majority of today's architects.

One of the best architects who experienced pluralism was Eero Saarinen. He started in a Miesian way, producing the General Motors Technical Center in Detroit, a rigid but quite correct scheme. At a certain moment, however, Saarinen became romantic. He came to Italy, and we often met in Rome. He was looking for the "mystical atmosphere" of churches. I asked him, "What churches, of what ages?" "All Churches," he said; actually we have quite a few churches in Rome, plus the Pope. At the end of his trip, Eero had decided that a church should be round, based on a circle, because the circle is perfection, and after all, God is perfect, otherwise he would not be God. Having discoverered this astonishing fact, he said that you needed a vertical element, I suppose because God is located in the sky and you have to point to him, not to the devil whose address is somewhere underground. Eero added that the material for a church or a chapel should be brick, as in the Romanesque period, and that you needed some kind of trembling light to give a mystical feeling to the inside. Out of this romantic and naive research, the chapel at MIT was built.

Later on, Saarinen seemed to embrace neo-medievalism. Back in Italy, he was looking for enclosed outside spaces, and something of Italy's piazzas can be found in the New Haven students' dormitories. Before becoming neo-medieval, however, Eero became "structural": the Yale Skating Rink and the Dulles Airport are among his best works. But he was not fully satisfied. All of a sudden, he felt that space in architecture should be given more importance. "Space plus structure will make architecture" was, more or less, what he thought. Out of it he produced the TWA Terminal at Kennedy Airport in New York. It was not really successful: the spatial fluency inside is beautiful and significant, even if slightly self-indulgent. The outside, on the other hand, is too much of a structural tour de force: he contorted the material, shaping and sculpting the reinforced concrete, going back to Expressionism, but without the rigor that exists, for instance, in the Einstein Tower designed by Erich Mendelsohn in 1921. If he had persisted in this research, Saarinen could have achieved first-class stature as an artist; but he was a pluralist, which means an eclectic, even if within modern trends. So he designed the most dissimilar buildings: the American Embassy in London, a failure; the Gothic-like CBS Building in New York; the Bell Telephone Laboratories at Holmdel, New Jersey, a huge glass wall, curious only because it is so huge.

Eero Saarinen was undoubtedly the best of the pluralists; this is why it is worthwhile criticizing him. He worked with great professional dignity, but lacking a principle or a method—one might say an ideology—never achieved the kind of consistent, rich, true variety that Frank Lloyd Wright did. Eero was searching all the time; he liked searching so much that he seemed to be almost afraid to find. From a didactic point of view, his influence was negative. He gave the impression that an architect could do anything, follow any idiosyncrasies whatever. Actually, Eero never disregarded the principles of the modern movement; he was only unable to select from among them. The others, however, felt that, if one could be an eclectic within the modern movement, then it was legitimate to be an eclectic without any limitations at all. Hence, the Lincoln Center, and what has been called "the vanguard of crayfish," that is, the vanguard of those who go backwards.

The modern movement, clearly, is besieged by two opposing forces. On the one side, the academy, monumentalism, and classicism are trying to bring us back to the old rules, the old proportions, a dictatorial architecture superimposed on society. Against this tendency is the pop line: no rules, no principles, no design, no order of any kind, in the end no architecture, total refusal. Two different ways to kill the modern movement and to commit suicide: the old box of classicism, or the chaos of pop architecture—perhaps one should call it beat architecture. This is the dilemma today, in a period when self-destructive forces seem to prevail over creative energies.

This, however, is not the whole picture. Fortunately, against the destructive forces, many architects in every country are fighting to defend and advance the modern movement. In closing, I will mention a few examples.

In Germany, Hans Scharoun and his "school" stem the spreading commercialism. Scharoun survived the Nazi reaction, and now is surviving the neo-capitalist reaction. His Berlin Philharmonic, both in the lobby and in the auditorium, is a masterly conception of space.

So far as Italy is concerned, there is not much authentic modern architecture to show. But a recent building in Rome, between Via Romagna and Via Campania, is quite interesting because it demonstrates how pluralism, or rather polyvalency, may work within the same structure. Commercial functions on the ground floor, offices in the middle, on top a series of "villas" designed with the same freedom which is generally applied only in the countryside. Breaking the box, you can have the most imaginative and logical function forms.

Of course Great Britain is leading in town planning and, I think, also in architecture. It is a country which has a long tradition in the modern movement and is going forward. But new countries have emerged in recent years, above all Canada. Until ten years ago Canada did not exist in the history of modern architecture. But now, especially for its new universities, it is becoming one of the most interesting and alive centers of architectural research in the world. I will not mention the Montreal Expo, but I feel sure that the Habitat built for Expo is going to remain a reference point during the next decades. I said at a recent press conference that the Habitat is to Montreal 1967 as the Eiffel Tower is to Paris 1889.

These few examples are enough. They testify that we have no need to destroy ourselves with a classicist reaction or with a beat escape. We can continue the tradition of the modern movement, which started with Michelangelo and Borromini and had its last genius in Frank Lloyd Wright. In Philadelphia, you can see Wright's last building: it is a synagogue, "a mountain of light," a symbol from a distance, of Mount Sinai. No monumentalism, just a monument that reminds us of Israel and the heroic people that recently saved mankind, all of us, from a Third World War.

HEBRAISM AND THE CONCEPT OF SPACE-TIME IN ART

IX Congress of the Italian Jewish Communities, Opening Speech, The Capitol, Protomoteca Hall, Rome, June 9, 1974

It is with some reluctance that I approach the theme "Hebraism and space-time in art." First, I am not quite sure that it is the most urgent argument for the opening of this congress. Second, despite the numerous contributions which have appeared in recent years—many of them recorded in our *Rassegna mensile di Israel*—this is a vast subject, still largely unexplored, and involving religious, philosophical, historical, psychological, aesthetic and semiological problems, a field of research to be tackled on an inter-disciplinary basis. Third, an audio-visual documentation would be necessary; music by Mahler, Bloch, Schönberg; slides of works by Chagall, Soutine and Modigliani, Lipchitz and Zadkine and Meldelsohn; snatches of Yiddish theater and of films of, at least, Eisenstein and Chaplin, all of which is impossible in this hall. For these reasons, I beg your imaginative indulgence as I proceed.

It has been said that Hebraism is a concept of time, that, while the divinities of other peoples are associated with places and things, the God of Israel is a god of events, and that Jewish life, nourished by the Book, is permeated with history, that is, with a time-related consciousness of human tasks.

In fact, Hebraic thought, in its dialogue across the centuries with the philosophical currents emerging in various and contradictory socio-cultural contexts, has always refused to espouse any dogma or fetish, including that of time. A most coherent, and cruel, proof of this attitude was offered, on October 17, 1910, by Carlo Michelstaedter who killed himself in Florence, at the age of 23, immediately after having handed in his thesis in philosophy. His reasoning was that, if historical life is alienation, if time is a sham, an awaiting the only sure thing—death in the future—it is cowardly to knuckle under to convictions and rhetoric: freedom from error and deceit lies in the refusal of time, that is, in the choice of death in the present. The metaphysical goal of the existential absolute leads, in Michelstaedter, to self-destruction of existence. A proof *ad absurdum,* paid in person coldly, rationally, by a young Jewish philosopher; or, as has been written, "a heresy splendid because of its anachronistic nature in a world which has become inferior to the possibilities of heresy."

On the other hand, a long time before the extreme case of Michelstaedter, three great thinkers, Philo, Maimonides, and Spinoza, proposed to seek a number of mediations between ontology and relativity. The time concept has always prevailed, however, since Hebraism cannot be reduced from any point of view to the concept of space. At the root core, the very Hebraic idea of God denies it.

A source of perennial and disconcerting wonder is the way in which God identifies Himself in the First Commandment. Among the innumerable titles He could have given Himself, He chooses that of a freedom campaign. He does not proclaim "I am the Lord your God who has created the universe, the world, man," he presents Himself as the leader of a revolutionary movement rather than as a god, almost as a chief of a partisan brigade who has fled from the siege by Fascist criminals. He says: "I am the Lord your God Who brought you out of the land of Egypt," out of a condition of slavery. The passport God shows to Moses on Mt. Sinai is given a visa by a specific historical event: not by an act but by an action; not by a miracle but by a pledge to fight against repression and obscurantism, a pledge carried out throughout time not only in the chronological sense but also in the dynamism of its execution, in the revolt against injustice, in the pursuit of a habit of freedom.

Let us suppose, for a moment, that God had been less modest and had, in that First Commandment, claimed His copyright to the creation of the world. We would be amazed, nonetheless, for the creation of the world was not an act but a time-consuming process. Why did it take God six days to create the world and a day to rest? After all, He did not have to do piece-work; He could take His time; He could have taken, who knows, a fortnight! This might not have been such a bad idea as it would have permitted Him a few touch-ups to the human psyche, male and female. Or, given the fact that He was not *a* God the Father but *the* God the Father, He would have created the world, if not in 24 hours, at least in five days and given Himself a long weekend. In any case, it took time. He did not create it in one thrust, He took pains which wearied Him, otherwise He would not have felt the need to rest; He worked out the product by stages, which is to say that He did not start from any *a priori*, from any preconceived and crystalized idea. He started His work empirically, without knowing exactly where it would end. He roughed it out in six days, then He stopped—and we should not exclude that, in His summing up, He was not too satisfied. Then, why not begin anew? Six days are few, indeed, even to reform the world, let alone create it: what was the hurry?

God, as such, could have framed the world in utter perfection, tidy, uncorrupted and incorruptible, where man, condemned to ecstasy, would have yawned to the point of nausea, feeling himself a futile, decorative element, a passive spectator perpetually applauding the same performance. Instead, God acted like an avant garde artist: He painted half the picture, He wrote half the script— or, perhaps, three quarters— leaving the task of completing the work to the user. He wanted man to cooperate with Him, even cursing when he does not seize His design or despairing when he becomes aware of its ambiguity.

Involved with God in a creative responsibility, not in the mere contemplation of the already-created, the Jew finds his life style measured by time. Our holy days are marked, in large part, by the seasons and by our memories. In the sabbath the religious identify the sanctification of time, of God, of existence. "The sabbaths are our great cathedrals," Heschel says, and he explains: "Jewish ritual as the art of significant forms in time, as 'architecture of time' . . . The essence of the sabbath is absolutely outside of space. During six days of the week we live under the tyranny of things in space; on the sabbath, we put ourselves in tune with the sanctity of time." "From the world of creation" we pass to "the creation of the world." Translated into lay terms, we place growth and becoming ahead of being, formation ahead of form as a completed entity.

Our history is antistatic, antispatial to a degree that has no parallel. It begins with a diaspora, a scattering, with exile into Egypt, with migration toward Palestine. The diaspora continues after the destruction of the second Temple and continues down the centuries with dramatic exoduses and systematic efforts to return. Nomads from the beginning, then wanderers until Theodor Herzl's dream was realized, as Nachum

Goldman noted, "in the 'galuth' we express our specific historical character, however paradoxical that might seem."

It is logical that this time concept, so experienced and suffered, should have decisive repercussions in all aspects of Hebraic research, from mathematics to art.

Awareness of space breeds idolatry, that of time underlies heresy. Jews are Jews in that they refuse the static nature of things and ideas, and believe in change and redemption.

In art, in the ancient world, the iconoclastic attitude is heresy. It depends not only on the will not to debase a principle whose content cannot be represented, but also on the judgement that the representative form is inadequate. The images of the ancient world, especially the Egyptian, are static. The Greek ideal represents the human being as an absolute, above history, beyond time—not man in the dynamics of daily living, but the human type, indeed the prototype. Such art could not be used to communicate the Hebraic message.

The thesis I submit to you may be stated in few words. Hebraism, in art, opposes three concepts: (a) classicism, (b) illuminism, (c) analytical cubism.

No to classicism because it is based on a priori orders.

No to the age of enlightenment because it propounds universal, absolute and absolutist ideas.

No to cubism because it makes abstractions from matter, it takes apart, superimposes and fits together forms in a process which is not really dynamic since it has no respect for the self-creation of form, and confines itself merely to the assembly of forms.

Hebraism in art emphasizes the anti-classical, the expressionistic de-structuring of forms; it rejects the ideological fetishes of golden proportions and celebrates relativity; it denies the authoritarian rules concerning what is beautiful, and opts for the illegality and disorderliness of what is true.

It follows that, for Hebraism, art is not a catharsis in the mythical, guilt-ridden sense. Rather, it opposes myths of whatever nature, whether transcendent or immanent, just as does science. On different levels, both Einstein and Freud are desecrators of myths. Schönberg is no less so: he opposes the octave, formulates the twelve-tone scale and even then renders the latter relative. In the field of literature, there is Kafka; in the visual, Soutine or Meldelsohn—substantially one single commitment to desanctify, laicise, break idols, destroy myths. The idol is the golden calf, the frightful, interminable, continuously self-renewing series of golden calves, dogmas, axioms, 'revealed' truths, rhetorical marble-heroes, before which Jewish history is one long plebiscite, reiterating *no,* with incredible critical and especially self-critical tenacity: a priesthood dedicated to time and development, to prosaic everyday behavior. "The teachings of Hebraism," says Heschel in a truly memorable passage, "consist in the theology of common action. The Bible emphasizes that God's interest is in everyday living, in the customs of daily life. The challenge is not in the organizing of great demonstrative systems but in the way we handle the commonplace." That is why our sanctuary may be a tent under the open sky, an ark-mobile which follows our itinerary: it is a temple called school because history is taught there, and it may be the peripatetic school of our wanderings, since history is in The Book which is in us.

Naturally, one finds a certain detachment between religion and art. For a rabbi like

Alexander Safran, "Hebrew time is sabbath time" and the Jew "must not reckon it as do other men. He computes it differently, in order not to fall, as a consequence of an easy calculation or of a lack of calculation, into the headlong wish to live or into a longing for death, still less into the free-and-easy ways of apathy toward existence." For the artist it is something else. His heresy is full of existentialist toil; time is a fleeting and consuming condition, quite often a belonging to the present. Time, for the artist, is not sabbath time but a time of anguish, if not of death, then of life. For Rabbi Simeon, "eternity is won by those who exchange space for time," and who, "instead of filling space with buildings, bridges and roads, understand that the solution lies in study and in prayer rather than in geometry and engineering." For the artist, it is completely different: he does not exchange space for time, he temporalizes space. Seen from this angle, the artist is more hebraic than the rabbi: he is like God who, dividing the time of creation into seven days, placed it in "intimate relation with space." Truly, the golden calf is everywhere: even in time, in the abstract. But the artist, embodying it through the experience of space, makes it concrete and human.

Let us consider some examples, among the innumerable ones available. The simplest is perhaps that of the two young Jewish people in *The Garden of the Finzi-Contini,* the novel by Giorgio Bassani. They are, virtually, in love, but they do not manage to realize their love, to live it in space. The imagination not so much of the "before" but of the "after" precludes it. The boy says: "For me no less than for her the memory of things counted more than their possession, memory in the face of which any possession must, in itself, seem banal, delusive, insufficient . . . My anxiety that the present must *immediately* become past so that I might love it and cherish it at my leisure was also hers, exactly the same. This was *our* vice . . ." This happens not only in the shadowy atmosphere of youthful love. The same phenomenon takes place in the boy's relations with his father: ". . . he spoke as if I and he were already dead and as if now, from some point outside space and time, we were talking to one another about life, about everything that in the course of our respective lives, could have been and had not been . . ."

What is the "vice" of these Jews who retain Jewish feelings no longer illumined by religion? The theology of the everyday is hampered, actions no longer related to rituals lose their meaning and tension; reduced to pretexts to be evoked at a later date, they become ineffective and paralyzing. Space is not annulled, but makes itself unreal, suspended as it is between a past which has not taken place and a presentiment of death.

In the Ferrara's and in the Italian context, in general, tragedy is somehow limited. The unreality of Modigliani's etiolated faces is not comparable to the maniacal deformations of those by Soutine. Thus the unreality of Bassani's characters appears tenuous and elegiac when compared with those of Kafka.

In Kafka, the contrast explodes between man's condition within space and the time sense of his soul's alienation. The breach is too wide to span: it leads to the monstrous, the absurd, to a negativity all the more desolate since the Jew has no taste for it and gets no romantic enjoyment from it; he cannot accept it either anthropologically or intellectually. Many of Kafka's stories, you will recall, begin with an awakening. An awakening from uneasy dreams which takes place not because of contact with some real experience but, on the contrary, because of a frighteningly glacial contact with the unreality of the human condition. No sooner is he awake than man is accused of something, tried for he knows not what crime, awaiting a verdict handed down by who knows what judge, in who knows what court building, standing for who knows what justice. Total ambush, an incomprehensible world, mad but fiercely organized according to efficient methods before which we stand defenseless and as if stripped of our humanity: we walk ahead like automata scarcely recovered from indescribable, hallucinating anxiety. If we adapt, if this anxiety leaves us, a metamorphosis takes place, space wins out over time, man-become-parasite truly changes into a repellent and disgusting insect; the trial stops only because the accused has been obliterated.

So a painful and fruitless awakening because we do not manage to recognize ourselves in space and in things. Kafka, for instance, visits a "restored" ghetto, looks at it without perceiving it, since its new spatial configuration has replaced time, the time sense of memory: "Within us the dark corners, the mysterious passages, the blind windows, dirty courtyards, noisy bars, boarded-up inns still exist. Today we walk through the broad streets of the rebuilt city but our glances and our footsteps are uncertain; inside, we tremble still as on the old streets of our distress. Our hearts as yet know nothing of the 'restoration' that has taken place. The old unhealthy Jewish quarter within us is more real than the new hygienic city all around us. Awake, we walk as in a dream, we too ghosts of time past."

Chagall's world is only in appearance antithetical to Kafka's. In fact, it is the same world but where the absurd is transformed into fairytale. For Chagall, too, man lives between two equally intolerable dreams, that of space, of the Jewish village with its huts, its pogroms, its isolation and hate, and that of time, with its topsy-turvy, ruinous skies. Man cannot live on the earth or in heaven but, thanks to the fantasy of the chassidim, he may provisionally occupy an intermediate zone immediately above the dreary hovels and below the tempestuous sky. In this imaginary and neutral zone, man wins out over the earth's gravity and the weight of the sky: all is harmony for there the absurd becomes reality, donkeys and violins, pendulum clocks and wedded couples are poised in the enveloping wind, larvae strangers to both life and death. If this mediating zone where opposites are reconciled should cease to be, that is, if one were to wake, then the sky would jolt down to meet the earth, as in the picture "The Doors of the Cemetery." If the transposition into fairytale ceases, Chagall's interval becomes Kafka's—between accusation and sentence, between condemnation and execution.

Saul Bellow is the same, in another key. *Mr. Sammler's Planet* is never synchronized with our planet. It is a planet *autre:* even when Sammler goes to Israel, his time is never reabsorbed and given peace in space. Instinctively drawn to fly to the land of his forebearers, where the centuries-old dream of return has been accomplished, he does not recognize it, as if it were too late for the bowed soul of the "just." Sammler says: "Life's many impressions and experiences seemed no longer to fit each into its niche in proper spatial order, each with its own recognizable religious and aesthetic importance, but human beings suffered—even Sammler speaks of man today in the past tense, as if of something that had ceased to exist—the humiliation of incongruent situations, of confused styles, of a long life that once contained many different, well separated lives. In fact, today each single life was obliterated by the flood tide of the entire experience of mankind, making all the historical ages simultaneous, forcing the fragile human being to receive and register, depriving him, with that volume, with that mass, of any power of leaving on it a trace of his own design."

What is implied by the characters of Bassani, Kafka, Bellow, by infinite others of Werfel, Zweig, Saba, Svevo, Malamud, Salinger and Roth, Babel and Agnon, not to mention those of Proust and Pasternak? What is this time-related anxiety, this existential anguish, this exhumation of memories either buried or removed to the realm of the unconscious, which is, after all, the motivation of Freudian analysis? It is quite clear: anguish arises from doubt and insecurity. The time factor prevails over that of space because man is uprooted. No spot on earth is immune from anti-Semitism, no place is safe, not even the land of Israel. Perhaps this is why the word "place" in Hebrew is often used to refer to God, which would be inconceivable in Greek philosophy.

Dazed by two equally unreal worlds, oscillating between the sour fantasies of dreams and the cruel nightmares of a reality even more indecipherable and foreign, the Jewish artist torments himself in his solitude, wounding both matter and ideologies. Only under exceptional circumstances, when the Hebrew tragedy coincides with that of the rest of humanity, can his repressed cry explode in the market-place. This happens in Zadkine's "Monument to the Martyrdom of the Destroyed City" in Rotterdam, a cry of horror at the atrocities perpetrated by the Nazi butchers which raises its invective in spasms to the sky. Only in such rare moments as during the anti-Fascist Resistance and revolutionary uprisings, when myths are overthrown and revolt is bred from oppression, can Jews be like others— only in emergencies, when tremendous disasters drive humanity from their lairs of cowardice and hypocrisy.

Otherwise, the Jewish intellectual and, to an even greater extent, the Jewish artist live in a state of incommunicability, suffering all the consequences of this condition. He cannot let himself be deluded, nor can he believe in even the most hypnotic and perfervid myths; he cannot believe in Illuminism nor, what is even worse, can he have faith in culture. In order to grasp Hebraism's contribution to art, such confrontations should not be ignored.

Illuminism, the idea of universal equality, of liberty, of equal rights for all, was meant to give a sense of security even to Jews. And how many of them embraced this ideal, fought for it. It took the death camps for Adorno to discover how Illuminism can logically debouch in Nazism: "There is no difference between the totemic animal and the absolute idea . . ." Adorno writes. "Myth is already Illuminism, and Illuminism becomes mythology . . . Illuminism is to things what the dictator is to peoples: it recognizes them in so far as it can manipulate them . . . Abstraction, the tool of Illuminism, works on its subjects just as did Fate, or Destiny, a notion which Illuminism eliminated: in order to liquidate them . . . The pure positivistic immanence, its end product, is nothing more than what we might call a universal tabu: nothing can be *outside* any longer, because the mere idea of an *outside* is a source of anxiety . . ." Now the Jews, and especially the Jewish artists, are always "outside," a sheet of litmus paper, living witness to the ways in which the worst wickedness can mask itself behind ideological abstractions. How can one believe in the principles of justice and democracy when they are humiliated by the first oil shortage? How can one believe in that myth of the Left, *pas d'ennemis à gauche,* in view of anti-Semitism in the Soviet Union? One cannot even believe in the autonomy of culture, for we have seen it enslaved by power.

No Jewish artist, in fact, no artist whether Jewish or not, provided he has received the Hebrew message, can forget what George Steiner wrote in *Language and Silence* a propos of German culture during the Hitler regime: "The cries of the doomed could be heard from the Universities, sadism walked the streets at the entrances and exits of theaters and museums . . . Ideas of cultural evolution and intrinsic rationality, elaborated from the time of ancient Greece and still intensely valid in Marx's utopian historicism and in Freud's stoic authoritarianism (two late exponents of Graeco-Roman civilization), can no longer be safely propounded . . . Today we know that a man may read Goethe and Rilke in the evening, may listen to or play Bach and Schubert, and then, on the following morning, return to his job at Auschwitz . . . In what way does this knowledge affect our hope that culture is a humanizing force, that the energies of the spirit are transferable to those of behavior? It is not merely the fact that the traditional tools of civilization—university, music, books— have not managed to put up adequate resistance to political bestiality: often they have lent themselves to welcoming and celebrating it."

It is not surprising that, against such a backdrop, Hebraism in art chose to manifest itself chiefly along Expressionistic lines. Expressionism was the only movement deter-mined to demolish all aesthetic and linguistic tabus without immediately erecting others, the only movement that could reduce them to zero degree, well aware that an apparently negative and destructive operation was, in fact, destructive but of idols and of golden calves. Indeed, it was the only movement that had the courage to destructure without restructuring, to achieve a time sense with the aim not of reaching an alternate spatial solution, but always somehow spatial, but of excluding any alter-native.

The burning slashes of Chaim Soutine are proof of this. "He paints instinctively, without paying the least attention to artistic trends . . ." Mario de Micheli wrote. "He is obsessed with his images, in which he pours out his invectives, his portents of disaster. Red dominates his canvasses, hot red, as thick as venous blood, a purplish red that burns as with a fever. And along with red there are greens, now the green of mold, now that of turgid vegetation. He paints his haunches of beef hanging from the hooks in butcher shops, his plucked chickens, almost obscene in their nakedness, just as you see them on the marble slabs of the poultry stalls. This butchered flesh, these poor defenseless shameless creatures, killed and laid out for show, achieve an emblematic quality. There is in them something like the distant echo of the pogroms perpetrated in the ghettos, the slaughter of wretched defenseless people. Like Segal, Soutine just grazes the centuries-old sorrows of his persecuted people. Thus we find infinite yet wounding tenderness in his paintings of boys, the little seminarians, the hotel runners, who offer their fragile innocence to the blows of fate."

The dynamic matter, the contortions of expression in the distraught faces are no more than the end result of the conditions and ethics of uprooting. And this end result is not limited to the psychological content or simply to its forms; it is evident in the very basis of communication, in language.

What Kafka states about Yiddish is highly pertinent to our subject, Yiddish in which so much of the theater, humor, self-irony of Jewish art is expressed. He notes that "it has not yet formed as clear linguistic structures as would be necessary. Its expressions are short and nervous. It has no grammar. Some amateurs have tried to write grammars, but Yiddish is spoken without a pause, and it finds no peace. The people will not give it over to the grammarians." Kafka's remarks could apply to the whole range of Hebrew art. "Yiddish is made up entirely of foreign words. These words, however, do not rest within its breast but keep the haste and vivacity with which they were first greeted. Yiddish is riddles, from one end of it to the other, by the migration of peoples. All that German, Hebrew, French, English, Slav, Dutch, Rumanian, and even Latin . . . it requires a certain amount of energy just to bundle all these tongues together in this way . . . And then, added to these various linguistic structures made up of arbitrary and fixed norms, there are the dialects, because all Yiddish is dialect, even the written language."

In the same key, we could analyze the music of Gustav Mahler, that great anthology of fragments, that magma of linguistic contaminations, popular songs, erudite comments, muddy illegitimate roots, satire, grimaces, funeral marches, sounds of nature— a congeries of mosaic tesserae which elude any pattern, made up of borrowings, anacronisms and inventions, aristocratic art and Kitsch, a hazardous montage impossible to reduce to syntactical and grammatical rules. An over-intensely composite hodge-podge it is, in which you may find anything and everything except the theme of the Nibelungen, whose place has been taken by that of the children's death.

Arnold Schönberg embodies Hebraism in art not only better than do Mahler and Bloch, but perhaps better than any other creative spirit in any form of artistic expression. What he called "the emancipation of dissonance" remains his major contribution, a discovery of incalculable importance which is at the root of every modern artistic research and, in fact, of all modern and fruitful ways of thinking and acting. The liberating of dissonance means the elimination of the last remnants of Illuminism and neo-classicism, the freedom from the gigantic apparatus of symphony and opera; and, further, the freedom from tonality, from everything hierarchical and authoritarian which presupposes a "before" and an "after." We do not need a symbolist interpretation to realize that the emancipation of dissonance coincides with the emancipation of the Jewish people, the most hated, derided and offended dissonant element of human culture. At that moment in which Schönberg proves that "music without constant reference to a tonic" is "understandable" and "capable of producing attitudes and states of mind, of provoking emotions, and is not without humour or gaity," at the moment in which dissonances are no longer exceptions or "special spice" of the assonances, and offer an alternative linguistic organism at once vital and autonomous, he accomplishes a revolution of Mosaic proportions.

He conducts this revolution in an extremely coherent manner, better than Kafka, Soutine and Chagall, better than Einstein and Freud, because he is not satisfied with merely stating the two unrealities that make human life impossible, and he does not seek a plausible compromise, but he proves the complete legitimacy and, what is more, the communicative validity of a structural state of contradictions. Ideally, the emancipation of dissonance reintegrates the Jews in the community of peoples, since it sweeps away those academic and formalistic hold-overs that had caused their ostracism. This takes place on many levels: by means of dazzling atonalism, by the "seismographic registration of traumatic shocks," as Adorno says, by the rigorous adherence to serialism stripped of any sonorous sensuality, by the most strained and hammered tones all the way to the brief and pale tones, by "multidimensional" sonorous space down to "radical music."

I should mention Segal, Werfel, Brod, and Zweig, along with many other artists, and folklore, Hebrew and Israeli dance; I should at least mention Einstein's concepts of the "extension of space" and of the "field," and Freud's notion of the coexistence of the successive phases of psychic development. But I shall spare you all this in order not to take advantage of your patience; moreover, my competence is inadequate in many of these areas and I should have to rely on the judgments of others. You will allow me, however, to dedicate the last minutes of my talk to a field in which I have some first-hand knowledge, namely architecture.

The theme "Hebraism and space-time concept in architecture" is especially interesting because it leads one to defy any ethnic and anthropological, not to say racial, ambiguity. In fact, this conversation is not entitled "The Jews and the space-time concept in art" but "Hebraism and the space-time concept," thus emphasizing that Hebraism, particularly in art, goes beyond the delimitation of the Jewish people. The Hebrew message influences many non-Jewish artists: this is especially noticeable in architecture, a field where, historically, the Jews have been few and far between.

The problem of space-time is highly complex in architecture because, for millennia, man has been terrified not only of time but of space, the void, the hollow places, that is to say, by the element that specifically characterizes architecture. For thousands of years, from pre-history to the Pantheon, space was considered a negativity, and man built temples and monuments giving primary importance to the plastic aspects—sculpture of vast dimensions—and neglecting or suppressing the "space within" element. Awareness of space was born late in history and in human experience: even today, the majority of so-called cultivated persons have no spatial perception; they stop at the outer shell, at "the box," without being able to "see" space itself.

When, with the Pantheon, space finally achieved artistic recognition, it was a question of static, spherical, closed immovable space which precludes any contact with the exterior, so that it receives light from a single, top-placed oculus. The time factor is totally bypassed. Time begins to affect architecture only in the late Roman era, when art is no longer monopolized by Greek plasticism and welcomes the Oriental style of "continuous narrative." The film-like stories of Trajan's and Antoninus's columns codify this change in sculpture.

How did the change take place in late Roman art? What eastern sources determined its new courses? This is still an open question. True it is, however, that the Hebrew paintings and mosaics discovered in the Middle East during the last decades are conceived as continuous narration, kinetic and time-linked. They are ascribed to the middle of the 3rd century, but they show such skill and maturity of language that they fully legitimize the supposition of preceding cycles which could have acted as inspiration for the art works of the late Roman period. Be that as it may, they clearly bespeak the Hebrew choice: negation of the immobile, static, classical, proportioned, and naturalistic; affirmation of the historical narrative, expressionistic, dynamic, fluid.

In architecture, a time-linked concept, anti-spatial to a metaphysical degree, took place only in an exceptional epoch: that of the Jewish and Christian catacombs. Then, underground passageways scores of miles long crossed and surmounted one another without geometric patterns: they literally corroded, undermined the very foundations of the great Roman city that stretched above them, monumentally spatial and static. The divine city of time went underground to burst the earthly city above. Architecture ceased to mean space. It came to mean wandering, measureless wandering without goal.

As soon as the church triumphed and took on the inheritance of Roman institutions, the compromise began between the Hebrew or Biblical trend and the Graeco-Roman world. The Christian basilica, in contrast to the Roman, organized its elements in such a way as to take into account man's ambulatory functions; that is, static space was revolutionized but within strict limitations, for man's movement was uni-directional, from the entrance to the altar; at the sides, the architectural framework remains essentially classical and spatial.

From those centuries on, architectural history is the account of the struggle to release space from its static constraint and make it time-conscious. Basic stages were the dilated spaces of the Byzantine world, the directional contrasts of the Gothic cathedral, the asymmetrical cavities, the circuits, the symbiosis between buildings, streets and squares in Medieval civilization, the urban dynamics and the compressed or exploded spaces in the Baroque period.

The struggle between time and space is the struggle between freedom and constriction, between inventiveness and academy, in linguistic terms between *paroles* and *langue,* in psychoanalytic key between the ego and the super-ego, in societal jargon between structure and super-structure. Golden calves, i.e. ideological space concepts, continue to turn up: we see them again in the Renaissance, when they were opposed by Mannerism, especially by Michelangelo who, on this very hill, the Capitoline, had the courage to realize an anti-perspective, trapezoidal piazza compressing, crushing space so as to charge it with energy. There were more golden calves after Michelangelo, and they were disposed of by Borromini; they came back, however, with neo-classicism and have been dispelled again by the modern movement. Architectural expressionism found its major exponent in Erich Mendelsohn whose buildings and visions seem to spring free by telluric motion from a lava-like boiling substance rising from the earth itself, propelled by its own force and caught in the instant of its dramatic self-making. In this moment, indeed, Hebraism found a Hebrew architect. However, most Jewish architects do not follow the time concept in the least: the cities of Israel are almost all rationalist, while the most Hebraic of architects is a non-Jew, Frank Lloyd Wright.

An American art historian, Norris Kelly Smith, has sought to explain the nature of Wright's genius in terms of a comparison between Hebrew and Greek thought. Essentially, Smith has applied to architecture the theories Thorlief Boman has expounded in his book, *Hebrew Thought compared with Greek.* Two ways of seeing the world and human behavior: the Hebrew, says Boman, is "dynamic, vigorous, passionate, often explosive"; the Greek "static, pacific, moderate, harmonious." To the Greek observer, the Hebrew way is "exaggerated, excessive, discordant, in bad taste;" to the Hebrew observer, the Greek way is abstract, alienated, impersonal, pedantically analytic, logical and rational in everything except what counts, that is, the root of the problems, the basis of thinking. For the Greek mind, it is enough "to be," as a concept, even if fixed and immobile. For the Hebrew mind, this mere "being" is "non-entity" for being without movement does not exist. The same applies to a house or a temple. For the Greeks a building means a house-object or a temple-object. For the Jews it is the object-as-used, a living place or a gathering place. As a result, architecture taking its inspiration from Hellenic thought is based on colonnades, proportions, refined moulding, a composite vision according to which nothing may be either added or eliminated, a structure defined once and for all. An architecture taking its inspiration from Hebrew thought is the diametric opposite. It is an organic architecture, fully alive, adapted to the needs of those who dwell within, capable of growth and development, free of formalistic tabu, free of symmetry, alignments, fixed relationships between filled and empty areas, free from the dogmas of perspective, in short, an architecture whose only rule, whose only order is change.

Boman, in analyzing the passages of the Bible concerned with building, notes that there is not a single description of the appearance— one might say, the photographic rendering— of the finished object. Noah's ark is documented every step of the way and in every detail of its construction, yet there is not a word given to how it looks when completed. Architecture is valid for its use, not for its image. Space not used by the community, such as we find in Egyptian temples and in the cell of a Greek temple, would be inconceivable to the Jewish mind. In fact, when Hebrew or Biblical thought came to influence architecture in the first centuries of the Christian era, we find that a revolutionary "happening" took place: the secret cell, kept for the statues of the gods and for the high priests but shut to the public, was thrown open. The columns which surrounded and enclosed the Graeco-Roman temples 'were brought inside so as to accompany man's itinerary. Thus, space wins out over the plastic shell, bending it to its proper form, and in this process is made temporal.

Wright detested Greek architecture, as it is well known, both in its content and in its forms. He saw its harmful consequences in the neo-classical rhetoric imported by the Paris Ecole des Beaux-Arts, where the majority of American architects was educated. A unitarian, actually son of a minister of that Protestant sect, he had a close acquaintance with the Bible. Refusing to have anything to do with the academy, "for the first time in history," Smith says, "Wright imbued the field of architecture— conditioned by "two thousand years of Graeco-Roman thought"—with Hebrew thought. Against an imperturbable and superstructural concept, he placed a consciousness of life as risk, as psychological involvement, as exaltation, an attitude that places man above things. His celebrated house Fallingwater and his helicoidal shaping of the Guggenheim Museum's cavity in New York, represent the victory of time over space, that is, the architectural incarnation of Hebrew thought, even more significant because it was fully realized by a non-Jew.

Like Schönberg's music, Wright's architecture is based in linguistic polarity, emancipated dissonance, contradiction; it is at once Expressionistic and rigorous; it applies Einstein's concept of "field"; it is multidimensional; it extols space by demolishing all fetishes and tabus concerning it, by rendering it fluid, articulated so as to suit man's ways, weaving a continuum between building and landscape. In linguistic terms, this means a total destructuring of form, denial of any philosophical a priori, any repressive monumentality: action-architecture, aimed at conquering ever more vast areas of freedom for human behavior.

That is all. I hope that this inquiry into the relations between Hebraism and art, although brief and cursory, will prove pertinent to the purposes of the Congress of Italian Jewish Communities. Heschel recognized that "to live in an upright fashion is like a work of art, the result of a vision and a struggle with concrete situations." Art is no other than life in extreme tension, and Max Brod said that "one can only live thanks to an almost superhuman tension." Hebraism rids this tension of any idolatrous, mock-heroic connotation and bends it to the day-to-day. But the day-to-day demands continuous vigilance and continuous renewal: in short, it demands a consciousness rendered timely by history and habits. "The knowledge of truth is not enough . . ." Einstein wrote. "It is like a marble statue standing in the desert, constantly threatened with being buried in sand. The workers on duty must always watch so that the statue may forever shine in the sun." Strangely enough, a Jewish scientist likened truth to a statue and not to a book. But, so be it. The Book, too, is constantly threatened with being buried in idolatrous sand. That is why you, we are the workers on duty.

200 YEARS OF AMERICAN HISTORY: WHAT DIFFERENCE HAS IT MADE?

Report on Architecture: Environmental Planning versus City Planning, the Development of New Architectural Language and Contemporary Research.

Paper prepared for the 1976 International Conference "The United States in the World," September 27–October 1, Washington, D.C. at The Smithsonian Institution.

In 1935 the Italian Novelist, Mario Soldati, published an account of his two years stay in the United States: *America primo amore.* Much later, in 1959, the book appeared in English with a different title. Instead of *America first love,* it read *When hope was named America.* The author explained the motive for the change: "Today we no longer go to America. It is America that comes to us."

Does this direction of trade, from the United States abroad, also hold true in architecture and urban planning? Only if we arbitrarily confine the American contribution to skyscrapers and super-highways, and note the spread of high-rise building and concrete ribbons all over Europe, Africa and Asia. But the most significant ideologies and achievements of the last two centuries were exported partially and often in a distorted form. In fact, for a long time, the United States lacked an efficient foreign policy in planning and architecture. Its image undulated in an emotional gammut ranging from mythical dreams to bitter disillusion and resentment.

In recent years, it has been almost the fashion for American intellectuals, many architects included, to warn the rest of the world: please, be careful, do not repeat our mistakes. Such an attitude is generous but somehow abstract, because what the

United States does with its cultural heritage is going to affect other countries in a radical way. That is why one cannot be detached and Olympian about the past 200 years of American architecture. There is a grandiose patrimony here waiting for full recognition, for the proper vehicle to carry its powerful message. In architectural terms, one could even risk saying: "When hope *is* named America" or, more cautiously, "When hope *might* be named America." The final balance of United States architecture 1776–1976 obviously depends on what we are ready, here and abroad, to do with it.

This paper concentrates on just three themes: (1) environmental planning versus academic city planning, (2) the development of a new architectural language emancipated from the Beaux-Arts, (3) contemporary research from pop and action-architecture to advocacy planning. Topics (1) and (3) mainly concern intentions, trends of thought, experiments and question marks. Topic (2), on the contrary, is based on real accomplishments and could have a world-wide impact.

The conclusion may be anticipated transposing to architecture what Alain Robbe-Grillet wrote a few years ago about literature. He compared the "fossil speech," continuous, unilinear, objective of the great French literature of the first half of the 19th century with the character of the Nouveau Roman, "discontinuous, mobile, aleatory, inclined to define itself as fictitious." He declared, "Bridge and chess have immutable rules. Our play is much freer. The point for us is to invent and destroy our rules with every game." It is not easy to embody such play in architecture, and avoid chaos and self-destruction. Yet quite a few ingredients of American culture suggest new approaches toward this purpose. Otherwise, it could well be the end of the play.

1. *Environmental planning versus city planning*

Everyone knows that the American attitude towards the traditional notion of "city" has been full of suspicion. The separation between town and country, as it grew from the territorial set-up in Europe, was considered obsolete in the U.S. much earlier than in other countries. From Henry Thoreau to Lewis Mumford the urge for an alternative is clearly expressed, although a new, global option was not found, either here or elsewhere.

Americans felt that a democracy could not expand within the urban structures typical of despotic regimes. Something different had to be invented. Utopian communities from the 17th century to the present prove the existence and the resistance, despite many failures, of a counter-culture in the field of the human habitat. Relevant factors in the same direction were the philosophies of men like Andrew Jackson Downing and Frederick Law Olmsted. It is not by chance that Olmsted's writings and the numerous books on him are now eagerly read everywhere. They are pregnant with hints that may help to give an answer to the urban crisis.

Landscape architects in the United States were not satisfied with the defense of the countryside beyond the city boundaries, nor with saving portions of the city areas from building. They looked for a kind of growth that would fuse town and environmental planning. As S.B. Sutton states, Olmsted "tried, above all, to civilize the city; his parks simulated nature in response to the needs of an urban population. He recognized the necessity of extensive planning to provide for logical development of the city as an environment where a man could lead a meaningful life; and he saw the seeds of our contemporary problems and tried to prevent them from germinating. Obviously, the task was too large for one man." Indeed, the park was for him an instrument to free both the city and its architecture from the bondage of uniform, degrading patterns. A few quotations may testify to his vision. "We should undertake nothing in a park which involves the treating of the public as prisoners or wild beasts." Even more significant, "It is a common error to regard a park as something to be produced complete in itself, as a picture to be painted on canvas. It should rather be planned as one to be done in fresco, with constant consideration of exterior objects, some of them quite at a distance and even existing as yet only in the imagination of the painter." In other words, the park system as envisaged by Olmsted, at least in his most genial intuitions, would have been the means to overcome the schism between town and country, to avoid bureaucratic zoning and community segregation. It would have encouraged the birth of a free architecture along the lines inspired by his friendship with H.H. Richardson. Olmsted said, "Openness is the one thing you cannot get in buildings. Picturesqueness you can get. Let your buildings be as picturesque as your artists can make them. This is the beauty of a town." Yet, probably his idea was that, in the integration of town and country, even buildings could achieve "openness." In any case, as Albert Fein writes, "The public park was one of those rare institutions embodying the spirit of a society: its utopian goals, specific social needs, and forms of expression . . . The image of an organic whole remained constant in Olmsted's planning and design theory."

Opposed to the Renaissance geometry heavily employed in French gardens, Americans generally adopted English landscaping, but in a more aggressive key that could create a different territorial panorama of human settlements. They looked for a scheme of open spaces which would liberate the town, leave it "unfinished" and guarantee its democratic quality.

This was the "American alternative." It failed for many reasons, partly because it did not find an architecture capable of implementing it. The Chicago School was deficient in urban vision, and the marriage between its architecture and the landscaping movement did not occur. What is worse, a sensational divorce took place at the Columbian Exhibition of 1893, when Olmsted's wonderful landscape was filled with classical and monumental buildings. At this point, landscaping became a subservient discipline, a corrective complement, though sometimes very important, to the traditional city. The environmental battle was largely lost.

Many historians now like to consider the Chicago Exhibition of 1893 as a positive or, at least, as an inevitable event. This is not the place to discuss the objections to such an interpretation. No matter how beautiful the "City Beautiful" might be, it denied the democratic option hypothesized by American culture at its most original.

The desire for an alternative, however, did not die. It keeps surging forth. It is enough to remember Wright's Broadacre City which, for a long time, was judged by the majority of us, historians and critics, as utopian, romantic, 19th century. It came as a real shock when, a few years ago, in an article published in *Architectural Forum,* Jonathan Barnett, Richard Weinstein and Jaquelin Robertson of the Urban Design Group of the New York Planning Department declared that Wright's thought was applicable even in tackling the problems of a great metropolitan area. Barnett wrote,

"The point of the Broadacre City formulation is not whether you like it or not, but that this kind of development has actually happened, and that we have missed much of the opportunity to give it a rational, ordered form . . . Jaquelin Robertson was on the AIA's National Growth Policy Task Force, and he points out that there is much in their report which was anticipated by Wright more than 40 years ago. Broadacre City's fundamental premise is that automobile-based settlement patterns require the total integration of the man-made and natural environment . . . Wright does not look as impractically romantic today as the planners who expected Americans to put their cars away and settle in tightly organized communities along the pattern of the English village". According to the author, "Wright's ideas of 1932 are also timely in other ways. If you read *The Disappearing City,* you will be surprised by how much of it would sound very up to date if it appeared, say, in the Sunday Magazine section of the *New York Times.* If there is such a thing as a 'counter-culture,' and if its denizens ever bothered to read anything, they would find Wright's outlook very congenial." Identifying the impact of modern mass communications on urban decentralization, and preaching the continuity of building and landscape, Wright also was seeking an American alternative to the European city and to suburban sprawl. As Norris Kelly Smith has shown in his excellent essay, *A Study in Architectural Content,* not even Wright was totally hostile to the city; otherwise, he would not have designed a symbolic mile-high tripod for Chicago. In 1931 he had warned, "You must choose between the car and the elevator. I choose the car." Later he also tried the elevator, proposing very few megastructures of such gigantic dimensions that they would save the land even if in a different, and in part contradictory, way than Broadacre. Both solutions aimed to avoid the urban catastrophe.

It is impossible to mention the many other contributions of American planners from the pioneers' time to the most recent research. Even touching on only a few examples, one has clear references to a rich and articulated philosophy embracing Los Angeles and Manhattan, the Green belts and the Farm Security Administration agricultural communities, the historical sections of towns to be preserved and the various theories on conurbation.

The outcome of this philosophy cannot be foreseen. However, the drive toward an "American alternative," a democratic human habitat on the land, is still strong and imaginative today, as many current experiments in United States cities and university investigations show. In Europe, too, we are striving for new processes in environmental design, for a new concept of "city region" or "city territory." In solving this enigma, American tradition is stimulating and inspiring.

2. *The development of a new architectural language*

The essential fact about Frank Lloyd Wright is not that he was one of the greatest architectural geniuses of all times, but that he elaborated the instruments for a new democratic language to replace the Beaux-Arts authoritarian precepts. This new language was not fully codified, however, and its effects consequently have been limited, failing to produce the general impact that they should have. It is almost a paradox: we possess a new language, ready to be used by everyone, to be "written" by architects and builders, to be "read" by art historians and critics, and to be "spoken" by the public. Yet, without a code, it does not achieve its full potential of communication.

The reason why Wright was able to create a new language is well known. He refused to have a Beaux-Arts education, and thus he had no need to fight against it, as his predecessors, Richardson and Sullivan, had to with much effort and without complete success. Being free from academic slavery, he could adopt the valid parameters of the 19th century architectural revolution: the new engineering, the Arts and Crafts movement of William Morris, Art Nouveau. He synthesized them in a different key (remember his famous lecture of 1902, *The Arts and Crafts of the Machine*), enriched by the merging of Western and Eastern cultures.

That Wright was the matrix of this new language is testified by H.P. Berlage, Mies van der Rohe, J.J.P. Oud, Erich Mendelsohn and practically all leaders of modern architecture, with the obvious exception of Le Corbusier. The De Stijl group in Holland would be inconceivable without Wright and his passionate disciple, Robert van't Hoff. The same is true for much of the German cycle up to 1933, notably with such personalities as Hugo Häring and Hans Scharoun. It is particularly significant that openly contrasting currents had a common inspiration in Wright, the Amsterdam School just as its antagonist De Stijl, Expressionists along with Functionalists. So vast was the range of Wright's language that each one could delve into it or refer to it. Even Le Corbusier, without admitting it, followed a Wrightian path in the Chapel in Ronchamp and subsequent works, when he understood that architecture is not only *le jeu savant des volumes assemblés sous la lumière* but, above all, the creation of spaces.

Why is it that a language was not derived from Wright, while we had so many mannerist trends based on Le Corbusier, Gropius and Mies? Mannerism implies the mistrust of stylistic rules and usually needs models to betray, orders to scorn. Wright is the anti-rule. He cannot be imitated, and he does not allow exceptions to the rules, simply because they are not there. Such a phenomenon is not unique in history. In some measure, Michelangelo as architect and Borromini—who were figures similar to Wright— created new languages which were not codified. Their influence, too, was very limited. Both were considered geniuses, almost superhuman artists, to be dutifully celebrated for a time, but to be shelved in the valhalla of heroes and forgotten as soon as feasible. Classicism prevailed again and, being the language of power, accepted only a few signs from Michelangelo's and Borromini's architecture, for use in a grotesque or decorative sense. Something analogous seems to be happening to Wright. So the greatest contribution of American architecture to the world runs the risk of becoming unfruitful.

This problem was discussed in a symposium organized by Frederick Gutheim last year for an *Architectural Record* book. I will try to summarize what seem to be the seven basic "invariants" or constant anti-rules stemming from Wright's most original messages.

The first could be called "list or inventory of contents and functions." It means "no" to all conventions, habits and ready-made phrases, to all aesthetic tabus such as classical proportion, rhythm, balance, to all preconceived grammars and syntaxes, to all dogmas about modular repetition. This is the fundamental principle that Wright derived from the preaching of Morris and from American vernaculars: an architecture descriptive of its human requirements, without any concern for a synthesis either a priori or a posteriori. It implies Zero Degree in architectural writing, destructuring of all the Greek, Roman, Medieval, Renaissance, Baroque and Enlightenment canons. Destructuring in order to rediscover what is specific in every element, be it a window, a door, a room, a community, and to disregard the notion of "series" of windows, of equilibrium between planes and voids, of symmetry. Even for Wright it took a lot of time to arrive at this Zero Degree, but he achieved it on every scale, from the small Prairie house to Fallingwater. This approach is perhaps the only one that can save architecture from perpetual oscillation between classicism and mannerism, rules and exceptions to the rules. It is a language which re-invents its own rules at every phase.

Dissonance is the second invariant, fully instrumental in expressing the diversity of contents underlined by the list or inventory. Classicism is based on uniformity, assonance, repetition, symmetry. It cannot admit that each opening, each room, each house may be radically different from all others, because lights, shapes and spaces have to be different. The modern language, on the contrary, exalts dissonances. It appropriates the musical lesson of Arnold Schönberg, who stated clearly that the problem was not to admit a few derogations from academic rules, but to establish the exception as a rule. From Art Nouveau to the Bauhaus, dissonances offered the method to avoid falling back on classicism. Yet, whereas in Europe and generally in the so-called International Style they were often used for their own sake, producing new formalisms (more vital, however, than the old ones), in Wright dissonances are always strictly bound to a creative interpretation of contents and functions.

Anti-perspective tri-dimensionality is the third invariant. Meaning the elimination of a privileged view-point, the moving of the observer around, above, under and inside the architectural object, the vanishing of facades and especially of the hierarchy of facades, it is attributed to Cubism's influence on architecture. However, while Cubism to achieve this objective destroyed the building mass, Expressionism obtained an anti-perspective, anti-Renaissance tri-dimensionality without renouncing the dynamic impulses provided by materials. Wright, as we have seen, inspired both the cubist and the expressionist architects, yet never reduced the building envelope to cardboard and never accepted the hysterical laceration of materials as if they were in a permanent state of incandescence. Now, many contemporary architects are tired with Cubism, and many with Expressionism. Some are going back to Expressionism and others to Cubism. Only a very few, in their best works, seem to have grasped the complex operation conducted by Wright.

Four-dimensional decomposition is the invariant that the De Stijl group took from Wright, and forms the substratum of Mies van der Rohe's European work. Though being the most serious attempt to give modern architecture a grammar and a syntax, again it was an intellectual reduction of Wright's language. It argued that, in order to negate Renaissance tri-dimensionality, there was no better escape than to go back to the two-dimensional, by breaking the building mass into slabs and re-assembling them in such a way that they could never reproduce the box. A code of mere slabs, however, is the denial of the structure and the tactile nature of materials. It is a unilateral interpretation of Wright's comprehensive approach, which could destroy four-dimensionally the box without giving up the third dimension.

Cantilever, shell and membrane structures. This is the engineering invariant acknowledged by every architect, but rarely integrated into architecture, at least not in normal building. The schism between structure and envelope, a dichotomy between bones and skin, is largely persistent. Wright's effort was directed at involving all architectural elements in the structural fabric, preventing the tremendous waste usually seen in construction. He did not always succeed, but this was his aim that later technologies were to implement and enrich.

Temporalizing space. Of the seven invariants, this is the most typically Wrightian. The Taliesin master worked with space from the very start. Space not to be contemplated as an abstraction, but to be lived in; space as the real receptacle of contents and functions, therefore a dynamic space; cavities which are no longer the void boxed in, where man feels extraneous, but shaped to his movements and his repose, made for work and recreation, for existential light and shadow. As Norris Kelly Smith saw, Wright rejected not only the static space of classicism, but also the compromise between the Biblical conception of time and the Graeco-Roman spatial concept. He adopted the spiral in the Guggenheim Museum as Borromini had in Sant'Ivo alla Sapienza, but again on a human, not only on a symbolic level.

The last invariant concerns building/town/landscape/territory reintegration or continuity. It means open scenery, ready to absorb and be contaminated by its surroundings, rather than isolated objects. It is related to Einstein's theory of "field."

My aim in the *Architectural Record* symposium was to submit the viability of transforming Wright's language into a popular idiom. His work has been a turning point, the major contribution to architecture produced in American history. This, however, is not enough. If we relegate his genius to a pedestal, removed from the daily life of common man, if we consider him like a God to be worshipped by a small minority and set aside by the rest of us, we would do a disservice to the progress of architecture. One may detest Wright as a personality, find him egotistical, self-centered, narcissistic, or whatever you want. One may dislike many of his buildings and judge the Guggenheim awful. That is not the issue. If we want to develop a free mode of architectural communication, a language is indispensable. Wright's code is not the final word, based as it is on anti-rules and not on "orders," on seven no's to all kinds of imposition. It is a starting point, like Schönberg's dodecaphony, a springboard with an even greater potential of liberation for new adventures. Yet, if we ignore it, the risk is regression, almost a hara-kiri. This, too, may be fun, but why?

3. *Contemporary research, from pop and action-architecture to advocacy planning*

Since the end of the Second World War, American art has become a dominant factor in international culture. In architecture, as we have seen, it was a fundamental guideline at least from 1910 on, but great stimuli have sprung from the United States in recent years, often re-orienting architectural trends abroad. Louis Kahn was "a hero" in Italy, just as in India and Japan, although the classical interpretation that many critics give his work—static spaces instead of fluidity, monumental accents, Beaux-Arts connotations—arouse doubts and suspicions, so as to make his hypnotic prophecies more illuminating than some of his later buildings.

The most significant messages from the U.S. in the last decades can be briefly indicated, though keeping in mind that no list could be complete:

—Jackson Pollock: his paintings may be seen as a sort of land/townscape, quite different than the geometric methods and procedures of Mondrian, Léger and other abstract artists. His "dripping" technique seems to suggest a flowing urbanization. For what we are seeking in the way of a new habitat, is there not a metaphor in his "aerial views?"

—Pop-art: this was perhaps the most provocative of the various pronouncements. It really changed our perception of urban and rural scenery, revealing the aesthetic value of the ugly, of the derelict, of the functionally useless, and so determining a radical turn in the attitudes of planners and architects in regard to the polyphonic cacophony that is beyond their control. Many felt, with Robert Rauschenberg, that "art is not enough and life is not enough"; our real task is not to compensate life with art, but to "fill the gap" between the two. All that had been excluded from architecture —barriadas and favelas, bidonvilles, barracks, slums and so on—became essential subjects to be studied. The "architecture of democracy" was sometimes identified with what, up to that time, had not been considered architecture at all. In the Vancouver Conference on Habitat, promoted by the United Nations, the competition for squatters was perhaps the pre-eminent initiative.

—Anonymous building: many events preceded, accompanied and followed the pop-art currents. Notable among them was Douglas Haskel's *Architecture and Popular Taste* of 1958, in which he attacked the critics' position on the so-called dreary, corrupt, hopeless environment that he saw as the symptom of a new "era of mass consumption," the triumph of the common man and of "democratic wilderness." Then there was Robert Venturi's and Denise Scott Brown's passionate and extremely acute revaluation of the signs and symbols of commercial vernacular and ordinary building. The slogan "Las Vegas is to the strip what Rome was to the piazza" had a tremendous reverberation in countries like Italy, since Rome itself is made up not only of piazzas, but mainly of magmatic suburbs whose existential value can be grasped better through Las Vegas' binoculars than through the telescope of Renaissance and Baroque ideologies. Of course, Bernard Rudofsky was decisive in a parallel line, with his *Architecture Without Architects* and other books. This kind of research did not always originate in the U.S. It imported elements from abroad, especially from Great Britain, but here it reached an intensity unknown elsewhere. Moreover, intellectual issues suddenly became a challenge for action. Jane Jacobs' *The Death and Life of Great American Cities* should not be forgotten even in such a rapid inventory. Indeed, the Architectural Heritage Year of 1975 in Europe could be interpreted as a version of the crusade conducted in the U.S.; and in our countries we have the obstacle of conservative groups always ready to defend a monument or a medieval hill town, but not to recognize the meaning of a slum or of a squatter village.

—Advocacy planning: in all its heterogeneous manifestations, it was an explosive incentive in the discovery of "subcultures," in the struggle for assuring the freedom of the user to manipulate his own environment against "professional imperialism." This populist movement had the effect of an earthquake on architects and students. The United States has exported the ever-expanding idea of a behavioral revolution in the relationship between architects and people. Despite the limits and exaggerations of its methodology, advocacy planning has infused new blood into a culture that was progressively becoming elitist and sterile.

There can be one reservation to these approaches. Too often they present themselves not as natural prolongations and enrichments of the modern movement, but in opposition to its so-called "functionalist dogmas" and "universal norms." They indict the whole modern movement instead of the esperanto, classical, pseudo-modern, boxy character of most contemporary building, which is in fact the antithesis of what the masters, from Wright and Mendelsohn to Le Corbusier and Aalto, stood for. The populists tend to deny the past on which their own conquests rest, in order to start all over again, rejecting the new architectural language, our only medium of communication. This risk should perhaps be mentioned: some avant garde architects, instead of exploring and popularizing the modern language, are sometimes going back to reactionary idioms.

That is why it is essential to evaluate the pertinence of American built-architecture, now excessively overshadowed by the sparkling hypotheses of the counter-culture movements.

Most of the American quality production which influenced the world during the last decades may perhaps be defined as mannerist, in the most positive sense of this term. The continuity of the modern movement and its developments from the 30s, 40s and 50s, have been due to the mannerists who sought a meeting ground among Wright, Le Corbusier, Mies and Aalto, though it is rather melancholy that Wright did not receive the attention deserved by his stature. In general, three mannerist streams may be distinguished:

(a) The first is similar to the historical Mannerism of the 16th century: a conceptual reflection on the work of the masters and of their initial progeny, like Giuseppe Terragni or Rudolf Michael Schindler. The New York Five have been the most coherent expression of this approach, and their resonance needs no comment. Their virtue rests on the fact that they defend architecture as a discipline and continue to refine the new language, even without trying to make it popular. They are not ready to abdicate and to abandon our modern heritage;

(b) The second, which frequently uses Louis Kahn as an alibi, is less clear in its intentions, because apparently it seems willing to rebuild a sort of classicism, in order to have something solid to rebel against. Such a process is obviously dangerous, as the modern movement is essentially anti-classical and to force it into academic schemata is an equivocal operation. In this context, the exhibition on the Ecole des Beaux-Arts at the Museum of Modern Art in New York had consequences remote from the aims of its promoters, if not opposite. Many architects and critics interpreted this show as a declaration of bankruptcy of the modern movement, and as an invitation to go back to classical architecture, emblematic of political and social authoritarianism. Fortunately, this attempt at revivalism has been dismissed also by the best followers of the Philadelphia School;

(c) The third is active and expansive. It is not satisfied to reflect on the lessons of the masters and, in general, rejects any deal with classical theories. It wants to go forward. From the late Eero Saarinen to Paul Rudolph and Charles Moore, just to mention only a few of the dozens if not hundreds of names one could cite, this kind of mannerism has been fertile, extrovert, pragmatic, unworried about making mistakes and thus able to correct them. From California to New England, it has been experimenting with new ways, demonstrating that the modern movement may be going through a neurotic and perhaps even a psychotic period, but this is because it is alive and conscious of the many problems we have to face.

"Action-architecture" is probably still the most comprehensive definition of the United States Message today. As G.M. Kallmann stated, "The revolt is directed not so much against the fundamentals of the modern movement as against more recent shallowness and abuses." The search is for "a harsher aesthetic than that of the present modish eclecticism," for "transcending the single finite form, self-enclosed and raised to universal significance," for interrelating buildings "in a complex scene" so that they appear "as mere passages in the unending game of space around them"; fluid images which revive "the aspirations of the early expressionists and futurists" (and one might add also the Russian constructivists) "now reinforced by the acquisition of mathematical and topological mastery"; a radical architecture, gestures "which are permitted to develop maximum impact without censoring limitations"; "shock therapy in galvanizing architecture out of its lethargy," a striving "for confirmation of identity and existence to counter the modern fear of nothingness."

Many of the impulses of "action-architecture" were nurtured by foreign experiences, British Brutalism in particular, or by the visual arts. In the U.S., however, they maintain in spite of their ups and downs a permanent vitality. Another architect worth quoting is John Johansen, especially for his philosophy as it is incarnated in the Mummers Theater of Oklahoma City, one of the buildings most discussed by architectural students abroad. "The Beaux-Arts is still very much with us, whether classically geometric or romantically amorphous," he complains; "formalism, centrality, ordered sequence and individuation of building design cannot deal with the demands that urban problems are now making upon the profession." Pleading for "permutational and open-ended programming, indeterminacy in which structures may not look the same from year to year, life-generated assemblages, components with subcomponents attached and then connected by circuiting systems," he stands for "surprise, unexpected juxtaposition, superimposition, crowding, segregation and confrontation of elements which accomodate the human movement patterns." In his opinion, "the concern is that of reality, immediacy" with unpredictable final appearance. "Facets, not facades result in bombardment of composite images," because "multiple simultaneous station-points" are outmoding "not only the axially fixed station-point of the Renaissance," but also "the moving station-point of Sigfried Giedion's space-time." Hence, "the relationship is organizational, not formal. Slang, not eloquence, is foremost."

The analogy between this kind of architecture and the new literature proposed by Robbe-Grillet in the passage mentioned at the beginning of this paper is quite evident. The players' rules cannot be static, they have to change with every game. Is this not the most profound and ironic lesson deriving from 200 years of American architecture?

Surely, too many items of equal if not greater importance have been omitted in this report. The difference that American history has made in architecture cannot be summarized in a few pages. Yet, even selecting three subjects—environmental planning versus city-planning, the new architectural language, and some recent research, from action-architecture to advocacy planning—one result emerges. The United

States imported all the goods that could be brought in from the West and the East, but its balance of trade is positive, because it stands against the dictatorship of dogmas, universal rules, styles, authoritarian principles.

We are now living in the era of "de-": de-planning, de-technology, de-architecturization, de-nigration of the modern movement. It is a chaotic, amusing experience, profitable even in its masochistic aspects. When the epoch of "re-" surfaces again, urging for a new re-integration, we will be able to rely upon a consistent American culture, centered on F.L. Wright. The leap will then appear even greater. How many nations have made more of a difference in the last two centuries? Truly, we might go back to the Italian account of 1935 and say, even about United States architecture today: *America primo amore.*

I.D.: MANY CHARACTERS IN SEARCH OF AN AUTHOR

X Congress, International Council of Societies of Industrial Design, Dublin, September 19, 1977

I have been wondering, during the last few months why the report on the identity of industrial design had been assigned to an architectural critic already worried enough about the identity of architecture in our present society. No clear answer has yet come to my mind, only some vague hints as to the possible reasons for this choice. I will tell you about them at the end of this talk.

My report is divided into three parts:

The first tries to justify the title "Many Characters in Search of an Author" on the basis of Pirandello's own explanation of his famous play, of his six characters, the Father, the Daughter, the Son, the Mother, plus the Manager and the Actors;

The second part concerns architectural design, its supposed crisis, and its real crisis that came as a consequence of the imagined one. Here I will be rather polemical in respect to the recent trend called postmodernism;

The last part is very brief, almost telegraphic. Instead of trying to offer a solution to the problem of identity either in industrial design or in architecture, I will point out the advantages, if not the glory, of non-identity, with an optimism only partially paradoxical.

It was Luigi Pirandello himself who explained the genesis of his "Comedy in the Making," of the six characters in the play he wrote:

> "Now, however much I sought, I did not succeed in uncovering a meaning to give them value . . . and I concluded therefore that it was no use making them live . . . I did all I could to put them away. But one does not give life to a character for nothing."

A critic could follow Pirandello's example. Considering that industrial design is still looking for its identity, one could be tempted to forget about it. But the I.D. characters —many more than six—are similar to Pirandello's six:

> They live on their own; have acquired voice and movement; have by themselves—in this struggle for existence that they had to wage—become dramatic characters, characters that can move and talk on their own initiative . . . And so let them go where dramatic characters do go to have life: on the stage. And let us see what will happen.

So, here we are, on this stage in Dublin, curious about what will happen, a bit afraid that nothing may happen, and in any case facing:

> The deceit of mutual understanding irremediably founded on the empty abstraction of words, the multiple personality of everyone corresponding to the possibilities of being to be found in each of us, and finally the inherent tragic conflict between life (which is always moving and changing) and form (which fixes it, immutable).

No critic or author would be ready today to give life and identity to the hundreds of I.D. characters. Our play too, consequently, will "not manage to get produced, precisely because the author" or critic whom we seek "is missing." All that a critic can do, at the moment, is to accept the industrial designers, like the six, "as rejected: in search of *another* author." Or, better, accept their "being" without "the reason for being." Therefore, as Pirandello stated, "The presentation of the drama in which such "characters are involved" will appear "tumultuous," will never proceed "in an orderly manner. There is no logical development, no concatenation of events."

In the field of industrial design, the situation is perhaps even more chaotic, because, in Pirandello's play, you have a very limited number of characters, all belonging to the same family, plus a manager who seems willing at times to have them perform even without an author, and the actors who do their best to fit the six characters' drama within the rules and conventions of theatrical drama. In our field, the satire is less "discreet" because designers need an author + a manager + the actors and, what is more important, a fairly complicated stage setting, namely the industrial complex with its machinery of production and marketing. Too often, we have splendid prototypes without products or products without valid prototypes.

The reaction to this tragi-comic situation, however, is more or less that of Pirandello's six characters. Indeed, some designers are stuck to ideologies, "almost in a ritual of self-punishment," like the Father. Others denounce their drama, "pushed by a feeling of revenge," like the Daughter. A few refuse to consider themselves characters and are "silent and suffer," like the Mother. Finally, half a dozen, at least, deny the drama, like the Son, "inasmuch as the author he seeks is not a dramatic author," much less an architectural historian or critic.

Now, let us leave Pirandello for a moment. In order to prepare this paper, I read as much material as I could concerning your previous congresses. I was particularly impressed by Professor Jean Baudrillard's speech, "Design Between Political Economy and Symbolic Exchange," delivered in 1973 at the 8th congress in Kyoto. Some of you will recall his conclusive point:

> No discipline can reach fulfillment nor, even more so, go beyond it, unless it puts itself to the supreme test and assumes its own death.

It should be recognized that some architects and designers have followed Professor Baudrillard's advice, not only jokingly assuming their own death, but also complacently indulging in their own funeral ceremonies. For instance, the theory of "de-architecturization" proposed by the American group SITE is based, in the words of its president, James Wines, on the assumption that an aesthetics of destruction is badly needed. Our monolithic institutions are crumbling under their inhuman weight; thus, only the "missing parts" are significant because they raise questions "against the a priori intolerant answers given by power." According to Wines, the missing parts are the positive interpretation of negativity, a proof of the search for less, in a world obsessed by more. In fact, the Sacramento showroom of Best Products is an object suspended between the act of construction and that of demolition, an example of the "architectural iconography of negation, subtraction, and fragmentation." The idea behind it is to un-build the building, or to build its ruins, archaeological pieces of rather uncertain and ambiguous identity. Through these negations, an attempt is made to "constitute a visual dialogue requiring the spectator to reconcile the known and the void as interactive events, to accept a dialectic of entropy and equivocation as the bridge between architecture and environment" and, finally, to find greater interest in "the intention of less" than in "the aspiration to more."

From the aesthetics of destruction it is easy to pass to the problem of identity as catastrophe. The theory of catastrophes appears significantly in the book *L'Identité* edited by Claude Levi-Strauss. A mathematician, Jean Petitot, holds that this theory is the only one that can represent the world and its phenomena without distortions, that it is the science of steady forms because, both in mathematics and in language, the structural invariants are offered by zones of catastrophe. Life is a continuous excursion out of these zones and a continuous relapse into them. Einstein's theory of relativity has denied the classical vision. That of catastrophes may well replace Einstein's.

If identity is mainly based on the "missing parts," on obstacles and difficulties, discontinuous zones, holes and wells, how is this going to affect our question, the identity of design?

As far as cities and buildings are concerned, the answer does not seem too abstruse, because facts and feelings have anticipated theory. What we can no longer tolerate is the completed object, the finished building or piazza or neighborhood, everything so totally defined in itself that it needs nothing around it—all monuments, self-affirmative, self-satisfied, which do not look for any interchange with their surroundings, and are not at all "in search of an author." The kind of architecture we reject is the classical, where nothing can be added or subtracted because there is no growth, no time process. We want the "un-finished" not only in the sense of Michelangelo and Mannerism—in order that the spectator may complete the image according to his own mood—but also because we like a city different from a cemetery, with its rows of independent marble monuments. We want buildings to communicate among themselves and with the users. To reach this dialogue, each component of the scenery must be somehow unfinished, unbuilt or partially demolished, must show its identity through the catastrophic hypothesis of its solitude and isolation, must require the other components' presence to identify itself.

Luckily enough, in this case designers have preceded grammarians and theoretical formulas. The Modern Movement started in an anti-classical key, with the neo-medievalist trend, which implied continuity of contrasting elements, interdependence, negation of the single finite object, flexibility, variety, missing parts, fragmentation and even romantic zones of catastrophe. What sounds new and surprising, if not down-right astonishing, in Jean Petitot's theory has been embodied in modern building design since the middle of the last century. The language of this design calls for a systematic, obsessive going back to the Zero Degree, to the assumption of death, to the relapse into earthquake zones. We identify ourselves by refusing to idolize classical, academic identity.

Here I have already entered into the second part of this talk, concerning architectural design, its supposed and real crisis, its indulgence in declarations of failure followed, wherever feasible, by actual failures. It is my impression that too many critics consider the Modern Movement dead long before they understand what this movement is all about. The fashionable, masochistic tendency nowadays, almost a conventional ritual, is to attribute to the Modern Movement the worst qualities and characteristics, all crimes, sins and faults of our society, so that one can feel quite safe in confirming its crisis and death. In order not to appear too reactionary, then, one leaps to the postmodern and takes delight in it. Postmodernism frees us from a heavy father complex and from the frustration of an unaccomplished task. There is a challenge in the Modern Movement. If we refuse to recognize it, we have killed the father, but are guiltless and happy.

Nothing to object to such a neurotic operation if it gives someone a better sense of identity. It probably does, as do all infantile acts of denial and ravage. But two questions arise and require an urgent answer:

1. Is postmodern equal to pre-modern, to the classical and eclectic trends against which the Modern Movement stood? Are we going back to the academy, to the architecture of absolutism? Has the Museum of Modern Art in New York become a museum of postmodern art just because it has organized the pre-modern show on the architecture of the Ecole des Beaux-Arts? If this were the case, the postmodern would not be as funny as it looks. In fact, it would be a bore. It would repeat, without any imagination, a phenomenon we have witnessed many times in history: a period of cynicism and regression, similar to those that dissipated the inheritance left by Michelangelo and Borromini. If that were all, best wishes to the postmodernists from us, the modernists, that is the post-postmodernists;

2. Does the postmodern concept oppose the modern because it has not reached its aims? Does it assume the same basic aims and reject the father because he has betrayed them? The risk, in this case, is the usual one of throwing the baby out with the bath water. Would it not be better strategy to say: a number of modern designers have stopped being modern and gone back to classicism more or less disguised behind pseudo-modern clichés. We are not ready to buy this operation as progressive. Therefore, we will start, once again, from zero, in order to reconquer and enrich the dissipated values of modern design. How can this be achieved? First, by codifying the modern in opposition to the pre-modern and the pseudo-modern, and secondly, by showing that everything valid in the so-called postmodern develops naturally within the modern code.

We could consider many recent essays and books on this subject published in various countries, in the U.S., in England, in Italy and in Spain, but I will concentrate my analysis on a very brilliant, much advertised booklet, *The Language of Post-Modern Architecture* by Charles Jencks. It consists of three sections: first, "The Death of Modern Architecture"; second, "The Modes of Architectural Communication"; third, obviously, "Post-Modern Architecture." But it is enough to read the introduction to find quite a few points that stir up controversy.

In the opening paragraphs, we read:

> An architect must master several styles and codes of communication and vary these to suit the particular culture for which he is designing.

And we learn with amazement that the author's approach "excludes the interiors of buildings with all those signs of comfort and habitation and daily life which are so important in giving meaning to architecture."

It is evident that, once you assume that an architect should go back to 19th century eclecticism and employ all the styles he likes, once you forget about the interiors of buildings taking care only of their exteriors, then to vituperate against modern architecture becomes too easy, if not banal. Interiors are the content of a building, the spaces within where people live, the original purpose and basic motivation of architectural design: if you dismiss them as secondary, only the box remains. And what should the box represent if not the content?

The Modern Movement arose to combat the Esperanto of academic architecture and its boxes decorated in Classical, Greek and Roman, or Gothic, Egyptian and Baroque dressings, altogether indifferent to the content but supposedly fit "to suit the particular culture" for which they were designed. If, instead of grasping these contents, the specific functions of a building, instead of inventing the building program, one is interested only in the exterior, then we are not post but pre-modern and this, of course, fully justifies eclecticism.

Another argument is that Rationalism, Behaviorism and Pragmatism are the philosophies of Modern Architecture, which is defined as "the son of the Enlightenment." Actually, neo-classicism was the expression of Illuminism, and one cannot understand how the movement that opposed neo-classicism can be condemned as a product of the Enlightenment. To be sure, the formula "classical modern architecture" is often used: but it is a contradiction in terms because whatever is classical cannot be modern, and vice versa.

It is certainly tempting to dwell only on the classical aspects of contemporary architecture, that is the examples where it ceases to be modern, and then deprecate their "univalent form" and "univalent content." For instance, Jencks attacks Mies van der Rohe for the Lake Shore Drive housing, the Seagram Building and the Illinois Institute of Technology, that is to say, for American work which became more and more classical; but no mention is made of the Barcelona Pavilion or the Tugendhat House. Likewise, the Chicago Civic Center is blamed because "you would not recognize the civic importance of this building, nor the various political functions that occur within"; but why neglect the Boston City Hall, which is not a "glass-and-steel box," and refuses to fetishize technology and building materials, or to adopt "universal grammar and universal contempt for place and function?" Again, Frank Lloyd

Wright fought all his life against the International Style based on machine metaphor; is it not a bit unfair and grotesque that he should be mentioned not for Fallingwater or the Guggenheim Museum, but only for the Marin County Civic Center at San Rafael?

Well, it so happens that the buildings selected by the postmodernists to confirm "the death of modern architecture" are not modern at all. In fact: (a) they care nothing about the listing of functions and contents, so that interiors are not even given consideration; (b) they are very often symmetrical and almost always assonant, constantly repeating the same modules; (c) they fully respect Renaissance perspective; (d) they do not destroy the box; (e) they may make a fetish of technology, but without involving the architectural elements in the structural play; (f) they offer no creative space, much less temporalized space; (g) they are complacent, finite objects, hostile to their surroundings, with no attempt at reintegration.

True enough, really modern buildings are few, while the pseudo-modern or classical-modern ones are innumerable. But this is no reason to jump to the postmodern, where no valid buildings exist at all. The urgent task in architectural design—and perhaps in industrial design as well—seems to be two-fold: first, to separate clearly the modern from the pre-modern and the pseudo-modern; second, to popularize the modern by codifying it in such a way that everyone can use it. In architecture we did not have a Schönberg able both to free music from the dogma of the octave and also to codify the process of liberation. The new architectural language is here, written and spoken by William Morris, the Art Nouveau masters, Wright, Le Corbusier, Gropius, Mies, Mendelsohn, Aalto and others, partially described by Futurism, Expressionism, De Stijl, Brutalism, Metabolism, action-architecture, but never codified in a few invariants transmittable to everybody. It must be added that my seven principles are not concerned with what architectural designers should do, but what they should avoid. They are seven No's, seven rejections of classicism. They do not aim at a style or a pluralism of styles, but at a democratic, daily-life language, a free expression of individual and social life, rather than of a capricious, exotic existence where you can only change the maquillage of the box in which you are imprisoned.

Consequently, "The modes of architectural communication" cannot be simply metaphors, iconic or symbolic. The axiom that "the architect must overcode his buildings, using a redundancy of popular signs and metaphors if his work is to communicate as intended and survive the transformation of fast-changing codes" cannot be accepted. You need a redundancy of metaphors when you have nothing to say. If you have something to communicate, as all real designers have proved, the authenticity and ambiguity of the message will survive the transformations induced by fast-changing codes. Jencks stated that "there was a devastating theoretical mistake at the very base of the modern language. It could not work the way the architect hoped because no living language can: they are all based on learned conventions, on symbolic signs." We should answer that the devastating theoretical mistake consists in applying mechanically the assumptions of semiology, as derived from verbal language, to the domain of non-verbal communication. These assumptions are subject to question today even in verbal language, and to force them into architecture and design is a desperate undertaking: it is not enough to be witty to get away with it!

The paradox of postmodernism is evident when from theory we get down to facts.

It mixes some excellent products, like Ralph Erskine's Byker Wall in Newcastle, with the most negative pastiches. Jenck's book ends with an apology for Antoni Gaudí, the Barcelona master, which seems rather superfluous, since his genius has been recognized for at least 30 years. But such an apology is significant because it shows that modern architecture is far from dead, and that in its patrimony, in Gaudí as well as in Wright and Le Corbusier, there are vital incentives for the future. The postmodern is either a development of the Modern Movement, strictly bound to its roots, or it is simply an evasion into the old academy.

I am sorry to have dwelled, perhaps too much, on architectural design. This is because it is the field I know something about, and also because many other fields of design, hard and soft, depend on it. The dichotomy between exterior and interior design in architecture, and the contradiction between the two, testify to our present crisis of identity. If the interior designer is not given creative spaces to work in, then he is justified in expressing stylistic idiosyncracies, now so fashionable. In fact, the postmodern tendency seems willing to extend the use of these idiosyncracies to the exterior, so that both interior and exterior are fake. At this moment, the search for identity becomes schizoid. To go back to Pirandello, any actor can play at random because the characters have been thrown off the stage.

There is no need to exalt the absurd. As the Father says, speaking to the Manager: "Oh sir, you know well that life is full of infinite absurdities, which, strangely enough, do not even need to appear plausible, since they are true." To the postmodernists one could say, like the Son: "Yes, phrases, phrases!" And one could even risk quoting the Father à propos of the crisis of modern design, which for many is an objective fact: "Very good, sir! But a fact is like a sack which will not stand up when it is empty. In order that it may stand, one has to put into it the reason and sentiment which have caused it to exist."

But who must fill the sack? The postmodern position is similar to that of the Manager who says: "All right . . . but here, my dear sir, characters do not act. Here the actors do the acting." Indeed, the postmodernists recognize that "eclecticism is in itself a senseless shuffling of styles, as incoherent as Purism, its opposite." Nevertheless, instead of promoting a language expressive of human and social content, they would like designers to be not characters but actors ready to adopt different codes according to an "ad hoc" arbitrary mood. Designers, however, the characters in search of an author, have the right to ask: "Who are you?" The Father states with great dignity: "A character, sir, may always ask a man who he is. Because a character has really a life of his own, marked with his special characteristics; for which reason he is always 'somebody.' But a man may very well be nobody."

Designers sometimes know better than their critics. They are searching for an author or, better, for a language, creative, democratic, pluralistic but not cynically eclectic, and refuse easy formulas which would bring them back to the pre-modern, to the academy. They prefer open questions to false solutions.

This could perhaps be the conclusion of my talk. If industrial designers or architects had a definite, fixed identity, they would be dead, just as classical and eclectic designers are. It is because they search for an identity every day, starting every day from zero, that they are alive. With their contradictions and doubts, they face the reality of our time more rationally and coherently than those who still follow Enlightenment myths or insist on romantic styling.

In your preceeding congresses, in your books, in your magazines, you have analyzed all the ideological, political, social, technological and aesthetic dangers inherent in any static design trend. The literature on industrial design is philosophically and intellectually superior to that on architecture. I can say that because I did not know much of it until a few months ago, and I have learned to admire your research and to appreciate your efforts. You are looking for an identity, risking non-identity every minute. This is splendid. Few other professions have the same courage.

By now, I trust, both architects and industrial designers have lost their infantile illusions. None of us believes anymore that a regime of austerity, as is expected in the developed countries, will coincide automatically with good design, because we know that economic crises very often generate not standardization and functionalism but the contrary: styling. None of us believes any more that the end of capitalism will produce better design, because we have seen the worst kind of monumentalism and the most unqualified design fostered in the name of Socialism and Communism. None of us believes anymore that the developing countries will stimulate decent design, because too often we have seen these countries accept and promote empty, meaningless and senseless versions of Kitsch.

From the outside, we still look like many characters similar to Pirandello's six, in search of an author. But, in fact, we are fully conscious that such an author—be it industry, neocapitalism, or communism, social democracy, trade-unionism, or whatever one can imagine and dream—simply does not exist. So, finally, architectural and industrial design have come of age. We know that we have to be authors of ourselves, authors and managers and actors of our own characters. We have to conquer our identity through a continuing process of non-identification, an endless series of contradictions, failures, defeats, catastrophes, insisting without rest on playing a game whose rules change every *manche*.

What is the real problem? Not to establish an identity, but to formulate a language that can be written by us, read by our clients, and spoken by the users of our products. A language based on few invariants or principles that do not prescribe what to do, but what to avoid: an anti-classical and anti-academic code. The architects, as I have mentioned perhaps too briefly, have begun to process this language of NO'S. The industrial designers may do the same, expressing as clearly as possible their linguistic alternative to reactionary and obsolete trends, whether neo-Art Nouveau, neo-Art Deco, neo-vernacular, and also neo-Bauhaus or neo-Ulm. In other words, we should not worry about our "being," even less about the "reason for being," but take pride in our "intention" and "urge" and "possibility" of being, formulating a language of permanent non-identity, a language that no grammarian can freeze into classicism.

As I said at the beginning of this talk, I have been wondering why the report on I.D. identity had been assigned to an architect. But, perhaps an answer can be found in one of the last articles by Misha Black, published in July 1976. Says Black:

> In the grey area between industrially-produced products and individual buildings, the architect has a special role. The design of underground railway systems, bank strongrooms, computer facilities and equipment for offices, requires the experience of the industrial designer and the sense of place and appropriateness which is the architect's

special contribution. Ideally, the architect and the industrial designer should work in close collaboration, but when the latter is not available to translate the architect's brief into economic practicality, the architect alone can bring his critical, humane and aesthetic capacity usefully to bear on industrial production.

I will simply add that the reverse is also true, as has been proved in many cases: when the architect is not available to offer convincing spaces, creative cavities for the industrial designer to translate and implement, then the latter alone can and must bring his critical, humane and aesthetic capacity usefully to bear on the architectural message.

ARCHITECTURE AND EINSTEIN'S SPACE-TIME

Museum of Modern Art, Tel-Aviv, 1979

Allow me to make a preliminary statement which some of you may consider unconnected with the subject of architecture. In his book *Language and Silence,* George Steiner devotes many pages to the experience of the inhuman, to the methodical organization of mass murder, to the technology of ideological massacre. Then he comments: "The ultimate of political barbarism grew from the core of Europe . . . Barbarism prevailed on the very ground of Christian humanism, of Renaissance culture and classical rationalism." I repeat: "on the very ground of Christian humanism, of Renaissance culture and classical rationalism."

We are here, at the end of the centennial of Albert Einstein's birth, and we must start from the crucial event of the age in which he lived, totalitarian savagery, its causes, the cultural context in which it occurred and which nourished it. Before going into the problem of Einstein's influence on art and architecture, a question should be raised, which is both agonizing and traumatic: in the 35 years between 1944 and 1979 has this cultural ground changed? Are our ways of interpreting the world, our existential behavior, our social and political customs based on something essentially different from Christian humanism, Renaissance bias and classical rationalism? Do scientific and artistic revolutions, after having affected laboratories, museums and books, manage to have an impact on day-to-day events and habits?

In our time, we have witnessed fundamental scientific and artistic revolutions. It will suffice to mention three: Einstein's relativity, Freud's analysis of the unconscious and Schönberg's dissonance theory. These revolutions have undoubtedly won out in their own disciplines, physics, psychology and music, but are still largely left out of our daily thinking and living, which continues to be based on millenialistic conceptions, on the abstract and compensatory ideals of harmony, consonance, proportion and on the dogmatic absolutes of illuministic origin. After 35 years, the cultural ground on which the technology of mass extermination emerged and flourished has remained substantially the same. Einstein's unappeased ghost looms threateningly in our consciences. Time is running short. Space-time even more so.

In this framework, and only in it, some remarks about architecture may perhaps be valid. The visual and physical environment belongs to our daily life and determine it. By evaluating the influence of Einstein on our homes, on our buildings, cities and landscapes, we can measure the distance still to be covered.

In appearance, Einstein's space-time concept has been assimilated into art and architecture. We can stress some chronological coincidences:

1905: Einstein sets forth the special theory of relativity. In the same year, Die Brucke is founded in Dresden and the Fauves organize a show at the Paris Salon d'Automne. In architecture also there are major achievements: Antoni Gaudí's Battló and Milá Houses in Barcelona; Otto Wagner's Postal Bank in Vienna; Josef Hoffman's Palais Stoclet in Brussels; the first monolythic reinforced concrete bridge on the Taranasa, Switzerland, by Robert Maillart; Hector Guimard's Chateau d'Orgeval near Morsang-sur-Orge.

1916: general theory of relativity. While Franz Kafka is writing *Metamorphosis,* Freud publishes the *Introduction to the Study of Psychoanalysis* and de Saussure holds his course in linguistics. In architecture, Eugene Freyssinet builds the hangars at Orly, Frank Lloyd Wright designs the Imperial Hotel in Tokyo, the National Service Act is passed in the United States and Theo van Doesburg develops the visual ideas which, one year later, will be publicized by the Dutch magazine *De Stijl.*

Let us consider Sigfried Giedion's famous treatise, *Space, Time and Architecture.* Einstein is quoted concerning Cubist research. We read: "Space in modern physics is conceived of as relative to a moving point of reference, not as the absolute and static entity of the baroque system of Newton. And in modern art, for the first time since the Renaissance, a new conception of space leads to a self-conscious enlargement of our ways of perceiving space. It was in Cubism that this was most fully achieved. The cubists did not seek to reproduce the appearance of objects from one vantage point; they went around them, tried to lay hold of their internal constitution . . . Cubism breaks with Renaissance perspective. It views objects relatively: that is, from several points of view, no one of which has exclusive authority. And in so dissecting objects it sees them simultaneously from all sides—from above and below, from inside and outside. It goes around and into its objects. Thus, to the three dimensions of the Renaissance which have held good as constituent facts throughout so many centuries, there is added a fourth one—time."

This interpretation of Einstein's space-time is rather rough and approximate from a scientific viewpoint. In general, architects learned about space-time not directly, but through the mediation of painting and the Cubist painters themselves had grasped it only superficially, to the extent that it could give their work a scientific look. Nevertheless, the theory of relativity implied a hiatus, almost an earthquake, in architectural vision. With the rejection of perspective, of its vanishing points and, even more, of its point of observation, the Renaissance's cultural structure collapsed, and, with it, the notion of architecture seen simply as a fine art, satisfied with the graphic representation of the three space dimensions on a two-dimensional sheet. Man, frozen in space, in fact paralyzed for centuries in a static vantage point, at last could walk around the building again, on every side and in all directions, inside and out. Consequently, the built structure suddenly produced a shock: it was freed from the authoritarian hierarchy of the monumental front—a typical reflection of social privilege. All points from which it could be observed were given equal importance. The closed, box-like volume was broken apart, it was raised off the ground to be examined also from the underside and its walls became transparent, thus establishing a continuous exchange between interior and exterior spaces. As is known, architectural rationalism between the two wars, that is the language of Le Corbusier, Gropius, Mies van der Rohe and their followers, reduced the walls to surfaces without thickness, exalted elementary geometry and stereometry, the cube, the sphere, the cylinder, the pyramid, the parallelepiped and, above all the right angle. It took the flesh off the building, breaking it into skeleton, structural framework and skin.

This is a reductive version of Einstein's thought. In fact, the box remained: a glass cube is different from a stone cube, but it is still a cube. This is why the Dutch De Stijl group destroyed the box, breaking it up into two-dimensional planes, and then reassembling them in such a way as not to rebuild a closed box. Thus, it drew closer to Einstein's space-time, but used a mechanical process which did not grasp its secret. Says Einstein: "So far, our concept of space has been associated with the box. It turns out, however, that the storage possibilities that make up the box-space are independent of the thickness of the walls of the box. Cannot this thickness be reduced to zero, without the 'space' being lost as a result? The naturalness of such a limiting process is obvious, and now there remains for our thought the space without the box, a self-evident thing, yet it appears to be so unreal if we forget the origin of this concept." This assumption, in architectural terms, may sound paradoxical because, if the walls have no thickness, the box no longer exists. This leads to an architecture without buildings which, in essence, is the true objective of the modern architectural revolution. The purpose is to desecrate the building as a symbolic entity of power, as an absolute value, and to shift attention to the life that takes place in it and which, too often, is choked and strangled, muffled and repressed by the building box. Architecture is a system for people, not things. One can design a park, which has no buildings. One can design folding tents or mobile houses, which do not alter the space continuum. Man could find again his nomadic impulse, inhibited for thousands of years: The question posed by Einstein, "the space without the box," postulates a liberating intention, a challenge for human freedom, which cannot be materialized through the artful mechanisms of the tendencies derived from Cubism. The limit of the Cubist operation becomes evident through another statement by Einstein: "Space-time is not necessarily something to which one can ascribe a separate existence, independently of the actual objects of physical reality. Physical objects are not *in space,* but these objects are *spatially extended.* In this way the concept of 'empty space' loses its meaning." This is a most important clarification for the architectural process. "The space without the box," or without buildings, is not an "empty space," lacking physical objects, for objects are not "in space," but are "spatially extended." They are not boxy buildings fixed three-dimensionally in space, with the time factor being just an added dimension created by the user's itinerary; on the contrary, space-time depends upon "the actual objects of physical reality" and becomes realized in them. In other words, the bodily object, ruled out by the Cubists as though it coincided with the box, regains legitimacy. Says Einstein: "The geometrical properties of space are not independent, but they are determined by matter . . . It appears to me that the formation of the concept of the material object must precede our concepts of time and space." Therefore, the Cubist dream of banning from architecture the bodily elements appears misleading and impoverishes the panorama of Einstein's philosophy.

Not by chance, Einstein's architect was Erich Mendelsohn, leader of the current opposed to Cubism. Mendelsohn's widow, Louise, has documented every stage of the conception of the famous Einsteinturm at Potsdam. The promoter of the project was Professor Erwin Finley-Freundlich, who was working as an astrophysicist at the observatory in Neu-Babelsberg near Berlin and was an assistant to Einstein from 1917 to 1921 as a member of the Kaiser Wilhelm Institute for Physics in Berlin. "Professor Freundlich was a friend of mine—writes Louise—and I had introduced the two men to each other in 1913 . . . A lifelong friendship developed between the two. Erich Mendelsohn and I were profoundly interested in the Theory of Relativity, which Freundlich tried to explain to us . . . It was Freundlich's idea to build a tower telescope to start research in solar physics. The tower telescope was necessary in order to verify the deviation of the sun's spectral lines predicted by the Theory of Relativity . . ." Mendelsohn was then drafted into the Army and spent one and a half years on the Russian front; in 1918 he was transferred to the French front. During this period, in the long night watches of the war, he developed, in hundreds of prophetic sketches, a new vision of architecture. "The first sketches for the tower were conceived during 1917 in the trenches in Russia." After his return from the war, at the age of 31, Mendelsohn continued to tackle with enthusiasm the theme of the Potsdam tower. "As can be understood, planning this building enticed and excited the young architect to the utmost. Here he could show for the first time his ideas of a new architecture, coinciding with an entirely new conception: the Theory of Relativity." The design work proved highly complicated, mainly because the laboratories, in the end, had to be placed underground. Inflation was raging; money, labor, materials and especially cement were scarce. "The erection of the building was a nightmare. Never had a structure been erected with curved surfaces as large as these. The building site looked like a shipyard. Personally, I was frightened and dreamt frequently that the entire building would slip down the hill . . . Thinking back, I believe the construction of the Einstein Tower was the most exciting, wonderful and nerve-wracking episode that I ever shared with Erich Mendelsohn. There it stood on a hill, overlooking the grounds of the Potsdam Observatories, overlooking all the old structures, like a monument to a new world . . . Einstein's opinion of the Tower was expressed in one word: 'Organic.' "

Completed in 1921 and inaugurated on December 6, 1924, the Einsteinturm is the masterpiece of architectural Expressionism, the antithesis of the Cubist vision. A turgid boulder, without any flat surface or right angles, it celebrates the material object that seems to build itself in time, as if rising out of the ground and exploding into the air. Earthly, telluric, incandescent matter, frozen at one instant of its growth, of its eruption—but not only matter. The inner and outer forces are spatial. Charged with energy to the point of spasm, they press on the boulder inwards and outwards, plasticize its contours and lacerate it in order to unite it. Doors and windows are not holes cut into the wall, but openings forced through by a dual stress, by a mighty drive of the landscape which strives to rush into the building and by an equal impetus of the architectual cavity which moves furiously to find its way through into the landscape.

Here, as in many of Mendelsohn's imaginary projects of this period, the notion of space, as an absolute system of coordinates, is cancelled out. The same applied to the notion of time as an absolute phenomenon, that is, says Einstein, "independent of the state of motion of the body of reference." And, elsewhere, he adds: "In order to arrive at the idea of an objective world, an additional constructive concept still is necessary: the event is localised not only in time, but also in space." The Einstein Tower is truly an event localized both in time and in space, a physical object not "in space" but "spatially extended," whose dynamic force penetrates every building fiber, from the dome to the basement. "Organic," Einstein defined it, that is anti-classical, alive, opposed to all kinds of absolutist axioms, relativistic and creative. Einstein states that physics is a logical system of thought in a state of evolution, whose foundations cannot be grasped by distilling lived experiences through some inductive method, but exclusively through free invention. Translated into architectural terms, this means architecture is "a logical system of thought in a state of evolution, whose foundations cannot be grasped by distilling lived experiences through some inductive method, but exclusively through free invention."

The Einsteinturm is still standing, has weathered the Nazi storm, the war and postwar calamities and is still efficiently used as an astrophysical observatory. It is unique in architectural history, for it combines the Sturm und Drang of Expressionism with Einstein's science, emotional and passionate extroversion with the most functional and rigorous logic. It can be read in Freudian terms and, in part, even in those of Schönberg, because if its clashing dissonance with the surroundings.

We have thus briefly considered the projections of Einstein's thought on two opposite currents of modern architecture: those of Cubism and Expressionism. What do they imply as human messages? To answer correctly, it is useful to go back to George Steiner, to the extermination camps and the technology of mass murder, to the sentence: "Barbarism prevailed on the very ground of Christian humanism, of Renaissance culture and classical rationalism." Well, the language of Le Corbusier, Gropius, Mies van der Rohe, and above all the syntactic proposition of Theo van Doesburg and the De Stijl group have undermined the foundations of one of these three pillars: that of Renaissance perspective. But rationalism was not overcome, although attempts were made to free it from classical connotations. Le Corbusier himself remained for a long time entangled in Renaissance-type research, based on proportion, Golden Sections and the Modulor. His Carthesian spirit led him to fight an anti-Beaux-Arts battle with Beaux-Arts weapons. Only after the Second World War, with the Chapel in Ronchamp, did he give up rationalism, turning to a sort of informal mannerism always ready to offend the classical, but not to destroy its code.

On the other hand, architectural Expressionism, with Antoni Gaudí and Erich Mendelsohn, has shaken the pillar of classical rationalism. But, like Futurism, it failed to develop transmissible instruments of communication. It remained an exception, a protest, a vital invective periodically re-emerging but incapable of offering a real linguistic alternative. There have been many attempts to create a bridge between Cubism and Expressionism: one can think of Hugo Häring, Alvar Aalto or Hans Scharoun, the author of the Berlin's Philharmonie. We could list quite a few architectural products somehow linked to the Potsdam Tower. However, the Einsteinian equation has always been reduced or betrayed, now denying matter, the bodily, more often reverting to classical schemes, to a rationalism of Illuministic if not of Renaissance descent. How many architects have assimilated the concepts of a "finite and yet unbounded" universe, of spherical-surfaces, of elliptical and spherical spaces? How many have fully grasped the meaning of the following statement: "The concept of space as something existing objectively and independent of things belongs to pre-scientific thought, but not so the idea of the existence of an infinite number of spaces in motion relatively to each other. This latter idea is indeed logically unavoidable, but is far from having played a considerable role in scientific thought?" Truly, this idea is almost ignored in architectural thought.

In any case, our review of the dialogue between architecture and Einstein's philosophy must go on and reach its final step, which goes beyond Cubism and Expressionism, which repudiates not only Renaissance culture and classical rationalism, but also the inhumane and barbarous. This means exploring the relationship between Einstein's space-time and the organic architecture embodied by the genius of Frank Lloyd Wright.

Wright was not tainted by Beaux-Arts education. When he was offered a chance to go to Paris to complete the studies which he had interrupted in the United States, he refused. Thus he never found himself in the position of having to eradicate the diseases of symmetry, proportion, consonance, perspective. Unlike Richardson and Sullivan, he could avoid the tremendous effort involved in discarding the burden of learned academic precepts. He did not need to discard, but he started from the zero degree and kept his independence even during the long apprenticeship with the firm of Adler and Sullivan. He hated "the Renaissance empty and pretentious forms, . . . that light at sunset that all of Europe mistook as if it were a dawn." He hated the Greek and Roman world, classicist no matter how packaged or concealed. For him, classicism and Renaissance were synonymous with an architecture of power, centralizing and repressive, with an antidemocratic architecture, hence firmly opposed to the libertarian and individualistic ideals of the American pioneers.

An even more significant and exceptional fact is that Wright was also immune from Christian humanism. His culture, as Norris Kelly Smith has shown in his book *A Study in Architectural Content,* sinks its roots into the Bible, the Old Testament. He opted for Hebrew thought, "dynamic, vigorous, passionate, and sometimes quite explosive in kind," as opposed to the Greek, which Thorlief Boman called, "static, peaceful, moderate, and harmonious in kind." In fact, the Greek world appeared to him abstract and alienating, impersonal, pedantically analytic, logical and rational in everything except what matters, the dynamics of living. Greek architecture, and even more the neo-Greek, denies growth and change; judging itself to be perfect, nothing can be taken away or added to it. This architecture that produces pure objects, is *le jeu savant, correct et magnifique des volumes assemblés sous la lumière,* according to Le Corbusier's definition. It is volume, container, refined and utterly sophisticated boxes that are lacking in content, in spaces made to be lived in.

Christian humanism stems from a compromise between Biblical anticlassicism and the Graeco-Roman heritage. In contrast to Imperial Rome's merely spatial and monumental rules, the Jews and then the Christians dug the catacombs, underground passages tens of miles long, superimposed and intertwined without any geometric rule, which corrode the very foundations of the city of power. But, as soon as the Church won and took charge of Roman institutions, the aimless and endless catacombs came to terms with classical structures, absorbing their orders, symmetries and conventions. The history of Christian architecture thus records the struggle between time and space, freedom and constraint, spirituality and materialism, inventiveness and academicism, risk-taking and discordant attitudes of a minority and the classical conformism of the majority. Needless to say, academic conformism always won, wiping out the revolutions of Brunelleschi, Michelangelo and Borromini.

This is enough to set Wright's contribution in its historical background. Free from Christian humanism, Renaissance culture and classical rationalism, he was the only one able to spontaneously get in tune with Einstein's space-time. Wright's experiences underlay both the Cubist and the Expressionist currents in Europe. However, his space-time is neither Cubist nor Expressionist. It does not even correspond to a hypothetical combination of Cubism nor Expressionism.

In his essay, *Organic Philosophy, Organic Architecture, and Frank Lloyd Wright*, Edward Frank has shown that the work of the American master embodies the most advanced positions in various disciplines, in theology as in biology, in psychology as in physics and botany. First of all, he was conscious that "the whole must always be considered as an integral unit," whose processes are functional to its overall requirements. "In organic building," Wright states, "nothing is complete in itself but is only complete as the part is merged into the larger expression of the whole." He, therefore, rejected the principle of decomposing the architectural object into parts, orders, modules, planes, which is typical of classicism in its ancient and modern versions, including Cubism. No component can be detached from the whole because, Frank says, "every part in an organic structure has this characteristic of being a point, plane or mass for the transmission of action." There is nothing static. Hence, Wright's assertion: "The law of organic change is the only thing that mankind can know as beneficent or as actual. We can only know that all things are in process of flowing in some continuous state of becoming." The physical environment is in permanent development and architecture fits into its dynamism, penetrating and enriching it with the human experience. Therefore, the continuity between building and environment, between interior and exterior space, constituted Wright's fundamental commitment right from the beginning. To the concepts of space and time, modern physics added that of motion, "not known a priori but only by experience," says Max Jammer. In Wright's architecture everything is in motion, man, volumes, spaces. As every site is different, every man is different, every life is different, so it is quite evident that every building must be different and there cannot be any uniform or standardized law, rule or precept. The landscape already suggests the building form, potentially already contains it, so as to become enhanced by it. But the landscape is not static. In fact, claims Wright, "Change is the one immutable circumstance found in landscape." Neither are building materials static: they record the flow of events, "they are all externally modified by time as they modify this earth in a ceaseless procession of change." Spatial field, human mobility, dynamic matter, interrelated with space and time. Think of Wright's masterpiece, Fallingwater, of the spatio-plastic context determined by the ravine, the cliff and the waterfall. How does architecture fit into this dramatic continuum of nature? Writes Frank: "By intersecting the counterflow of space and matter, the structure actively engages the latent dynamic properties of the field and becomes, in effect, its vortex, wherein spatial and plastic directional energies are gradually transmuted into their opposites. Thus, the dense lithic matter of the cliff, extended into the structure as natural masonry piers, is increasingly fragmented by its progressive impact with the powerful spatial flux channeled by the ravine. Conversely, the cantilevered concrete balconies project into and pierce space, drawing it into the depths of the structure to be humanly defined, compressed by the gathering pressure of the masonry planes and ultimately absorbed by the cliff beyond. Fallingwater thus presents the simultaneous image of drawing back into its hillside as it reaches out into space. Wright's solution for Fallingwater, which transcended the dichotomy of space and matter in architecture by effecting their integration as polar elements of an encompassing dynamic field, is akin to a development in modern physics." At this point, the author directly quotes Einstein: "The victory over the concept of absolute space . . . became possible only because the concept of the material object was gradually replaced as the fundamental concept of physics by that of the field." And Jammer adds: "Because matter cannot be understood apart from the knowledge of space-time, then matter as the source of the field will become part of the field."

Wright's architecture stems from the dynamic interplay between environmental field and live-in space, is morphogenetic and relates continuously to the law of change. Therefore, it unfolds itself into nature, contrary to all architecture that retires into itself, defends itself, locks itself up in its own avarice, barricades itself against man and life, behind the false idols of academic dogmas, bowing to the golden calves of symmetry, proportion, perspective, abstract harmony and consonance.

Einstein's lesson coincides with that of organic architecture in a philosophical, scientific and artistic key. For, on the one hand, it relates buildings, space-time and human existence to the ecologic context, to the universality of phenomena; but, on the other hand, it advocates freedom, an exuberant unfolding and creative courage. Man is no longer the center of the universe, his laws are no longer axiomatic and absolute; but, just at the time when these laws become relative, man's slavery to them comes to an end. The individual regains his independence, which was repressed for centuries by millenialistic conceptions, brutalizing rules and regulations, metaphysical visions and illuministic myths.

I conclude as I began: "Barbarism prevailed on the very ground of Christian humanism, of Renaissance culture and classical rationalism," that is, on the ground of an architecture which offends both the environment and human freedom. This kind of architecture is still ruining our landscapes and our cities. Of course, there are quite a few architects who are courageously fighting this suicidal trend. Among them, Ralph Erskine, Reima Pietilä, John Johansen and others. But the heritage of Einstein, Freud, Schönberg and Wright, which derives from the heritage of the Bible and of Jewish thought, has not yet been taken up in a living culture of the built environment capable of translating its conquests in terms of daily actions. This is the challenge that the first centennial of Einstein's birth, now at its end, is making to the decade of the 80s. It is a challenge against "authoritarian and social prejudices," "acritical automatisms and acquired habits," academic idolatry. The alternative leads to extermination and self-extermination.

ARCHITECTURAL LANGUAGE AND THE CRITIC'S ROLE

Meeting of the Comité International des Critiques d'Architecture, Buenos Aires, 1980

Discussing the functions of criticism in his fundamental book *Language and Silence,* George Steiner states: "The critic has special responsibilities towards the art of his own age. He must ask of it not only whether it represents a technical advance or refinement, whether it adds a twist of style or plays adroitly on the nerve of the moment, but what it contributes to or detracts from the dwindled reserves of moral intelligence. What is the measure of man this work proposes? It is not a question which is easily formulated, or which can be put with unfailing tact. But our time is not of the ordinary. It labors under the stress of inhumanity, experienced on a scale of singular magnitude and horror; and the possibility of ruin is not far off. There are luxuries of detachment one should like to afford, but cannot."

It is now rather fashionable to stand against morality in architecture. The Modern Movement is accused of being holistic, preoccupied with the social and human conditions of the present and of the future, ready to sacrifice individual expression on the altar of a common purpose. I have two objections. First, the Modern Movement is full of great and very different personalities; it has nothing to do with the International Style, its classicist corruption. Second, the immoral attitude is perhaps more compelling than the moral one, as it has to confirm the authority of morality in order to betray it. Like the Mannerists, the new Beaux-Arts revivalists and the Post-Modernists are "traitors" with a guilty conscience and are obliged to produce either the obsolete or the evasive, the funny, the curious, the ironic, in any case something that becomes boring very soon. However, the 16th century Mannerists had a positive influence because they popularized the languages of the masters of their age; while our revivalists and Post-Modernists are simply dilapidating the modern masters' languages. With all its drawbacks, morality in architecture stands for life. Immorality stands for escape and death: it is the ideology of despair, dressed sometimes with tragic humour.

The problem of language, and its meanings, in architecture is somewhat connected with that of morality. A city or a building communicates its messages only if its expressive code has some consistency and can be understood. To be sure, the hypothesis of applying Roland Barthes' "zero degree of writing" to architectural phenomenology seems quite useful and fertile. But it is historically a moral idea, as its mythological aim is to destroy all conventions and precepts in order to express reality without any linguistic mediation. Atonality and chaos are necessary in some phases of history. They are revolutionary instruments to annihilate the official, mummified code of power and to resemanticize the lexicon, disregarding grammar and syntax. To go back to the Beaux-Arts or to preach confusion just for fun, however, is not revolutionary. It is still an Enlightenment cultural lag, even more so when it is presented in Marxian terms.

In recent years, a notable effort has been made in the field of architectural semantics, linguistics, and semiotics. The results are excellent from one point of view, and rather poor from another. The use of the semiotic and linguistic vocabulary in architectural criticism is positive as it has legitimated architecture in the circuit of modern criticism. But this operation has been largely done by applying mechanically to cities and buildings the critical apparatus developed in the study of verbal communication. The artificiality of such a method is evident: the semiotic description of architecture is too often reductive, especially for what concerns the inside, lived space, the basic constituent of cities and buildings.

Architecture is a language or, if you like, an expressive system whose structure has to be analyzed on its own process, taking into account the verbal, musical, pictorial processes but not trying to transfer them automatically into architectural terms. I have elaborated this point in the book *The Modern Language of Architecture,* and there is no need to repeat its arguments here.

In what senses is architecture a language? In as many senses as its possible interpretations. Juan Pablo Bonta has brilliantly listed the numerous ways of "reading" Mies van der Rohe's Barcelona Pavilion of 1929. Ambiguity, plurality of senses, are a characteristic of any true work of art, whose messages can be received in a multiplicity of different and even contradictory ways. A poem, in architecture as in any other art, is such because its interpretation can be constantly enriched, according to the critical angles of its observers. In fact, every age has to read anew the past, underlining the aspects of it that are more stimulating for the present. Even today the most urgent task does not concern the history of modern architecture, but the modern history of architecture. Too many people are still bound to Banister Fletcher's textbook. This depends on the lack of a systematic collaboration of the architectural historians and critics among themselves, and with the profession at large.

The need for such a collaboration is now strongly felt. The *Comité International des Critiques d'Architecture* was founded, within the professional framework of the International Union of Architects, to fill this gap. Its purpose is not to find a common denominator on which all critics can agree. On the contrary, we want to stimulate disagreement by comparing our quite different positions. To that end, I believe that the following, very controversial, points could be useful to start a debate:

1. Classicism stands for conventional rules, for the architecture of power, oligarchy, bureaucracy, dictatorship and totalitarianism. The prize of its apparent "urbanity" is social and individual repression. The International Style version of contemporary architecture is classicist as it reiterates vertical and horizontal boxes in a Beaux-Arts manner. A box remains a box even if it is enveloped in glass instead of in stone. Classicism, stylistic or pseudo-modern, is conservative and reactionary. It stands for the *status quo* or, better, for the *status quo ante.* Any attempt to revive it is both pathetic and ridiculous.

2. The Modern Movement is not based on a single language. Between the expressive systems of F.L. Wright and Le Corbusier, for instance, the differences are enormous. However, they have in common the revolt against Classicism. When such a revolt does not exist, a contemporary classicist monument like the Seagram Building is possible, but outside the Modern Movement. Symmetry, consonance, proportion, perspective, static spaces, boxy volumes, a priori integration are the main Beaux-Arts precepts and dogmas against which the Modern Movement arose. We have to recognize that,

during the last decades, architectural criticism was unable to establish a clear line of separation between truly modern and pseudo- or classical-modern. In the end, in order to fight the pseudo-modern and the classical-modern too many critics have started a battle against the Modern Movement. The results are dangerous abortions: neoacademism and postmodernist eclecticism.

3. The linguistic revolution of modern architecture cannot be a permanent revolution. The daily search for novelty is a weak and naive aspect of its culture. It was unable to grow, to become mature. It was not institutionalized except in its classical-modern, International Style version. It was not codified, and therefore it could not achieve a state of cultural stability. But who is to be blamed? The architects or the critics? Arnold Schönberg created a new musical language, and then codified it. He was an artist and a critic, at the same time. But Brunelleschi, Michelangelo, Borromini, Wright, Le Corbusier have created new languages without codifying them. So it was rather easy for the classicists of the 15th, 16th and 17th centuries to root out their words and meanings, to disfigure their works (Santo Spirito, San Pietro, San Giovanni in Laterano) and to make their messages untransmittable for centuries. Will it happen also to Wright, Gropius, Le Corbusier, Mies, Mendelsohn, Aalto, Scharoun? It is up to architectural critics to answer. If they are unable to codify the new language, we will assist to an *nth* wave of classicism and eclecticism. Rarely in history has the critics' responsibility been greater than now. If they abdicate, architectural criticism will become mere tautology.

4. As known, the modern language of architecture has no rules, it destroys all academic rules, in a certain sense it continuously destroys itself. Hence, it is difficult to codify. One can enumerate its anti-rules (asymmetry, dissonance, anti-perspective, disintegrated volumes, fluid spaces, etc.) which can never become "rules with an opposite sign" because an anti-rule can be interpreted in infinite ways (one of which, among thousands, can also be the rule). This is why modern criticism, both of the new and the old architecture, is rather complicated. It is concerned with the process more than with the products, with circuits more than with objects. One could say that it belongs to the process and its circuits; codification must be extremely flexible, each case being a different case. Yes, codifying freedom and democracy is more difficult than codifying classicist dictatorship. This is our task, whatever the obstacles can be. A new language implies a new kind of criticism, a different codification.

5. The question whether our criticism should be "descriptive" or "prescriptive" is not too relevant. If the critical action is concerned with the creative process and is developed within it, the descriptive moment coincides with the prescriptive. The same can be said for the supposed dilemma between "personal" and "collective" interpretations of architecture. Criticism cannot abdicate with the alibi that what is important is the people's response to a city or a building. This response is too often conditioned, and the critic's duty is concerned with removing anachronistic taboos and psychological conditionings. As we can learn from history, in certain circumstances the critic has to find the courage to be alone.

6. If the modern language is different from the classicist, the use of academic methods cannot be fruitful. Classification according to building types or morphological classes seems dated, as it tends to lose what is specific and original. Fletcher's comparative

method may be partially unavoidable, but we should try to eliminate it as much as we can. Theodor Adorno has demonstrated how the Enlightenment goes from Voltaire to Hitler. J.P. Bonta, in *Architecture and its Interpretation,* shows with admirable precision the Hegelian component of Mies van der Rohe's American production. He comments: "This is a government of laws not of men: with all its Enlightenment assurance this was surely a statement almost prewritten for Mies. It is one of the crucial American statements; and is it not an entirely reasonable/unreasonable dictum which, incidentally, will always promote classicism?" Well, types and classes belong to the Illuministic way of thinking.

7. Finally, the role of the architectural critic should probably change or, at least, should be integrated with a more systematic participation in the design team. The profession badly needs this participation in the design process. It is rather absurd that an architect who has received a constant criticism during five years of school, once he has a degree should renounce for the rest of his life the presence of the critic. Of course, all architects are irritated with critics, just as students are with teachers. But, if they are really useful, teachers are accepted and respected, and so could be the critics. The real problem is that criticism in school is institutionalized, while in the profession it is not. Perhaps CICA's main challenge is the invention of an international center of critic consultants at the disposal of the profession. Let's remember: a) that the best architectural criticism is done not through books and essays, not through words, but through design instruments; b) that much of architecture is not creative and poetic, but critical, it is architectural thought and therefore it incorporates criticism.

These points are meant for discussion and disagreement. It is often repeated that the age of the avant garde is finished. This may be a positive event, which can bring us to maturity, to a better equilibrium between history and creativity. But let's avoid creating the avant garde of regression. Morality or not, our time "labors under the stress of inhumanity."

THE ZERO DEGREE OF ARCHITECTURAL WRITING: MIRAGE OR CHALLENGE?

Session on Architectural Criticism, XIV World Congress of Architecture (International Union of Architects), Warsaw, June 17, 1981

As this is the first of four sessions organized for the Congress by the International Committee of Architectural Critics (CICA), I believe it useful to explain briefly why this committee was founded and how it operates. The idea was Pierre Vago's, honorary president of the International Union of Architects (UIA). Three years ago, he felt that there was an unjustified and dangerous distance, almost a state of incommunicability, between architects and architectural critics. Therefore, he invited a group of architectural critics to the UIA Congress of 1978, held in Mexico City, and asked them to study ways of overcoming this situation. A large audience, both of architects and critics, was present at our meetings in Mexico City. After a long debate, the committee was founded on the basis of a declaration of principles, whose main points were reported and discussed in the architectural press of every country. These principles are threefold:

1. The purpose of the committee is to underline the existing differences of opinion, and compare them in the most frank and even polemic way. While the UIA, representing the whole profession, is often condemned to making declarations full of platitudes and ambiguities, the critics' committee offers a platform for disagreement and open confrontation of individual opinions. This platform is necessary, because too many critics are satisfied with their sophisticated and sometimes hermetic monologues which, in general, have a negative influence on the profession. In more than one case, as you know, the new labels of architectural tendencies in recent years have been invented by critics, while architects, for fear of not being up to date, have passively adopted them. It is therefore urgent to analyse these labels, the retro/pre/post/late/post-post modern and check their consistency or vacuity.

2. CICA, is an independent body within the UIA. Why? It is independent because it is free from the bureaucracy of the national groups of UIA, but it is in this framework because it interprets architectural criticism as an activity belonging to the creative process of architecture in all its phases, from the building program to the last detail, from a chair or a television set to a regional plan. Architectural criticism, states the Mexico declaration, is no longer conceived as a tribunal where the critics are the judges and the architects are judged, rejected or praised. The critical operation is part of the creative procedure, and thus the critic is an essential component of the design team. This brings some of us to believe that architectural criticism should in some way be institutionalized, that critics should serve as consultants in architects' offices, that they should be involved in a more active and provocative role than the one of judging after the work is finished. This is the key to a better use of criticism.

3. Finally, the Mexico declaration considers criticism as a stimulus for freer and more courageous architectural expression. The critic's task is to defend and foster individual and collective imagination against rules and regulations, against a red tape mentality that tries to establish meaningless standards, and to mortify and kill the creative power of architects. The critic's main function is to persuade the architect that, as history demonstrates, he is never daring enough, that he should not be so afraid of new ideas and new experiments. It is the critic's duty to defend the architect's original work, to be its advocate against anachronistic institutions and obsolete professional bodies.

These are the three main characteristics of CICA: It is a platform for disagreement and discussion among critics and architects; it views criticism as a permanent factor within the architectural process; finally, it sees criticism as incentive for more emancipated and courageous creativity.

And now I come to the subject of the Architectural Writing Zero Degree. Before entering the theoretical field, I want to stress that the Zero Degree is a notion well known in art history. It may be called primitivism, destruction of grammatic and syntactic instruments, disintegration of a code, or other names. What it means is that, in certain periods of history when formalism prevails, when linguistic dogmas exclude a real evolution, when it is necessary to reconquer the semantic value of words in order to fight the habit of ready-made phrases, the Zero Degree becomes the essential instrument for injecting new blood and vitality into the exhausted language.

Perhaps the most convincing example of the Zero Degree in the history of painting is the early Christian frescoes found in the catacombs. Were they as primitive as they look? Made by incompetent craftsmen who ignored the classical techniques of Roman realistic art? That is what was believed for many centuries until art historian, Franz Wickhoff, the founder of the Viennese School, studied the early Christian painting and discovered that it represented an extremely mature phase of expression, a step forward from the classical tradition. Artists, at that time, felt that the classical language was worn-out and paralyzing, that they had to annihilate its grammar and its syntax, and start again from Zero.

In architecture, we had a similar experience. Against the huge static spaces and the theatrically closed volumes of Roman monumental scenery, the Jews and the Christians built endless hypogeal tunnels, a Zero Degree architecture no longer to contemplate, but to move through.

The Zero Degree was also evident in the Middle Ages, between the crisis of the Byzantine language and the birth of the Romanesque. Here again, because architects felt that the mechanism of the Byzantine code was no longer creative, they destroyed its grammar and syntax, abolished its superimposed decoration, and started once more from Zero, with simple, elementary buildings revealing their brutal materials and free from any law of symmetry and proportion.

The Modern Movement, as you know, started with the same approach. On the one side, the engineers and, on the other, the Arts and Crafts Group led by William Morris proclaimed the obsolescence of all neo-Renaissance and neo-Baroque stylistic taboos. They did not try to substitute the old styles with a new one. They preached an architecture free from rules of any kind, able to express social contents and functions without the filter of academic devices.

Many other examples could be mentioned of the Zero Degree in history. But most important is to remember that, in general, all creative architects, in one way or another, return to the Zero Degree. They are creative, and therefore they cannot express their ideas within the framework of a limited, standardized, official language. They reject it and go back to the fundamentals of architecture, to "Adam's house on paradise," as Joseph Rykwert would call it, to a legendary primitivism which, of course, is not primitive at all, because it presumes the mastering and surpassing of a complex culture. Le Corbusier, even more Erich Mendelsohn, most of all Frank Lloyd Wright are examples of architects who created new languages in opposition to all previous scholastic and bookish culture. For obvious reasons, one has to be very cultured to reject the cultural establishment. Think of Le Corbusier: he had to travel for years in the Orient and Greece in order to elaborate a Zero Degree language; and later on, after World War II, he had to make a terribly consuming effort to deny, with the Chapelle in Ronchamp, the very language he had helped codify, and go back to the Zero Degree of informality.

Now, there is reason to believe that the majority of architects today are rather annoyed and disgusted with what is being done by the small sophisticated élite which dominates a large part of the architectural press. Quite rightly, they are fed up with the International Style, which is the classicized version of the Modern Movement, that is its betrayal; but, at the same time, they look with suspicion and mistrust at the two or three therapies which have been proposed to overcome it. We have seen these therapies in action at the last Biennale at Venice. The first is the retro tendency, a Beaux-Arts revival. The second is postmodern, a decorative, arbitrary, bizarre evasion in façade design. The third is regionalism, pseudo-vernacular idioms. These three therapies provoke great confusion in the profession, which is not convinced at all of their validity, and continues to work in the path of the modern movement, but without the support or the feedback of a consistent group of leaders. People do not know anymore how to design a building. The whole situation is rather absurd. In this vacuum, in this sterile battle of superficial, empty stylistic fashions, one thinks automatically about the hypothesis of a Zero Degree of architectural writing, and at this point it may be useful to discuss Roland Earthes' idea.

Barthes was one of the pre-eminent intellectuals of our time, and more. After his death, it was discovered that, following a trip to Japan, he had devoted part of his time to painting. There was an exhibition of his work in Rome, and it was clear that he had tried to translate the Zero Degree from literary to figurative writing. The question then arises: suppose that Barthes were interested in architecture, in which direction would he have looked for the Zero Degree?

The answer can be found in his famous essay, written between 1947 and 1953, reprinted many times in spite of the mental reservations of its author, who defined the Zero Degree as "a mythology of literary language." Quite true. Also when applied to architecture the Zero Degree is a mythology of architectural language. It therefore has great relevance, because it is a permanent challenge, an ideal that cannot be fully realized, but should never be dismissed.

Let us analyze how this ideal was born. It derives from two exclusions, two refusals. The refusal of "the great literary language, that extends from Racine to Claudel, a language flattered, embalmed, official," which is "compromised, anachronistic, it is by now the language of the landlords, of the feudatories of thought." And, at the same time, the refusal of "the language in revolt, which fights, from the Surrealists to Queneau, against all formal conformism with fury and with irony." In architectural terms, this position implies the refusal of two trends: the academic one and, even more, the neoacademic; and the postmodern which becomes "ornamented, emphatic: nothing is more theatrical than anarchy." In this double refusal lies, according to Barthes, the drama of today's writer, "a suicide in constant delay." The architect may appear more cheerful but his drama is not very different.

The contrast between the classical and modern approach is underlined throughout the whole essay. "The relations between thought and language are reversed. In classical art, a ready-made thought generates an utterance which 'expresses' or 'translates' it. Classical thought is devoid of duration . . . In modern poetics, on the contrary, words produce a kind of formal continuum from which there gradually emanates an intellectual and emotional density which would have been impossible without them." Words, with their full semantic meaning and their dynamic continuity, instead of the static, ready-made formulae of classicism. In another passage, Barthes writes: "The function of the classical poet is not to find new words, with more body or more brilliance, but to follow the order of an ancient ritual, to perfect the symmetry or the conciseness of a relation, to bring a thought exactly within the compass of a meter. Classical conceits involve relations, not words: they belong to an art of expression, not of invention." While modern poetry attempts "to eliminate the intention to establish relationships and to produce instead an explosion of words. For modern poetry destroys the spontaneously functional nature of language, and leaves standing only its lexical basis."

What is the way out of this paralyzing dilemma between classical and modern? How can we disengage the architectural language from the idiosyncrasies and absurdities of the academic, the postmodern, the vernacular trends? How can we defend the invention of words, without renouncing the establishment of relationships? In a most difficult page, Barthes states: "In the same attempt towards disengaging literary language, here is another solution: to create a colorless writing, freed from all bondage to a pre-ordained state of language. A simile borrowed from linguistics will perhaps give a fairly accurate idea of this new phenomenon: we know that some linguists establish between the two terms of a polar opposition (such as singular-plural, preterite-present) the existence of a third term, called a neutral term or zero element: thus between the subjunctive and the imperative moods, the indicative is according to them an amodal form. Proportionately speaking, writing at the Zero Degree is basically in the indicative mood or, if you like, amodal . . . The aim here is to go beyond Literature by entrusting one's fate to a sort of basic speech . . . This time, form as an instrument is no longer at the service of a triumphant ideology; it is the mode of a new situation of the writer, the way a certain silence has of existing; . . . it deliberately foregoes any elegance or ornament . . ." And finally: "When the writer follows languages which are really spoken, no longer for the sake of picturesqueness, but as essential objects which fully account for the whole content of society, writing takes as the locus of its reflexes the real speech of men. Literature no longer implies pride or escape, it begins to become a lucid act of giving information . . . We can see taking shape, by this means, the possible area of a new humanism: the general suspicion which has gradually overtaken language throughout modern literature gives way to a reconciliation between the logos of the writer and that of men. Only then can the writer declare himself entirely committed, when his poetic freedom takes its place within a verbal condition whose limits are those of society and not those of a convention or a public."

But "architect" in the place of "writer," "academic architecture" in the place of "literature," "postmodern" in the place of "elegance or ornament," "regionalism" in the place of "picturesqueness," and you will arrive at Barthes' proposal for our field. The idea of an architectural writing "freed from all bondage to a pre-ordained state of language," no longer "at the service of a triumphant ideology," which rejects "picturesqueness," "elegance or ornament," and follows "a sort of basic speech," "the languages really spoken" by common people, is rather fascinating. It is the way out of the dilemma "pride or escape," it produces "a lucid act of information." It is, more or less, what the profession is looking for: an architecture no longer subject to academic retro and postmodern anarchy, a simple, direct expression of the needs of the users and of society, and of the creative ability to interpret them.

In my mind, the Zero Degree is an essential and constant value of the modern movement. When I think not about the International Style, which is a vulgar, commercial, classicized version of the Modern Movement, but about the work of the masters and of their honest followers, I see that the notion of the Zero Degree has always been present. The modern masters invented a new language based on the Zero Degree, they refused the idea of making a new style out of it, that is of codifying this new language, because they were afraid that people would imitate the exterior forms of their messages, and not their substance. Modern architecture is a play in which the rules are changed all the time; every game, in some way, has to return to the Zero Degree. As soon as the International Style made a formula and a formalism out of it, the masters were horrified. Le Corbusier and especially Wright violently attacked the International Style at least half a century before the so-called postmodernists. It was clear to them that classical-modern was a contradiction in terms.

A codification of modern architecture can be done only by constantly remembering that its first and basic principle, from which all others derive, is the Zero Degree: a free description of contents and functions, without any worrying about achieving a synthesis, be it a priori or a posteriori. We can learn more from cave dwellings than from many authoritanian monuments of classicism. Here you have a continuum of words, that is of human facts and needs, without any grammatic or syntactic bondage. Thus, the necessity to reconquer the exact semantics of every word, be it a space, a volume, a light, a wall, a window, a door or a handle. Nothing can be gratuitous, nothing customary, nothing can be "finished" once and for ever in modern architecture. As in the caves, there are no fixed models, no fixed types to refer to.

Surely, other principles or "invariants" can be derived from a century and a half of modern research, starting with asymmetry and dissonance, and ending with reintegration of building, city and landscape. These other principles, however, do not concern what you have to do, but what you have to avoid and reject. They are "No"s to the Beaux-Arts dogmas, to symmetry, assonance, proportion, privileged points of view of perspective, visual stasis based on old structural conditions, volumetric enclosure, that is "boxes," self-sufficient spaces, isolation of the building from its context. These "No"s are the products of the positive experiences of the Arts and Crafts, of Art Nouveau, of Expressionism, of Rationalism and particularly De Stijl, of informal, pop and action-architecture and mainly, as far as dynamic space is concerned, of organic architecture.

Today, the neoacademics and the postmodernists blame the International Style, repeating what has already been stated, a long time ago, by the masters of the modern movement. They never mention Frank Lloyd Wright, Le Corbusier, Erich Mendelsohn, Hugo Häring, Hans Scharoun or Alvar Aalto. They know that, if they did consider the work of these masters, the fashionable thesis that modern architecture is dead would sound simply ridiculous. The Modern Movement may well be in crisis, it has always been in crisis, like all vital movements that cannot rest on what they have achieved and want to advance. I believe that postmodernism was buried at the Venice Biennale of last year, and that neoacademism was obsolete from its very beginning. The future is not with pre-modern, anti-modern or post-modern, three different tendencies that collaborate in an attempt to reaction, so much so that they are reevaluating the architecture of Hitler, Stalin and Mussolini. The future rests with modernity, with social responsibility, with the problems we have to face at the present, and not with the consolations and compensations of the past.

In any case, Barthes' idea of the Zero Degree should never be forgotten, because creative people must check and verify continuously, and must have the courage, whenever necessary, to get away from passive habits, formalisms and stylisms, starting all over again, from the Zero Degree, from an ethical and artistic platform able to renew itself every day. This seems to be the only scientific approach for architecture in the epoch of Einstein, Freud and Schönberg, that is in the age of relativity, psychoanalysis, dissonance and information. The Zero Degree represents a mirage and a challenge, both at the same time. I see no alternative, except for a shameful retroguard or an equally disgraceful, irresponsible escape.

ARCHITECTURE SINCE 1932: FROM AVANT-GARDE TO OFFICIAL STYLE

Speech given at the conference "The International Style: Architecture Since 1932," Harvard Graduate School of Design, Cambridge, Massachusetts, April 17, 1982

Let me tell you first why I am so glad to discuss the 1932 exhibition and its influence. And why I do not consider this Conference as a funerary service fifty years after, but as a most joyful event.

Believe it or not, I am a remote offspring of this exhibition, a testimony of its cultural relevance.

The story goes back to 1936 when, in Rome, I entered the School of Architecture. The dean was Marcello Piacentini, leader of fascist classicism, and the other professors were worse than mediocre. The Italian modern movement had been disbanded in 1931 by order of Mussolini, and we were only vaguely informed about it; Sartoris' Encyclopaedia was a photo collection with no critical structure.

Belonging already to the anti-fascist underground of the university, I hated all that was taught in the school, passionately looking for an alternative.

One day, unexpectedly, a young assistant professor, who had been an exchange student at Columbia University in New York and knew my political standing, called to me in a mysterious manner, looked around to be sure that nobody else was in the classroom, then gave me a well wrapped book, saying: "Be careful, do not open it here."

We were used to receiving clandestine books, particularly the publications of the Italian refugees in Paris. But you can imagine my surprise when, at home, I opened the parcel: it contained the catalogue of the 1932 exhibition.

For me it was an experience of vast importance. I studied English to read this catalogue, I learned it by heart, I matured on the basis of its illustrations and texts, even if later on I criticized most of them. For me it conveyed a revolutionary message, and I used it in the school, especially in relation to Lewis Mumford's essay on housing, as a weapon to fight dictatorship.

A telegraphic appendix to this episode: In 1940 I landed here at Harvard. After a few weeks, at Robinson Hall, I met Philip Johnson. Of course, my impulse was to tell him this story, to express my appreciation for his role in making the exhibition. But I could not, I had no time to do it. Immediately, we started quarreling about politics, ethics, behavior, philosophy, art and architecture.

We have been constantly quarreling for the last 42 years, and I suspect that we will continue for the next 42. However, this is finally a good occasion to thank Philip for this undertaking, certainly one of his best among so many mistakes and misdeeds, from the Seagram Building to postmodern horrors.

Perhaps the 1932 exhibition was less influential than it is supposed to have been. But its catalogue had a widespread international importance, and it helped a group of 18-year-old Roman students in their struggle for democratic freedoms.

I come now to the subject of this session. My feeling is that its title could perhaps be reversed. Instead of "From Avant Garde to Official Style" it could read "From Official Style to Avant Garde" because, after the recent paranoid banquet of neo-academicism, postmodern, neo-vernacular, eclecticism, idiosyncrasies, revivals and copyisms of all kinds, modern architecture is happily becoming once again a minority report.

Actually, it was always a minority report, as the truly modern buildings of the last 50 years are very few in comparison to the mass of classical, academic boxes of steel and glass. But the confusion between modern and pseudo-modern was so great that a building like the Seagram—to mention the best of its kind—could be considered by many critics as a masterpiece of modern architecture. It is symmetric, rigidly hierarchic—in having a main front, secondary sides and a back—it is conceived in terms of Renaissance perspective and proportion, it does not communicate any of its contents and functions, it is made of closed, static volumes and of boxy, static, meaningless spaces. Perhaps it is a masterpiece. I doubt it. But in spite of its elaborate corners it does not embody one single basic principle of modern architecture.

Now, how did it happen that the Official Style could be interpreted, for such a long time, as modern architecture? One can identify at least two reasons for this colossal misunderstanding.

The first has often been referred to during this conference. It relates to the historiography of modern architecture that gave a distorted, unidimensional image of its origin and development, extolling its Cubistic components, from Corbu's Purism to Dutch De Stijl, playing down or forgetting its permanent Expressionistic counterpart, and totally devaluating the organic approach of Wright and his international followers.

The responsibility for this unidimensional vision can be abscribed only partially to the 1932 exhibition. It is mainly due to Giedion's *Space, Time and Architecture* of 1941, where Gaudí and Mendelsohn, Steiner, Häring and Scharoun are not even mentioned.

In the last four decades, a lot has been done to correct Giedion's misinterpretation of modern architecture. However, in our historiography, the classical pseudo-modern still largely prevails over the organic trend. In Giedion's book, Fallingwater and the Johnson Wax Building are illustrated 100 pages before the Villa Savoie at Poissy.

Well, even today only a few historians understand that, linguistically, they should be dated a century ahead of modernism, and a millennium ahead of postmodernism.

The second reason is more specific and highly controversial.

The modern language of architecture was not codified. Consequently, it could not be transmitted except to an elite.

Schönberg invented a new music, and then codified it in such a clear way that all composers, including the most modest, could use the dodecaphonic system.

In contrast, William Morris, the Art Nouveau masters, Wright, Le Corbusier, Gropius, Mies and Mendelsohn invented a new architecture, but were unable or unwilling to codify it. They trusted that their buildings could communicate the new principles without any mediation, and they were afraid that a codification would kill the vitality of the modern language, reducing it to another academic style. Thus, we had a lot of formulas and cliches, promulgated also in the catalogue of the 1932 exhibition, but not a true code.

The result was that, lacking a system of communication for the new language, architecture, quite often without even knowing it, went back to the only available code, the traditional, Beaux-Arts, classical system.

I submit to you that even today, in spite of so many books, magazines, radio and television programs, conferences and symposiums, not only the public at large but also the intelligentsia and many, many architects ignore what the modern architectural language is about, its code of dissonances, articulated volumes and creative human spaces.

The majority of people, including cultivated people, could not tell the difference between Avant Garde and Official Style, while they would be ashamed if they did not know the difference between traditional, tonal music and dodecaphony, or between academic painting and abstract, expressionist and pop art.

In my opinion, there is no escape from this dilemma. Either we elaborate a valid new code, or the Beaux-Arts system will continue to wear out the modern language, making it pseudo-modern, Official Style, as it did with all original languages of the past.

The classical, Beaux-Arts system produces "orders," impositions, paradigmatic rules, starting with symmetry and assonance, perspective and proportion, regularity and repetition. The modern language, instead, is based on freedom from canons, dogmas and idolatric taboos. It is based on what Schönberg called "the emancipation of dissonance," that is on derogations and anti-rules.

The "emancipation of dissonance" coincides with Einstein's theory of relativity, with the scientific principle of indetermination, with what Wright proclaimed as "the law of change."

We must recognize that this immense patrimony of revolutionary ideas has not been fully assimilated by architecture, because it was not translated in efficient architectural terms. As a consequence, the modern movement since 1932, and especially since the last war, was mainly represented by manneristic tendencies, from neo-expressionism to New Brutalism.

I have nothing against mannerism. I admire it in the 16th century and in the contemporary versions, like the Boston City Hall. But mannerism, as you know, has this limit: to offend the classical rule, to falsify and destroy it, it needs that rule; it has to put the Golden Calf on a pedestal to knock it down and crash it. In other words, it depends on its enemy for its own existence.

Well, the majority of architects, including some of the best, have not as yet understood that such a dependence is no longer necessary today, that dissonance is no longer a piquant dressing of assonance: it is emancipated, independent, free. As Schönberg stated, it can communicate and move in its own right, autonomously.

Thinking back to what happened since 1932, we can better grasp the present situation.

Modern architecture is in a state of flux, conflict and crisis; therefore it is vital. Academic and eclectic architecture never faces a conflict or a crisis, because it is a corpse.

The modern movement is in constant change, it can never become an Official Style except by suicide, reverting to its contrary. In fact, there is a greater difference between the flexible, fragmented, non-homogeneous buildings designed by Erskine, Kroll, Renaudie, Pietilä, Fehling and Gogel, just to mention a few European names, and the "pure," orderly, doctrinaire exhibited in New York in 1932, than there is between Borromini and Arnolfo or Brunelleschi.

But the modern language of architecture still has to be explored in all its complex and splendid implications. It can and must be codified in an anti-classical, anti-Beaux-Arts manner, based on disorder, choice and participation, so as to become a really democratic value, a language that everybody can write, read and speak.

This is perhaps the major challenge facing architectural culture in the eighties.

I started with a personal memory. Let me close with another one, which is a tribute to this school where I graduated in 1941.

On the whole, it was a rather good school, but many of us were not satisfied with its teaching methods. I had come from Europe full of illusions, and was particularly polemical.

In the cellar of Robinson Hall, we held numerous night meetings to discuss the school and, in general, the state of architecture. At the end, a group of us published a provocative pamphlet titled "An Opinion on Architecture." Not knowing whether the library kept a copy of it (actually it has two) I brought one with me back from Rome.

I have re-read it on the plane. It attacks the Official Style, the pseudo-modern boxes, the academic tendencies already emerging then; and, with the same vigor, the evasive, playful, irresponsible alternatives to eclecticism. It speaks of the genius of Frank Lloyd Wright, a giant figure almost forgotten at that time at Harvard. It fights for an organic conception of architecture against all styles, old or new, and implicitly it calls for a codified re-statement of the modern principles against pseudo-modern formulas and clichés, idolatric certainties and obsolete escapes. It is an aggressive, heretic, controversial pamphlet. It makes me feel 41 years younger, still a restless member of this school. Thank you.

Biographical notes

1918 Born, January 22, Rome. A few months later, the family moved to Via Nomentana 150, where Zevi still lives and has his office.

1931 Bar mitzva at the Via Balbo Synagogue, Rome.

1936–
1939 Student at the Faculty of Architecture, University of Rome. Involved in anti-Fascist activities of the University underground movement.

1939 Attended the Architectural Association School, London as a third year student. Worked for the Italian anti-Fascist resistance.

1940 In Paris, joined the anti-Fascist group *Giustizia e Libertà*. Returned to Italy for two weeks before emigrating to the U.S. to attend the School of Architecture, Columbia University, and then the Graduate School of Design, Harvard University. Married Tullia Calabi, December 26, New York.

1941 Studied with Walter Gropius at Harvard. Received the degree of Master in Architecture, Harvard University.

1942 Editor of the anti-Fascist publication, *Quaderni Italiani,* which was smuggled into Italy. Led the U.S. branch of *Giustizia e Libertà*. Made anti-Fascist radio broadcasts, from Boston, then from NBC in New York.

1943 In March, returned to Europe, with three other members of *Giustizia e Libertà,* Alberto Cianca, Aldo Garosci and Alberto Tarchiani, to fight for the liberation of Italy. Made clandestine broadcasts for *Giustizia e Libertà*. Worked as an architect in the U.S. Army Headquarters, London.

1944 Returned to Rome. Joined the *Partito d'Azione,* a liberal-socialist party. Founded the "Association for Organic Architecture" (APAO).

1945 Co-editor of the architectural magazine *Metron* (until 1955). Doctorate in architecture, University of Rome. Editor of the "Technical Bulletins" published by United States Information Service in Rome. Director of the town planning office of the Undersecretary of Fine Arts, during the first democratic government of post-war Italy.

1946 Editor, *Manuale dell'Architetto,* published by U.S.I.S. and the Italian Council for Research. Campaigned for the *Partito d'Azione* in the administrative elections of Rome. Opened an architectural office with Luigi Piccinato, Enrico Tedeschi, Cino Calcaprina and Silvio Radiconcini. Lectured at the University for Foreign Students, Perugia. Mother died August 26.

1947 Taught architecture and planning at the School for Social Assistance in Rome. Birth of daughter, Adachiara.

1948 Won national competition for the Professorship of Architectural History. Taught Architectural History at the Institute of Architecture, University of Venice (until 1963) and History of Modern Architecture in the Faculty of Letters and Philosophy, University of Rome (until 1955).

1949 Birth of son, Luca.

1951 Won the European Ulisse-Cortina Prize for *Architecture as Space*. Received an honorary degree in architecture from the University of Buenos Aires, and honorary membership to Society of Argentinian Architects. Appointed Academician of the Academy of Fine Arts in Venice. General Secretary of the Italian Institute of Town Planning (until 1969), under the presidency of Adriano Olivetti.

1952 Member of the Townplanning Section, High Council of Public Works.

1953 Campaigned for *Unità Popolare* against the coalition of rightist parties.

1954 Appointed architectural columnist of the weekly *Cronache.*

1955 Editor of the monthly magazine *L'Architettura - Cronache e Storia.* Appointed architectural columnist of the weekly *L'Espresso.* (Still holds both positions.)

1956 Organized an exhibition on Biagio Rossetti, the 15th century planner and architect of Ferrara.

1957 Member of the Advisory Committee of the Venice Biennale.

1959 Founded the National Institute of Architecture (In/arch), and was elected vice-President (a post he still holds).

1960 Winner of the first national competition held in Italy for the chair of full professor in Architectural History. Founded and directed the Institute of Architectural History, University of Venice. Appointed Academician of San Luca, Rome.

1961 Architectural Office, with Errico Ascione and Vittorio Gigliotti. Key-speaker, A.I.A. convention, Philadelphia.

1962 Member of the National Commission for Economic Programs of the Italian Government. Academician, Academy of Design, Florence. Key-speaker, Congress of Landscape Architects, Haifa.

1963 Assumed the chair of full professor of Architectural History, University of Rome. Honorary member of the Royal Institute of British Architects.

1964 Organized the anniversary of the fourth centenary of Michelangelo's death.

1965 President of the Consulting Committee of the Jewish Community of Rome (until 1976). Member of the Central Committee of the Unified Socialist Party.

1967 President, International Technical Cooperation Centre, based in Israel (until 1970).

1968 Honorary Fellow, American Institute of Architects. Grand Officer of the Italian Republic for Cultural Activities.

1969 After the schism between the Socialist and the Social Democratic parties, resigned from the Socialist Party.

1970 Founded and directed the Institute of Operative Criticism in Architecture, University of Rome (until 1979). Member of the World Committee for Jerusalem.

1975 Death of father, November 15.

1976 Founded *Teleroma 56,* the first independent Roman television station. Report on Architecture at the international conference, *The United States in the World,* held for the U.S. Bicentennial at the Smithsonian Institution, Washington, D.C.

1977 Walker-Ames lectures, University of Washington, Seattle. Opening report at the 10th International Congress of the Council of Societies of Industrial Design in Dublin. Honorary Professor, Universidad Nacional Federico Villarreal, Lima. Honorary Professor, Universidad Nacional de San Antonio del Cuzco, Cuzco. Organized the exhibition *Brunelleschi anticlassico* in Florence.

1978 One of founders of C.I.C.A. (International Committee of Architectural Critics) at the 13th World Congress of the International Union of Architects, Mexico City. Registered again in the Italian Socialist Party. Editor, series of books *Universale di Architettura,* Dedalo Libri, Bari.

1979 Elected President of C.I.C.A. Doctor honoris causa, Istanbul Academy of Fine Arts. Resigned from the University of Rome, as a protest for its inefficiency and eclectic teaching.

1980 Member of the Consulting Committee for Planning, Chamber of Deputies, Rome.

1981 Co-director, exhibition "From Design to Habitat" in Bari. Founder, Club Rosselli, Rome. Directed C.I.C.A. sessions at the 14th World Congress of the International Union of Architects held in Warsaw.

1982 Medal for Architectural History and Criticism, Académie d'Architecture, Paris. Panelist at the Conference "The International Style in Perspective: 1932–1982" held at the Graduate School of Design, Harvard University.

Essential Writings on Bruno Zevi

Jorge Romero Brest, "Bruno Zevi y la apreciación de la arquitectura," *Ver y Estimar* no. 18, 1950, Buenos Aires.

André Corboz, "Bruno Zevi et l'architecture organique," *Dire* no. 3, 1960, Geneva.

Juan Daniel Fullaondo, "En torno a Bruno Zevi," special issue of *Nueva Forma* no. 105, October, 1974, Madrid.

Giovanni Klaus Koenig, *Analisi strutturale delle sette invarianti zeviane,* Editrice Fiorentina, Florence, 1976.

Rubén Pesci, "Bruno Zevi y la arquitectura como lenguaje," *CEPA* no. 5, 1977, Buenos Aires.

"Las invariantes de Bruno Zevi," *a/mbiente,* separata 1, March 1980, La Plata.

Zevi as consulting critic: buildings and townplans

Restoration of Villa Aurelia, American Academy in Rome (1946)

Flats in Via Monte Parioli 15, Rome (1947)

Townplan of Montagnana (1950)

Flats in Via Pisanelli 1, Rome (1952)

Housing "Pastena," Salerno (1955)

Townplan of Perugia (1960)

Railway Station of Naples (1963)

Library "Luigi Einaudi," Dogliani (1964)

Italian Pavilion, Expo, Montreal (1967)

New Directional Centers for Rome (1970–75)

Townplan of Benevento (1979–82)

Selected Bibliography

1945 *Verso un'architettura organica,* Einaudi, Turin. In English, *Towards an Organic Architecture,* Faber & Faber, London, 1950.

"Per un'architettura organica in Italia," *Mercurio,* no.13, September.

1946 "Per un centro di pianificazione urbanistica e edilizia nell'organizzazione delle Nazioni Unite," *Metron,* no.6, January.

"Town Planning as an Instrument of American Foreign Policy," *Journal of the American Institute of Planners,* January-March.

1947 *Frank Lloyd Wright,* Il Balcone, Milan. In English, "Frank Lloyd Wright and the Conquest of Space," *Magazine of Art,* May 1950.

"Gustavo Giovannoni," *Metron,* no.18, August.

"Quattro riforme nell'insegnamento della storia dell'architettura," *Metron,* no.19–20, September-October.

"Note sul corso di 'Caratteri stilistici e costruttivi dei monumenti'," *Metron,* no.21, November.

"Urbanistica e architettura per gli assistenti sociali," *Educazione Sociale,* March.

1948 *Saper vedere l'architettura,* Einaudi, Turin. In English, *Architecture as Space,* Horizon Press, New York, 1957.

Erik Gunnar Asplund, Il Balcone, Milan.

Lezioni di storia dell'architettura italiana: dal Paleocristiano al Gotico, Ferri, Roma.

"L'architettura organica di fronte ai suoi critici," *Metron,* no.23–24, January-April.

"Riforma e contro," *Metron,* no.25, June-July.

"Invito alla storia dell'architettura moderna," *Metron,* no.30, December.

1949 "Franz Wickhoff nel guarantennio dalla sua morte," *Instituto Universitario di Architettura,* Annual, Venice, 1948–1950 *(Zevi su Zevi,* Magma, Milan, 1977).

"On Architectural Culture: Message to the International Congress of Modern Architecture," *Metron,* no.31–32, February-March.

"Realtà dell'architettura organica," *Metron,* no.35–36, November-December.

1950 *Storia dell'architettura moderna,* Einaudi, Turin. Totally rewritten and expanded for *Spazi dell'architettura moderna,* Einaudi, Turin, 1975.

Architettura e Storiografia, Tamburini, Milan. Revised edition, Einaudi, Turin, 1974. In English, Part Two of *The Modern Language of Architecture,* University of Washington Press, Seattle, 1978. Paperback edition, Van Nostrand Reinhold, New York, 1981.

"Mies van der Rohe e Frank Lloyd Wright, poeti dello spazio," *Metron,* no.37, July-August.

"Un genio catalano: Antoni Gaudí," *Metron,* no.38, October.

"Sulle tradizioni moderne," *Comunità,* no.6, January-February.

"Lo spazio interno della città ellenica," *Urbanistica,* no.3, January-March.

"Architettura per il cinema e cinema per l'architettura," *Bianco e Nero,* August-September.

"Historia de la arquitectura e historia para la arquitectura," *Canon,* no.1, Buenos Aires.

"La metodologia nella storia dell'urbanistica," VII National Congress of Architectural History 1950, *Soprintendenza ai Monumenti,* Palermo, 1956.

"Los valores espirituales de la arquitectura moderna," *Ver y estimar,* July, Buenos Aires.

1951 "L'arte e la critica," *Comunità,* no.12, October.

"De Architectonische Cultuur van Her Moderne Italie," *De Gids,* no.9–10, September-October, Utrecht.

"La quarta dimensione e i problemi della proporzione," *Domus,* no.264 –265, December.

"Charles Rennie Mackintosh, poeta di uno strumento perduto: la linea," *Metron,* no.40, April.

1952 *2 Conferencias,* Faculty of Architecture and Urbanism, University of Buenos Aires.

"Guido Costante Sullam (1873–1949)," *Istituto Universitario di Architettura,* Annual, Venice, 1951–1952.

"Fine di un istituto di cultura," *Metron,* no.46, October.

"Benedetto Croce e la riforma della storia architettonica," *Metron,* no.47, December *(Zevi su Zevi,* Magma, Milan, 1977).

"Rapporto sull'organizzazione del IV Congresso di urbanistica," *La Pianizione Regionale,* Istituto Nazionale di Urbanistica, Rome.

1953 *Poetica dell'architettura neoplastica,* Tamburini, Milan. Revised edition, Einaudi, Turin, 1974.

"Commemorazione di Aldo della Rocca," *Giornale del genio civile,* September.

"L'architettura d'oggi," *Ulisse,* no.19, Autumn, Rome.

1954 *Richard Neutra,* Il Balcone, Milan.

"Auguste Perret," *Metron,* no.51, May-June.

"Il rinnovamento della storiografia architettonica," *Annali della Scuola Normale Superiore di Pisa,* Vol.XXII, Vallecchi, Florence.

"La conquista di una moderna tradizione architettonica," *Quaderni ACI,* no.13, Turin.

1955 "The Reality of a House is the Space Within," *House Beautiful,* November.

1956 "The MIT Auditorium Criticized," *Architectural Forum,* March.

"L'architettura moderna ha cento anni," *Rivista Tecnica della Svizzera Italiana,* no. 475.

"Una nuova 'philosophy' urbanistica nell'economia americana: downtown come San Marco," *Urbanistica,* no.20, September.

1957 *L'architettura paesaggistica di Roberto Burle Marx,* Galleria d'Arte Moderna, Roma.

"Milaan—de roem en de miskenning van de moderne italiaanse architectuur," *Forum,* no.9–10, Amsterdam.

"Rapporto sull'organizzazione del VI Congresso di urbanistica," *La pianificazione intercomunale,* Istituto Nazionale di Urbanistica, Rome.

1958 "Alberti, Leon Battista," *Enciclopedia Universale dell'Arte,* Vol.I, Istituto per la Collaborazione Culturale, Venice-Rome. In English, *Encyclopedia of World Art,* Vol.I, McGraw Hill, New York, 1959.

"Dibattito sull'architettura messicana," *Arquitectura Mexico,* no.62, June.

"Italian Architecture Today," *Atlantic Monthly* supplement, December.

"La città del futuro," *Epoca,* no.404, June 29.

"Longhena," *Les Architectes Célèbres,* Mazenod, Paris.

"Palladio," *Les Architectes Célèbres,* Mazenod, Paris.

"Architettura," *Enciclopedia Universale dell'Arte,* Vol.I, Istituto per la Collaborazione Culturale, Venice-Rome. In English, *Encyclopedia of World Art,* Vol.I, McGraw Hill, New York, 1959. Edited as a book, *Architectura in Nuce,* Istituto per la Collaborazione Culturale, Sansoni, Florence, 1960.

1959 "La dinamica delle strutture urbane," *Módulo,* no.16, Brasilia.

"Le Corbusier, poeta senza storia," *Forme e tecniche nell'architettura contemporanea,* Editalia, Rome.

"Problemi di interpretazione critica dell'architettura veneta," *Bollettino del Centro Internazionale di Studi d'Architettura Andrea Palladio,* no.1, Vicenza.

"Prognosis Reserved: A New Launching of Modern Architecture," *Italian Quarterly*, Vol.2, no.7–8, Fall-Winter, Los Angeles.

1960 *Biagio Rossetti, architetto ferrarese, il primo urbanista moderno europeo*, Einaudi, Turin. Revised edition, *Saper vedere l'urbanistica*, Einaudi, Turin, 1971.

"Inchiesta su Brasilia: sei interrogativi sulla nuova capitale sud-americana," *L'Architettura*, no.51, June.

1961 "Culture of the City," *AIA Journal*, June.

"L'architettura moderna ad una svolta," *Ingegneri Architetti Costruttori*, Bologna, January.

"Architettura contemporanea," *Ausonia*, Istituto Italiano di Cultura, Athens.

1962 "The Modern Dimension of Landscape Architecture," *IFLA Annual* and *Athos*, no.3, September, Zürich.

"La crisi dell'insegnamento architettonico," *Ulisse*, March, Rome.

1963 "Palladio, Andrea," *Enciclopedia Universale dell'Arte*, Vol.X, Istituto per la Collaborazione Culturale, Venice-Rome. In English, *Encyclopedia of World Art*, Vol.X, McGraw Hill, New York.

"Architettura e Società," *De Homine*, no.5–6, June, Sansoni, Florence-Rome.

1964 "Attualità di Michelangiolo architetto, Le Fortificazioni Fiorentine, Santa Maria degli Angeli," *Michelangelo architetto*, Einaudi, Turin.

"Sanmicheli, Michele," *Enciclopedia Universale dell'Arte*, Vol.XII, Istituto per la Collaborazione Culturale, Venice-Rome. In English, *Encyclopedia of World Art*, Vol.XII, McGraw Hill, New York.

"L'architettura nell'età dell'informale," *Quaderni di San Giorgio*, no.23, Sansoni, Florence-Venice.

1965 "History as a Method of Teaching Architecture," *The History, Theory and Criticism of Architecture*, Marcus Whiffen, ed., MIT Press, Cambridge, Mass.

"Michelangiolo e Palladio," *Bollettino del Centro Internazionale di Studi di Architettura Andrea Palladio*, no. VI, Vicenza.

"Ipotesi di un nuovo professionista: il consulente linguistico di architettura," *Settecolli*, September, Rome.

1966 "El coloquio de Le Corbusier con la historia," *La Torre*, no.52, January-April, Puerto Rico.

"Esiste un'arte ebraica?" *La voce della comunità israelitica*, June 5, Rome.

1967 *Attualità del Borromini*, Accademia Nazionale di San Luca, Rome.

1968 "Arte popolare come architettura moderna," *Arte popolare moderna,* Cappelli, Bologna.

"Architecture 1967: Progress or Regression?" *Man and his World,* The Noranda Lectures, University of Toronto Press.

"El Modernismo Catalan, problema abierto de la cultura arquitectónica," preface to *Arquitectura Modernista* by Oriol Bohigas, Lumen, Barcelona.

1969 "Theo van Doesburg To-morrow," *Bouwkundig Weekblad,* no.4, Amsterdam.

"Ferrara non-finita," *Ferrara, il Po, la Cattedrale, la Corte,* Alfa, Bologna.

"La matrice razionalista dell'architettura contemporanea in Italia," *L'Architettura,* no.163, May.

1970 *Erich Mendelsohn: opera completa,* Etas/Kompass, Milan.

"La sfortuna critica di Palladio nell'età dell'architettura moderna," *Bollettino del Centro Internazionale di Studi di Architettura Andrea Palladio,* no.XII, Vicenza.

"La veglia per Israele al Portico d'Ottavia: 28 maggio 1967," *Scritti in memoria di Enzo Sereni,* Sally Mayer Foundation, Jerusalem.

1971 "Viatico urbatettonico," *Messaggi Perugini,* IBR, Perugia.

"A Foggy Colloquy," *The Architectural Review,* September, London.

1972 *Saper vedere l'urbanistica,* Einaudi, Turin. Expanded edition, 1973.

"The Architecture of the Museum," *Ariel,* no.29, Jerusalem.

"Storia illustrata della città italiana," *Parlare italiano,* Laterza, Bari.

1973 *Spazi dell'architettura moderna,* Einaudi, Turin.

Il linguaggio moderno dell'architettura, Einaudi, Turin.

"Filippo Brunelleschi," *Die Grossen der Weltgeschichte* Encyclopaedia, Vol.IV, Kindler, Zürich.

1974 "Organique (architecture)," *Encyclopaedia Universalis,* Vol. 12, Encyclopaedia Universalis France S.A., Paris.

"Rationaliste (architecture)," *Encyclopaedia Universalis,* Vol.13, Encyclopaedia Universalis France S.A., Paris.

"Urbanisme et Architecture," *Encyclopaedia Universalis,* Vol.16, Encyclopaedia Universalis France S.A., Paris.

"Wright, Frank Lloyd," *Encyclopaedia Universalis,* Vol.16, Encyclopaedia Universalis France S.A., Paris.

"Ebraismo e concezione spazio-temporale dell'arte," *La Rassegna Mensile di Israel,* June, Rome *(Zevi su Zevi,* Magma, Milan, 1977).

Raffaello architetto by Stefano Ray, preface by Bruno Zevi, Laterza, Bari.

"Un crítico confrontando su obra," *Nueva Forma,* no.105, October, Madrid.

1975 "A Language after Wright," *Frank Lloyd Wright: In the Cause of Architecture*, Frederick Gutheim, ed., Architectural Record Books, New York.

"Urgenza di poesia architettonica nella città-regione," *Quaderni del Centro Culturale "Merolla,"* Vol.2, Aversa.

1976 *Architecture by Sert at the Miró Foundation*, Polígrafa, Barcelona.

"L'a-historicisme de Bauhaus et ses conséquences," *C.I.E.R.*, Université de Saint-Etienne, France.

Kibbutz + Bauhaus by Arieh Sharon, foreword by Bruno Zevi, Krämer, Stuttgart and Massada, Israel.

"L'architecture muette à la recherche d'un language," *Architecture*, no.395, February, Paris.

1977 *Zevi su Zevi*, Magma, Milan.

"Industrial Design: Many Characters in search of an Author," *Dublin Congress on Industrial Design*. Unpublished.

1978 "The Italian Rationalists," *The Rationalists: Theory and Design in the Modern Movement*, Dennis Sharp, ed., Architectural Press, London.

"Avanguardia, retro- e neo-avanguardia architettonica," *Ulisse*, May, Rome.

"Brunelleschi anti-classique et anti-Renaissance," *Filippo Brunelleschi 1377–1446*, C.E.R.A., Paris.

The Modern Language of Architecture, University of Washington Press, Seattle, 1978. Paperback edition, Van Nostrand Reinhold, New York, 1981.

1979 *Editoriali di architettura*, Einaudi, Turin.

Frank Lloyd Wright, Zanichelli, Bologna.

Architecture and Einstein's Space-Time, Tel-Aviv Museum.

"Teoría y crítica de la arquitectura," *Nueva Visión*, Buenos Aires.

"Governo-ombra e università di massa," *Argomenti radicali*, no.12–13, April-September.

1980 "The Poetics of the Unfinished," *SITE—Architecture as Art*, Academy Editions, London.

"¿Es la arquitectura un lenguaje, y en qué sentido?" *CAYC*, Buenos Aires.

Giuseppe Terragni, Zanichelli, Bologna.

1981 "Architectural Theory and Criticism since 1945," *International Handbook of Contemporary Developments in Architecture*, Warren Sanderson, ed., Greenwood Press, Westport, Conn., and London.

"Architettura," *Trattato di Estetica* by M. Dufrenne and D. Formaggio, Mondadori, Milan.

"The Degree Zero of Architectural Writing," *International Union of Architects Congress,* Warsaw.

"The Influence of American Architecture and Urban Planning in the World," *For Better or Worse - The American Influence in the World,* Allen F. Davis, ed., Greenwood Press, Westport, Conn., and London.

1982 *Erich Mendelsohn,* Zanichelli, Bologna.

The weekly articles by Bruno Zevi in *Cronache* and in *L'Espresso* have been published in book-form, under the title *Cronache di architettura,* Laterza, Bari, 1971–1981. In the most recent edition, there are 24 volumes, with the following sub-titles:

1. dal Memorial alle Fosse Ardeatine a Wright sul Canal Grande (1954–55).

2. dallo sconcio dei Lungarni alla Chapelle de Ronchamp (1954–55).

3. dalla celebrazione di Biagio Rossetti alla polemica su Sant'Elia (1955–56).

4. dall'Interbau berlinese all'Opera di Utzon a Sidney (1956–57).

5. dall'Expo mondiale di Bruxelles all'UNESCO parigino (1958–59).

6. dalla scomparsa di F.Ll. Wright all'inaugurazione di Brasilia (1959–60).

7. da La Tourette corbusieriana ai Laboratori Medici di Louis Kahn (1960–61).

8. dal piano di Kenzo Tange per Tokyo alla battaglia per la diga sullo Jato (1961–62).

9. dal concorso di Tel-Aviv/Jaffa alla Philharmonie di Scharoun (1963–64).

10. dal recupero dell'espressionismo al piano regolatore di Roma (1964–65).

11. dalla scomparsa di Le Corbusier al piano Pampus per Amsterdam (1965–66).

12. dal centro civico di Cumbernauld all'Habitat di Moshe Safdie (1966–67).

13. dalla ricostruzione di Gerusalemme ai segni di James Stirling (1968–69).

14. dall'utopia del gruppo Archigram agli scioperi generali per la casa (1969–70).

15. dall'apologia di Las Vegas al Mummers Theater di Johansen (1970–71).

16. dalle obliquità di Claude Parent al londinese Brunswick Centre (1971–72).

17. dall'inedito di Umberto Boccioni all'autolesionismo della Triennale (1973–74).

18. dai "Five Architects" newyorkesi a Bernini plagiario (1974–75).

19. dalla conferenza di Vancouver alla scomparsa di Aalto (1975–76).

20. dal Bicentenario americano al Centre Beaubourg (1976–77).

21. da Brunelleschi anticlassico alla Carta del Machu Picchu (1977–78).

22. dalla National Gallery di I.M.Pei alla polemica sui "falsi" bolognesi (1978–79).

23. dal "rifiuto" dell'università al concorso per Les Halles (1979–80).

24. dal fallimento del Post-Modern all'impegno sociale del design (1980–81).

The analytical indexes of the 1379 articles are published in a special volume, *Cronache di architettura - Indici,* Laterza, Bari, 1978 (articles 1–1180, volumes 1–20), and *Cronache di architettura* (articles 1181–1379, volumes 21–24).